MOON HANDBOOKS

COLUMBIA
RIVER GORGE

west of Hood River

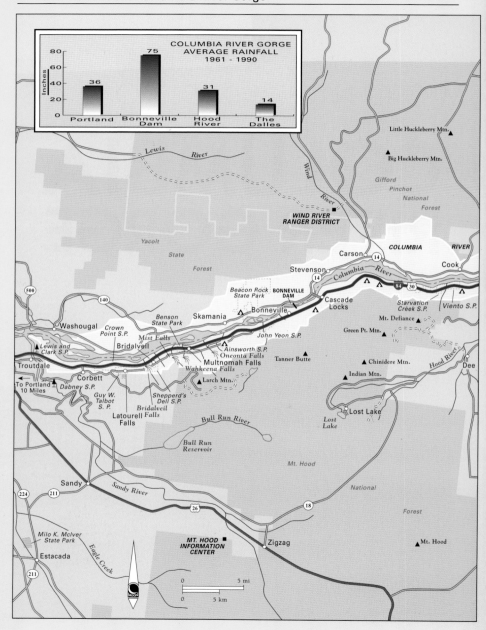

COLUMBIA RIVER GORGE
AVERAGE RAINFALL
1961 - 1990

Portland	Bonneville Dam	Hood River	The Dalles
36	75	31	14

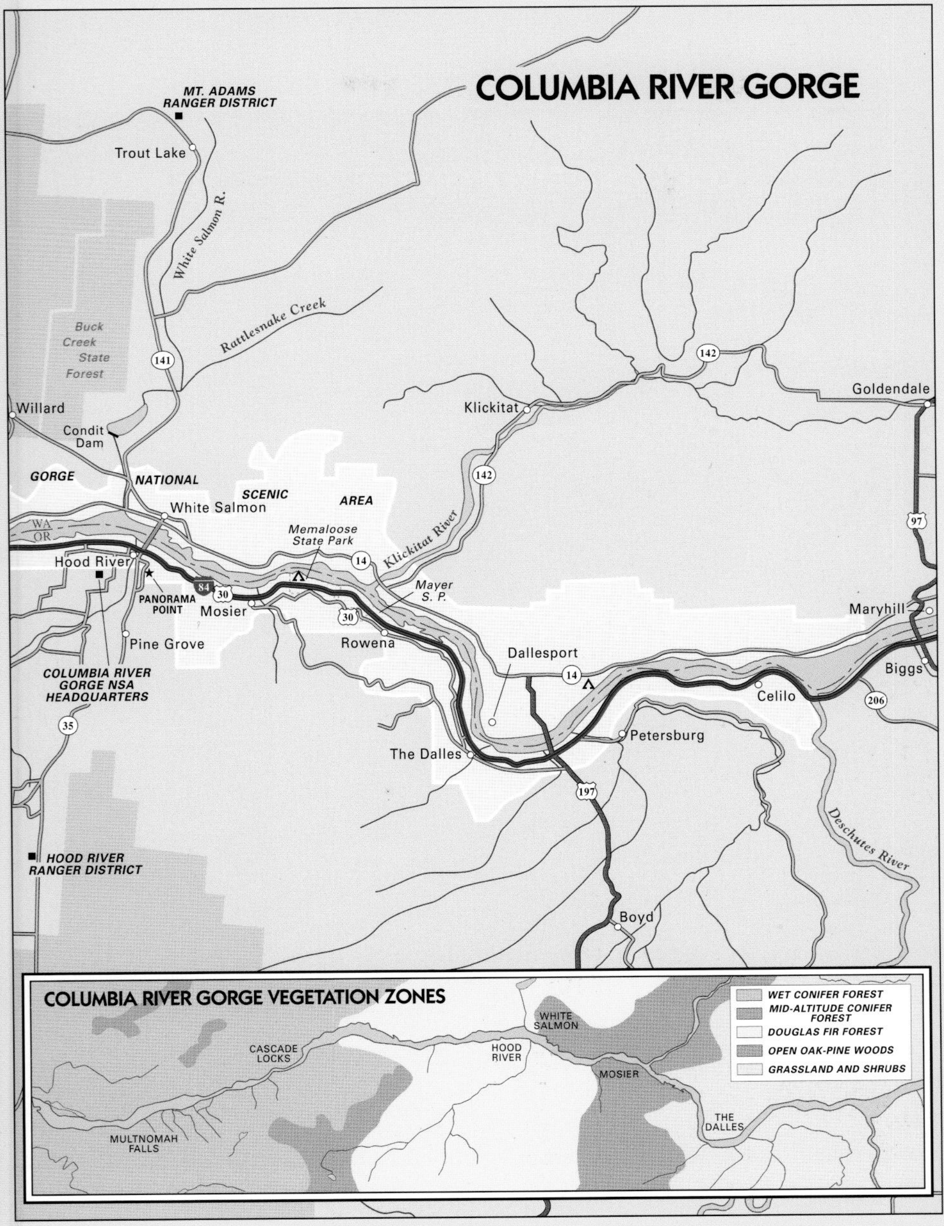

COLUMBIA RIVER GORGE

MT. ADAMS
RANGER DISTRICT

Trout Lake

White Salmon R.

Rattlesnake Creek

Buck
Creek
State
Forest

141

Willard

Condit
Dam

GORGE   NATIONAL

White Salmon

SCENIC   AREA

Klickitat

142

142

Goldendale

97

Memaloose
State Park

Klickitat River

14

WA
OR

Hood River

30
84

PANORAMA
POINT   Mosier

Pine Grove

COLUMBIA RIVER
GORGE NSA
HEADQUARTERS

35

Rowena

Mayer
S. P.

30

Maryhill

Dallesport

14

Biggs

206

Celilo

The Dalles

Petersburg

197

HOOD RIVER
RANGER DISTRICT

Deschutes River

Boyd

COLUMBIA RIVER GORGE VEGETATION ZONES

	WET CONIFER FOREST
	MID-ALTITUDE CONIFER FOREST
	DOUGLAS FIR FOREST
	OPEN OAK-PINE WOODS
	GRASSLAND AND SHRUBS

CASCADE
LOCKS

WHITE
SALMON

HOOD
RIVER

MOSIER

THE
DALLES

MULTNOMAH
FALLS

© AVALON TRAVEL PUBLISHING, INC.

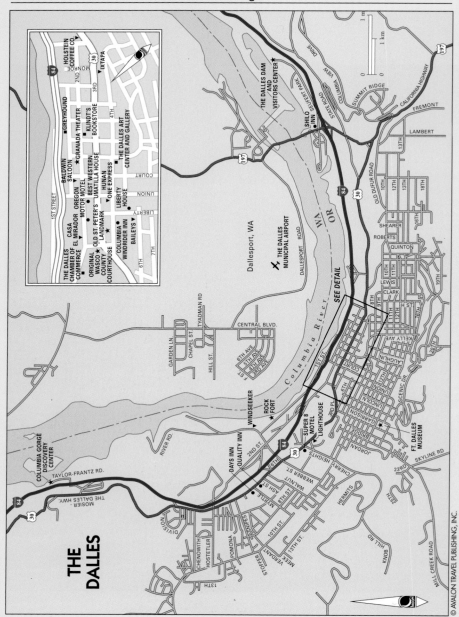

THE DALLES

THE DALLES CHAMBER OF COMMERCE
CASA EL MIRADOR
ORIGINAL WASCO COUNTY COURTHOUSE
OLD ST. PETER'S LANDMARK
BEST WESTERN UMATILLA HOUSE
OREGON MOTOR MOTEL
BALDWIN SALOON
GREYHOUND
HOLSTEIN COFFEE CO.
GRANADA THEATER
KLINDT'S BOOKSTORE
IXTAPA
HUNAN
ONE EXPRESS
THE DALLES ART CENTER AND GALLERY
LIBERTY HOUSE
BAILEYS
COLUMBIA WINDRIDER INN

THE DALLES DAM AND VISITORS CENTER
SHILO INN
THE DALLES MUNICIPAL AIRPORT
Dallesport, WA
SUMMIT RIDGE
FREMONT
LAMBERT
SHEARER
ROBERTS
QUINTON
LEWIS
CLARK
KELLY AVE
LAUGHLIN
LINCOLN
UNION
GARRISON
JORDAN
FT. DALLES MUSEUM
SCENIC DR.
SKYLINE RD
HERMITS
HILL RD
MILL CREEK ROAD
KNOX
CALIFORNIA HIGHWAY
OLD DUFUR ROAD

CENTRAL BLVD.
TYADMAN RD.
GARDEN LN.
CHAPEL ST.
HILL ST.
6TH AVE
5TH AVE
4TH AVE
3RD AVE
WINDSEEKER
ROCK FORT
SUPER 8 MOTEL
LIGHTHOUSE
DAYS INN
QUALITY INN
Columbia River
DALLESPORT ROAD
SEE DETAIL

COLUMBIA GORGE DISCOVERY CENTER
TAYLOR-FRANTZ RD.
MOSIER
THE DALLES HWY.
RIVER RD.
2ND ST.
WEBBER ST.
WALNUT
ASH S.
MYRTLE
DIVISION
CHENOWITH
HOSTETLER
POMONA
VERDANT
STOTHER
MEEK ST.
13TH
10TH ST.
HAZEL ST.
HILL ST.
CHERRY HEIGHTS

© AVALON TRAVEL PUBLISHING, INC.

MAP SYMBOLS

Symbol	Description
——	Divided Highway
——	Primary Road
——	Secondary Road
=====	Unpaved Road
╈	Railroad
🛡	U.S. Interstate
◯	U.S. Highway
◗	State Highway
◯	City
○	Town
✕	Airfield/Airstrip
★	Point of Interest
●	Accommodation
▶	Restaurant/Bar
■	Other Location
⌂	Campground
▲	Mountain
◀	State Park
⛳	Golf Course
⤵	Waterfall
〰	National Scenic Area
▓	National Forest

HOOD RIVER

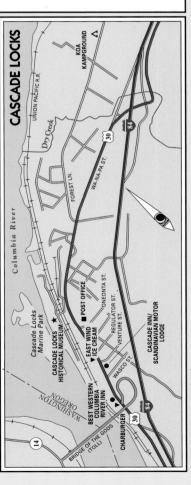

CASCADE LOCKS

looking west from Ruthton Point

MOON HANDBOOKS

COLUMBIA RIVER GORGE

FIRST EDITION

INCLUDING COMPLETE COVERAGE OF PORTLAND

STUART WARREN & BRIAN LITT

AVALON
TRAVEL

**Moon Handbooks: Columbia River Gorge
Including Complete Coverage of Portland**

First Edition

Stuart Warren & Brian Litt

Published by
Avalon Travel Publishing
5855 Beaudry St.
Emeryville, CA 94608, USA

Printing History
1st edition—March 2002
5 4 3 2 1

Please send all comments, corrections,
additions, amendments, and critiques to:

**Moon Handbooks:
Columbia River Gorge**
AVALON TRAVEL PUBLISHING
5855 BEAUDRY ST.
EMERYVILLE, CA 94608, USA
email: atpfeedback@avalonpub.com
website: www.moon.com

ISBN: 1-56691-367-5
ISSN: 1536-3147

Editor and Series Manager: Erin Van Rheenen
Copy Editor: Emily Lunceford
Graphics Coordinator: Melissa Sherowski
Production: Amber Pirker, Jacob Goolkasian
Map Editors: Naomi Adler Dancis
Cartographers: Suzanne Service, Mike Morgenfeld, Landis Bennett
Indexer: Vera Gross

Front cover photo: © John Elk III

Distributed by Publishers Group West

Printed in China through Colorcraft Ltd., Hong Kong

ABOUT THE AUTHORS
Stuart Warren

When Stuart dropped out of the University of Oregon's journalism grad school to become a travel agent, tour planner, and tour director, his wanderlust resulted in *Moon Handbooks: Oregon*. This well-received work inspired him to pen a book about his favorite part of the Pacific Northwest, the Columbia River Gorge. He found the perfect collaborator in Brian Litt, a friend from graduate school whose longtime residence and government service in the Gorge would prove invaluable.

When he isn't writing, Stuart works for Tauck World Discovery as a tour director. In addition to sharing the most fantastic places in the world with several dozen travelers each trip, he particularly relishes the comedy that seems to accompany this job. While details of such experiences as helping a naked lady catch up to her luggage on a cruise ship will have to await future publication, the following incident best captures the essence of Stuart's "other vocation."

It was July 4th in Wasilla, Alaska. Stuart's group had already been delayed en route to the lunch stop there and was eager to break bread at an old hunting lodge. However, several miles from their destination, a holiday parade stopped traffic. A parade marshal informed Stuart that only floats and vintage cars could continue down the road to the restaurant. After a brief negotiation, Stuart donned a moose hat and sunglasses and climbed out the hatch onto the roof of the bus. With a sign saying "Alaska Tourism," the coach joined the parade and headed to lunch, following a school of giant crepe-paper salmon atop several pickup trucks.

Stuart lives in Portland with Kathleen, another Gorge hiking enthusiast. His free time is spent teaching chess in Portland public schools and discovering Mexican restaurants with his son Phineas.

ABOUT THE AUTHORS
Brian Litt

Brian Litt lives in the heart of the Columbia River Gorge, in Hood River, Oregon. He has been a Gorge resident and a planner for the Columbia River Gorge Commission since 1988. This is Brian's first co-authorship of a travel book, though he was a contributing writer to *Moon Handbooks: Oregon.*

Brian grew up adjacent to an off-ramp of the Long Island Expressway, in the suburbs of New York City. This may help explain his lifelong passions for travel and nature, which led Brian to constantly badger his parents into taking as many vacations as far from home as possible. Early exposure to the wilds of Cape Cod, the Catskill Mountains, and the Pennsylvania Dutch Country fueled Brian's growing wanderlust.

In recent years, Brian has traveled extensively through western Europe and Brazil. His international experiences were further enhanced by forays into Israel and Thailand. "Each time I return home from overseas, I'm struck by what spectacular beauty I have the privilege of enjoying every day here in the Columbia Gorge," Brian notes.

Working on this book held some beneficial surprises for Brian. He explains, "I discovered a number of hidden treasures right in my own backyard. This was particularly true with respect to local history. For example, learning that the first "talkies" west of the Mississippi debuted at the now-restored Granada Theater in The Dalles gave me an appreciation of the building's significance that is a dimension beyond its impressive Moorish architecture."

Brian is also a guitarist and singer specializing in traditional country blues and rags on his well-worn Gibson acoustic guitar. He regularly performs at various Columbia Gorge venues. He enjoys ethnic cuisine when he can't actually travel abroad, as well as hiking, symphony concerts, and cooking for loved ones. His faithful black lab, Buddy, can be seen shadowing him through the back alleys of Hood River.

Contents

Map Contents

Keeping Current

We strive to keep our books as up to date as possible and would appreciate your help. If you find that a resort is not as we described or discover a new restaurant or other information that should be included in our book, please let us know. Our mapmakers take extraordinary effort to be accurate, but if you find an error, let us know that as well.

We're especially interested in hearing from female travelers, RVers, outdoor enthusiasts, and local residents. We are always interested in hearing from the tourist industry, which specializes in accommodating visitors to the Columbia River Gorge and all of Oregon. Happy traveling! Please address letters to:

Moon Handbooks: Columbia River Gorge
Avalon Travel Publishing
5855 Beaudry St.
Emeryville, CA 94608, USA
email: atpfeedback@avalonpub.com

Abbreviations

AARP—American Association of Retired People
AYH—American Youth Hostel
BLM—Bureau of Land Management
CCC—Civilian Conservation Corps
F—Fahrenheit
Hwy. (plus number)—state highway
I (plus number)—Interstate highway
MAX—Metropolitan Area Express
mph—miles per hour
NFS—National Forest Service
NRA—National Recreation Area

NWR—National Wildlife Refuge
OMSI—Oregon Museum of Science and Industry
OR—Oregon
POVA—Portland Oregon Visitors Association
pp—per person
RV—recreational vehicle
U.S. (plus number) —federal highway
USGS—United States Geological Survey
WA—Washington
WISTEC—Willamette Science and Technology Center

Introduction

To native tribes it was the great gathering place. To Lewis and Clark and Oregon Trail pioneers, it was the gateway to the Pacific. To first-time visitors, the Columbia River Gorge is the Northwest they always imagined—towering waterfalls, rainforests, and orchard country backdropped by snowcapped volcanoes.

While most visitors confine themselves to the western Gorge's moss-draped cliffs and dense arboreal canopy, a surprise awaits the newcomer venturing east from the Portland–Vancouver area. Halfway through this cleft in the Cascades, the greenery parts to reveal buff-colored gently sloping grasslands and sage-covered semiarid desert under a big sky. It soon becomes apparent that this 80-mile long, five-mile wide, 4,000-foot-deep chasm has as much variety in climate, topography, and vegetation as terra firma can muster.

However compelling this rainforest-to-desert diversity may be, the region is more than a montage of ecosystems or a marine borderline between Oregon and Washington. Humans have trod the earth here for at least 10,000 years. Their presence is given voice by petroglyphs, pictographs, prehistoric village sites, the Lewis and Clark Expedition route, the Oregon Trail and the first paved public road in the Pacific Northwest, the Historic Columbia River Highway. Visitors also revel in the world's largest concentration of high waterfalls as well as one of the more diverse botanical communities on the planet. An abundance of roadside markers, interpretive centers, and museums, caption the stories behind the scenery. Add a recreational menu that can include skiing in the morning and windsurfing in the afternoon for a recipe to sate mind, body, and spirit.

Unfortunately, this recipe for a peak travel experience is not so secret. As weekend wilderness to the 25th largest urban area in the country, the strains on the Columbia River Gorge are palpable. The added impacts of tens of thousands of

the view east from Cape Horn

full-time residents and air- and riverborne pollution from urban neighbors have taken enough of a toll that the peace of nature coexists with an environmental battleground. The 1997 inclusion of the Columbia River on a list of the most endangered watersheds in the country compounded the impression of an ecosystem under siege. In addition, debates over land use, mining, timber practices, salmon preservation, and other issues that have taken center stage in Oregon and Washington rage most fiercely in the Gorge.

And why not? The Gorge is the Northwest's primal landscape, a veritable microcosm of its ecology and the location of its most important historical sites and pioneer thoroughfares. The campfires of Lewis and Clark and Oregon Trail emigrants may be gone now, but ground-breaking trails are still being blazed here today in the thickets of legislation and jurisprudence.

The Land

GEOLOGY

If there's one word to describe the forces that created the Columbia River Gorge, it's *cataclysmic*. This adjective applies with equal emphasis to the volcanic activity, flooding, and landslides that sculpted the present-day contours of this fjord-like border between Oregon and Washington.

While eons-old mud and lava flows are visible throughout the Gorge, and ancient avalanche scars still mar the land, there is a dearth of visual clues about the primary agent of landscape alteration here—floods of biblical proportions. Scientists now estimate there were at least 40 mega-inundations here between 12,000 to 19,000 years ago conforming to periodic cooling and warming cycles at the end of the last big Ice Age.

Bretz's Theory

Despite the magnitude of these phenomena, this idea was not even suggested until Harlen Bretz proposed his "Genesis" theory during the 1920s. To further confound the geologists of the time, he said "glacial erratics," a term referring to rocks moved far from their place of origin due to glaciers, were the best evidence for these Ice Age floods. Massive boulders, distinct geologically from other Gorge rocks, were found on bluffs as

Halfway through the Gorge, it becomes apparent that this 80-mile long, five-mile wide, 4,000-foot-deep chasm has as much variety in climate, topography, and vegetation as terra firma can muster.

high as 1,200 feet above the river. Bretz theorized that they were transported to the region from the area of the present-day Canadian border encased in waterborne icebergs during the largest floods known to humankind. Such thinking was decried as implausible "catastrophism" by the earth science establishment for much of the 20th century until aerial photography and radiocarbon dating made it easier to substantiate cataclysm theories. When eroded terraces from an ancient lakebed encompassing 3,000 square miles were discovered in the area of present-day western Montana, Bretz's theories began to be considered worthy of attention, finally gaining widespread acceptance in the second half of the 20th century.

Prehistoric Lake Missoula contained approximately 500 cubic meters of water. The melting of an ice dam released a wall of water several thousand feet deep exceeding 50 miles an hour en route to the Columbia River Gorge. These torrents entered the eastern Gorge at depths as high as 1,200 feet, exiting the western extremity of the region at approximately 400 feet above sea level. The floodwaters submerged what is now Portland and then headed 120 miles south and west, depositing rich alluvial sediments in the Willamette Valley where it formed a temporary lake extending 3,000 square miles near present-day Eugene.

At press time, moves were underway to establish a National Geologic Trail paralleling the course of these ancient floodwaters. Consult www.nps.gov/iceagefloods for more information.

Waterfalls

The flood scoured the Gorge's three-mile thick crust of hard-to-erode basalt lava and mud, leaving sheer basalt cliffs. Feeder streams for many of the region's 77 waterfalls today were left on top of these promontories. Unable to cut a chasm in their streambeds, these ribbons of water had nowhere to go but down.

The Gorge possesses the largest concentration of roadside waterfalls in North America including such giants as Multnomah Falls (620 feet), Elowah Falls (289 feet) and Wahkeena Falls (242 feet). Eleven waterfalls visible from the roadside here exceed 100 feet.

The Gorge's 80-mile long break in the mountains is the only such divide in the cordillera of Cascades and Sierra Nevada peaks extending between the Canadian and Mexican borders. More impressively, only one other river in the world

(the Brahmaputra in the Himalaya) cuts through a major mountain range at sea level.

The Columbia River

While the Columbia no longer exerts so pervasive an influence on the topography here, it still is more powerful than any river in the United States except the Mississippi. This 1,243-mile long waterway flows south and west from Canada's Kootenay Range to eventually release a quarter-million cubic feet of water per second into the Pacific Ocean after draining 259,000 square miles, an area larger than France. Lake Columbia in British Columbia is the primary source. Glacial runoff and snowmelt plus such impressive tributaries as the Deschutes and Snake Rivers guarantee a fairly consistent flow year-round. This flow peaks in spring and early summer, coinciding with irrigation needs.

Another leading use of the Columbia is the hydropower produced by the eight dams on the river in Oregon and Washington. As a result, the current incarnation of the Columbia is in stark contrast to the white water that filled its channel prior to the dams. Back in that era, spawning salmon had to jump over several sets of roiling cascades and shipping was a hazardous enterprise. Floods were commonplace; the flood of

© LIPSCHUETZ & KATZ

Horsetail Falls is 208 feet high.

1894 inundated the downtowns of Hood River and The Dalles.

Despite stretches of the river today that resemble a windsurfing pond-cum-shipping canal, there are still moments that conjure the power unleashed by the fabled "River of The West" in the days of Lewis and Clark. When you see five-foot swells created by 40-mile-an-hour gusts here or dam spillways unleashing high white thunder, you'll know what I mean.

CLIMATE

The disparity between the wet western Gorge and the dryness of its eastern edge can be best understood within the larger context of regional precipitation patterns. Because rising air cools three degrees Fahrenheit every 1,000 feet, and cooler air can't hold as much moisture as warm air, Cascades summits can catch more than 200 inches of rain yearly from eastward moving cloud masses, leaving much of the eastern side of the range desert dry. The dryness happens because air descending the lee slopes becomes warmer and loses humidity. Larch Mountain (4,058 feet) and Mt. Defiance (4,960 feet, highest in the Gorge) are sometimes the rainiest places in Oregon, yet cactus can grow less than 50 air miles away in the eastern Gorge.

When the thick, rainforest-like growth in the west is supplanted by the wide open spaces of cowboy country in the east, it's like you've left the Pacific Northwest and entered the Old West. A transition zone begins a few miles east of Hood River, where a 19-inch drop in annual precipitation occurs within a dozen miles—dry enough for oaks and grasslands to replace conifers. Beyond this oak savanna, the sagebrush and other semiarid desert vegetation take over.

Given these contrasts, it's not surprising that the convergence of weather systems at mid-Gorge often results in meteorological bedlam. Early pioneer journals repeatedly described the weather around present-day Cascades Locks as prone to violent outbursts of wind and rain. Bonneville Dam recorded the state's one-day record for snowfall, 39 inches in January 1980.

Wind

Ask any local about Gorge weather and it's likely that the subject of wind will come up. High pressure systems west of the Cascades are drawn eastward by low pressure systems on the other side of the mountains, causing winds to move faster the farther east you go. Thus, a five-mph wind in Portland can become three or four times that strong by the time it reaches the eastern periphery of the Gorge. This phenomenon is known as the "Venturi effect" and is driven by prevailing Pacific westerlies filling the vacuum left by sun-heated eastern desert air rising.

Temperature

Portland and Vancouver share a latitude with Green Bay, Wisconsin, so it may surprise you that west of the Cascades, winter lows seldom dip below freezing. A notable exception to this happens when frigid winds originating in the Colorado Rockies blow through the Gorge in winter. The eastern Gorge experiences more dramatic temperature variations than the western Gorge's more maritime conditions. Wintertime lows below 20°F and summer-time highs over 90°F are not uncommon east of the Cascades.

Silver Thaws

This area also generates hazardous "silver thaws," a storm that covers roadways with black ice and coats tree branches and power lines with icicles heavy enough to send them crashing to the ground. This phenomenon occurs when icy winds from the east blow down the Gorge beneath the warm rains moving inland from the Pacific. As the resulting super-cooled drops fall, they freeze. When such a storm blows into Portland, as it did on Christmas of 1996, it brings traffic to a standstill.

Weather Information

A good phone number for wind and weather conditions Gorge-wide is 541-386-3300. Windsurfers can find out about conditions at www.windance.com.

Flora and Fauna

FLORA

As you drive Interstate 84 from west to east in the Gorge you'll see mixed conifer ecosystems with Douglas fir and western hemlock between Portland and Hood River. Deciduous big leaf maples (which blaze orange-red in late October) and alder also occasionally assert themselves among the conifers.

Riparian environments in the Gorge are dominated by willow and black cottonwood. A lush understory of ferns covers the lower reaches of western Gorge waterfalls. Thimbleberry (a species of wild raspberry) and blackberry are also common during late summer.

Pockets of **white oak** and **ponderosa pine** begin to show up east of Bonneville Dam on the way to Hood River. Just outside Mosier, this oak "savanna" dominates the landscape until sagebrush, rabbitbush, cheatgrass, and other chaparral define the beginning of the semiarid desert east of the Cascades Range. This transition begins farther west across the river on SR 14 due to the Washington Gorge's south-facing slopes.

Leaf Peeping

Fall foliage in the Gorge tends to peak late October to early November. In the western Gorge, Angels Rest offers one of the best vantage points on the brilliant bigleaf maples across the river in the hills above Prindle, WA. The region around Multnomah Falls displays these trees as well as cottonwood and Oregon ash against a conifer backdrop. Throughout the western Gorge, red vine maple and other smaller shrubs add diversity. The Hood River Valley country adds more color to the mix. To the east, the Historic Columbia River Highway and I-84 between Mosier and The Dalles show off a more muted montage.

Perhaps the best fall color near the Gorge can be enjoyed in the Cascades. By traveling south and west from Hood River and Dee over Lolo Pass Road past Lost Lake (see the Hood River section of the Oregon Gorge chapter), you can enjoy splashes of red and gold from vine and bigleaf maples broken up by a scarlet huckleberry understory. This is a great fall foliage drive if undertaken before the first snows, usually early November.

Poison Oak

Poison oak is rampant in the understory of Gorge oak forests. Detailed recommendations on dealing with this hazard are offered in this book's Health and Safety section in the Essentials chapter. Gorge hikers should be especially vigilant at Tom McCall Preserve at Rowena Crest near Mosier, as well as across the river at Dog Mountain west of White Salmon, WA. These two sites of the most visited regional wildflower displays also are inundated by the three shiny leaves of poison oak. Other frequently visited areas that mandate caution include the Mosier Twin Tunnels and the upper reaches of Catherine Creek between Bingen and Lyle, WA.

Edible Delights

While the thorny brambles of blackberry and raspberry might be another hiker hazard, they might also alert you to the feast that awaits. Here in the Gorge you can find wild mountain blackberries, Himalaya blackberries, blue elderberries, blue serviceberries, salmonberries, gooseberries, salal, huckleberries, blackcap raspberries, wild strawberries, and thimbleberries. Chanterelles, a yellow fluted mushroom prized in gourmet eateries worldwide, pop up every so often after the first rains of autumn in mixed conifer forests.

Wildflowers

The variety in climate and vegetation habitats is paralleled by a diversity of flowering plants, rich enough to merit its own reference volume. *Wildflowers of the Columbia River Gorge* by Russ Jolley (Oregon Historical Society Press, 1998) identifies 744 of the more than 800 varieties of the area's flowering shrubs and wildflowers, singling out 14 "endemics," plants found nowhere else in the world.

These unique species, some of them survivors from the Ice Age, are found among plants that typically thrive in a Rocky Mountain subalpine biome. Thirty-one plants usually encountered at 4,000 feet above sea level are found in the Columbia Gorge at elevations almost always below 1,600 feet. The damp, cold air that gets trapped in the shadows of cliffs sustains such aberrations.

A number of Ice Age orphans are located in **Oneonta Gorge** just east of Multnomah Falls where sheer 100-foot-high basalt walls frame a creek. Moisture and cool air trapped in the canyon walls here support dozens of flowering plants and enough endemics to be a designated botanical area. If you're willing to wade through this boulder-and-log-strewn cold creek in a 20-foot-wide chasm for about 45 minutes, other rewards include a seldom-seen 80-foot waterfall and a small beach.

A riot of color awaits flower lovers at **Tom McCall Reserve** atop Rowena Crest with balsamroot, shooting stars, Indian paintbrush, camas, penstemon, wild lilies, desert parsley, and many more. While May is the Gorge's peak wildflower month, rotating blooms can be enjoyed from summer through fall. An even greater variety exists on Dog Mountain halfway between Stevenson and Bingen, WA.

A map published by the Forest Service and the Gorge Trust has color photos of prominent species and information on notable displays. It's sold throughout the Gorge as well as at Powell's in Portland. Also recommended is the National Forest Service website (www.fs.fed.us/r6/columbia/), which lists the Gorge's 14 endemics, their habitat, time of bloom, and locations in the Gorge.

It's worth noting that the Gorge's earliest wildflower displays are not, as you might expect, near the milder Willamette Valley, but instead are east, where the oak woodlands and grassy slopes are more exposed to the Northwest's first extended period of sunshine. The first big show takes place in March at **Catherine Creek** near Lyle, WA, across the river from Rowena Crest. The arrival of sunshine here brings yellow bells, orchids, prairie

fir

stars, grass widows, and Barrett's penstemon as well as a view of Mt. Hood looming over Gorge cliffs across the river on the Oregon side. At this time, trillium can be seen near Horsetail Falls on the Historic Highway and glacier lilies on the Eagle Creek Trail.

In addition to wild species, the spring blossom festvials in Gorge orchard country (see the Hood River and The Dalles sections of the The Oregon Gorge chapter) and the floral fantasia planted around Oregon's Bonneville Dam visitor center and The Columbia River Gorge Hotel add color to the landscape. In this vein, the first apple tree in the Northwest reportedly got its start at Fort Vancouver in 1924—planted by a ship captain from England at this one-time British outpost. That same tree still produces fruit today at the Washington portal of the Gorge.

Those interested in following the species-filled trail of botanical discoveries made by Lewis and Clark should read the sidebar Lewis and Clark's Botanical Legacy in The Oregon Gorge chapter.

Old Growth Forests

While old growth can be found on many Gorge trails, an extensive ancient forest atop Oregon's Larch Mountain on the periphery of the Gorge can be reached by car (see The Oregon Gorge chapter). Besides 400-year-old noble firs, white-blossomed beargrass will catch your eye here in June and July.

This is also a good place to see spotted owls, a bird considered by some biologists to be the indicator species of a healthy old growth forest. This bird is federally classified as an endangered species, mandating protection of the old growth fir forests where it likes to nest in hollowed-out snags. It is also a source of controversy in many Gorge towns that once enjoyed healthy resource-based economies.

FAUNA

The archaeological record indicates that saber-toothed cats, giant beavers,

THE COLUMBIA RIVER GORGE SCENIC AREA

Recognition of the necessity to protect the environment in the Gorge goes back to 1915, when a 14,000-acre Recreation Reserve was created around the cliffs and waterfalls surrounding the Columbia River Highway. The latter was complemented by private philanthropists purchasing other roadside real estate here such as Crown Point and Multnomah Falls for protection and public recreation.

In the 1930s, the federal government completed the first comprehensive study recommending conservation of the entire Gorge. The study came in reaction to the threat of outside industrialists, lured by the promise of Bonneville Dam's cheap hydropower. While the Pacific Northwest Regional Planning Commission ruled out national park status because Gorge railroads, highways, and dams were already in place, it still was able to deter the establishment of a smoke-stack economy here by addressing potentially adverse impacts of proposed development. More importantly, committee members formally asserted the need for a regulatory agency addressing both human and environmental needs here.

This 1937 study set the stage for Oregon and Washington to create their own Gorge Commissions two decades later. Unfortunately, these commissions were advisory bodies bereft of power to regulate counties who routinely ignored their recommendations. When 1970s proposals for large housing developments and open-pit mining threatened to mar sensitive landscapes here forever, activists advocated a new kind of jurisdiction combining the preservationist philosophy of a national park with the "multiple use" orientation of a national forest. A citizen advocacy group for federal protection, **The Friends of the Columbia Gorge,** was established in 1981. Another faction, popular in Washington where there is more private property than in Oregon's Gorge, wanted control in the hands of a bi-state commission composed largely of area residents. Oregon Senator Mark Hat-

field's proposal of a governmental infrastructure combined both orientations, resulting in the 1986 passage of The Columbia River Gorge National Scenic Area Act. The act designated a 292,500-acre area of Gorge land as a scenic area subject to both land use controls as well as provisions for environment-friendly development. This development is largely confined to Gorge towns in order to protect the region's scenic, cultural, recreational, and natural resources. Decisions on preservation and use are meted out by a two-agency partnership. In addition to the U.S. Forest Service, the Columbia Gorge Commission—made up of delegates from Gorge counties and both states—plays an integral role in decision-making. These entities put the Scenic Area Act's goals into practice with a management plan they crafted in 1991. Guidelines protecting forest and farmland from residential development, tribal access to traditional hunting and gathering sites, and the region's archaeological treasures exemplify concerns in the Plan. Along with conservation, economic development was fostered by millions of dollars in federal grant money helping to fund such enterprises as Skamania Lodge and The Columbia Gorge Discovery Center. These monies are only distributed in counties adopting local ordinances implementing the management plan.

The Scenic Area Act and 1991 Management Plan's commitment to both economic development and preservation has made it a frequent target of controversy. Add such situations as advocacy of increased recreational access to the Columbia River, where many protected tribal activities and cultural resources are located, and it's easy to understand why conflicts are inevitable. Nonetheless, this system of governance reflects the ecological and cultural diversity of the Gorge landscape. Without it, population and development pressures would result in paved-over patrimony and environmental desecration of this special place.

grizzly bear, mastodons, ancient horses, and camels once roamed parts of the Gorge. In 1805, Lewis and Clark noted a condor flying above a Columbia practically overflowing with salmon near the mouth of the Wind River. Perhaps the Lewis and Clark bicentennial can spur the reintroduction of this bird with a nine-foot wingspan back to its original nesting ground. The explorers also complained of an inability to sleep in the western Gorge due to the cacophony of birds in the area. Their journals mention wolves, mountain goats and even seals as far upstream as The Dalles. While the wilderness that supported the numbers and variety of these species has largely disappeared, you'd still be hard-pressed to find a region this close to a major urban area with rattlesnakes, spotted owls, cougars, bald eagles, black bears, seals, pika, Roosevelt elk, and other species that occupy the modern-day Gorge. Wildlife viewing opportunities are noted in the chapters to follow.

Living Fossils

Two living fossils, the **mountain beaver** and the **white sturgeon,** also exist in this watershed. The mountain beaver (called a "boomer" by locals), is a primitive species of rat found only in western North America that resembles a beaver minus the flat tail. It was first mentioned in print by Meriwether Lewis whose February 26, 1806 journal entry spoke of his fascination with the animal and his unsuccessful attempts to procure one from the Indians. The fossil record of this species dates back 65 million years, making it the world's oldest living rodent.

In like measure, the white sturgeon, a creature that can measure longer than 10 feet and weigh more than 1,000 pounds, has not changed structurally in 200 million years. It's North America's largest freshwater fish. These Gorge inhabitants offer scientists valuable perspectives on evolution.

SALMON

Despite sporadic resurgences, the Pacific salmon is a species in decline. Just as native peoples of the

Gorge considered the salmon the totem animal of the inland watershed, biologists consider it an indicator species whose well-being reflects the health of the environment. The salmon's decline underscores why the American Rivers Association ranked the Columbia River ecosystem the country's most endangered in 1997.

The Columbia Basin salmon run has consisted of less than a million fish for much of the 1990s. By contrast, an estimated 10–16 million Columbia River salmon were caught by Native Americans annually in the 1800s. During the 1880s, 55 canneries operated on the Columbia fueled by new technologies such as the salmon wheel, a Ferris wheel–like scooping device that extracted salmon from the river in such large numbers that the wheels were banned in the first decades of the 20th century. Thereafter, perhaps the greatest scourge of salmon populations were introduced here: the hydroelectric dam and the hatchery system.

Salmon Hatcheries

The era of modern river management is thought to have begun with the first hatcheries on the Columbia in 1887. The hatcheries took advantage of the salmon's homing instinct. Hatchery managers could extract the roe, fertilize it with milt (salmon sperm), and let the eggs hatch. Once the baby salmon grew to roughly the size of a finger, they could be released, sure to return to the site years later, after migrating as much as several thousand miles. Today, 90 percent of the fish on the Columbia are raised in this way, and some scientists say salmon aquaculture undermines the species' natural vigor. Hatchery naysayers further claim these fish are more prone to disease and less able to handle the manmade obstacle course created on the present-day Columbia.

Chinook salmon

BOB RACE

The Threat from Dams

The advent of large hydroelectric dams in the 1930s introduced a tremendous threat to salmon survival. First, damming slowed the river sufficiently enough to increase the exposure of ocean-bound baby salmon to predation and disease. Nitrogen bubbles created by dam drawdowns suffocate the fish and unscreened turbines chop juveniles to bits, rendering the eight dams on the Columbia/Snake River system in Oregon and Washington a murderer's row. The altered flow of the river has also created higher water temperatures (salmon thrive in colder free-flowing water) and degraded spawning conditions.

While some of these impediments to salmon survival have been mitigated by recent refinements in fish management, other factors make the long-term outlook not so sanguine for Columbia River chinook, chum, and sockeye salmon. (Steelhead, for years considered a trout but recently reclassified as a species of salmon, have also been adversely affected.) These factors include such culprits as overfishing and spawning stream siltation due to logging and cattle grazing in the watershed. The increase in federally protected salmon-eating species such as seals, sea lions, and Caspian terns, along with industrial pollution, have also cut into the river's fish population.

With zealous eyes being cast on the Columbia River hydroelectric power by a growing population, the dams versus salmon debate will not go away.

After decades of steady and dramatic decline, the healthiest returning Columbia River chinook runs here since 1938 took place in spring 2001. Some oceanographers attributed it to a cyclical phenomenon known as the "Pacific oscillation," ocean currents (connected to climatic cycles) causing the upwelling of colder nutrient-rich water. Other scientists point to the release of dam water in previous years to help speed the seaward migration of baby salmon. Less time in the river means less exposure to predation. Whatever the explanation, one thing is for certain: with zealous eyes being cast on the Columbia River hydroelectric power by a growing population, the dams versus salmon debate will not go away.

Conservation Issues

Recent government listings of many Columbia River species as threatened or endangered add to the legal arsenal of save-the-salmon advocates, many of whom call for breaching several hydroelectric dams near the spawning grounds. Opponents brand breaching impractical because of resulting electricity rate increases and disruption of irrigation and commercial barge traffic. Other observers feel that the runs are so damaged that nothing can restore populations to an ecologically significant level. Treaty guarantees of a tribal fishery might have the last word in this controversy. The Treaty of 1855 gave Gorge tribes access to traditional fishing venues and rights to pursue their salmon catch in a "reasonable and accustomed manner." Some contend the depleted runs since the advent of the dams make this impossible (see History, following).

Polls continually reassert the desire of a large majority of Pacific Northwest residents to restore the salmon runs, even if financial and other sacrifices are involved. It's as if the people hold a shared realization echoing the traditional Native American belief—after the salmon, we're next.

Buying Salmon in the Gorge

Columbia River salmon can be bought at a good price directly from Native Americans who are allowed to sell fish from the surviving runs in a special federal program each fall at the dams, Bridge of the Gods, and other heavily trafficked venues. Native fishermen are not subjected to the catch limits of the rest of the population due to 1855 treaty guarantees mandating their right to catch fish in traditional areas such as the Gorge. When there's a healthy spring spawning population, these sales may also take place. Call 888/BUY-1855 for details.

Viewing Salmon Spawning

The spawning phenomenon, despite its decline, can still be enjoyed at the **Bonneville Dam** fish viewing windows and hatchery as well as at **Oxbow Park** (see Portland—Gateway to the Gorge chapter). Even on a diminished scale, it is still a life-affirming spectacle. The best time to view the returning salmon at these venues is during the fall, even though there are also smaller spring runs. During the mid-October spawning festival at Oxbow Park, interpreters are frequently on hand to explain what is known about this archetypal cycle of the Pacific Northwest.

History

FIRST PEOPLES OF THE GORGE

When American explorers Lewis and Clark first came through the Columbia River Gorge in 1804, they found a gathering of the tribes near present-day Wishram, WA and The Dalles, OR whose numbers and variety surpassed any native trading center on the continent. Chinook-speaking natives of the wet western end of the Gorge came to barter with their brothers from the dry east. Artifacts unearthed during archaeological excavations indicate that native presence on both shorelines dates back more than 10,000 years, probably predating the floods that sculpted the present-day contours of the Gorge. In fact, archeological digs indicate that Wishram, WA, and Celilo (near The Dalles) are among the oldest continuously occupied village sites in the 48 states.

During eons of living along the Columbia, it's likely that Gorge natives had contact with visitors from other continents, evidenced by Chinese ceramic pottery shards dating back to 5 B.C. found at the mouth of the river. Explanations for this include theories ranging from Asian nomad hunters crossing the present-day Bering Straits when it was a land-ice bridge at the end of the last Ice Age (between 10,000 and 12,000 years ago) to Asian boat migrations. In addition to shipwrecks of ancient oriental vessels and Asian artifacts found all along the Pacific Coast, correspondences in art, ritual, dialect and dental records point to East meeting West. In later centuries, Lewis and Clark encountered evidence of foreign contact on the Columbia River from such disparate sources as a Chinook tribal chieftain with red hair and Gorge natives with British swords, coins, Hudson's Bay blankets, and other European goods.

The region hosted indigenous peoples from distant regions such as Alaska and the Great Lakes who would come for barter fairs during salmon fishing season. Gambling, races, and potlatches (parties where individuals gave away possessions to gain status) supplemented trade and fishing. This exposure to foreign cultures was reflected in Gorge native dress and the Chinook trade jargon, an overlay of English, Nootka, French, and other tongues in addition to the native Chinook dialect. This lingua franca exerted an influence from Alaska throughout the American West and probably beyond. Certain artifacts suggest trade with natives from as far away as present-day Michigan and the southwestern United States. Not surprisingly, Chinookan currency consisted of shells from Vancouver Island and blankets crafted by the English Hudson's Bay Company rather than indigenous articles.

KENNEWICK MAN

The 1996 discovery of Kennewick Man, the oldest and most complete skeleton ever found in the Northwest, introduced the possibility that Caucasians were present 150 miles upriver from the Gorge 9,300 years ago. Native Americans who claim their people have been here forever take umbrage at this suggestion. They also regard the remains found at Kennewick, WA, as tribal property and their disinterment as grave-robbing. Kennewick Man is currently housed at the Burke Museum on the University of Washington's Seattle campus. The skeleton's dental and bone structures are being analyzed in an attempt to determine Kennewick Man's ethnic origins.

NATIVE AMERICAN DECLINE

It's difficult to find many descendants of the Gorge tribes living in their homeland today. Most were moved to reservations outside the Gorge as a result of treaties enacted in 1855. The flooding of ceremonial fishing sites at Celilo by The Dalles Dam in

1957 also had this effect. The Wascos, for example, a tribe that greeted Lewis and Clark in 1805, currently live at the Warm Springs Reservation in central Oregon. Native acquiescence to the 1855 agreements came after measles, a malaria-like disease, and smallpox epidemics reduced their population to a small fraction of the 13,500 natives counted in the region in 1811. Even before these epidemics, other massive die-offs occurred here in the previous century due to the diseases of civilization contracted from foreign traders at the mouth of the Columbia.

While the arrival of settlers on the Oregon Trail brought about some isolated conflicts with Gorge tribes, far more damaging to the long-term survival of native cultures here was the diminished presence of such regional dietary staples as wapato—a nutritious starchy tuber that grew in the Columbia shallows (killed by accidentally introduced carp)—salmon, and other elements of a rich natural ecosystem.

THE GORGE NATIVE LEGACY

The rich native culture of Gorge tribes can be appreciated today in area museums and in the excellent photo essay and narrative by Chuck Williams, *Bridge of the Gods* (Friends of the Earth, 1981). In 1999, the literature on Gorge natives gained a self-published classic, *Naked Against the Rain,* by Rick Rubin. It can be found in such independent Portland bookstores as Powell's or from the author at 2147 NW Irving, Portland, OR 97210, 503/227-4207.

At the many acclaimed Gorge interpretive centers you'll find artifacts, tapes of oral presentations by descendants, photos, and exhibits articulating a complex and sophisticated culture. Most petroglyphs, pictographs, cemeteries, and other indigenous cultural landmarks have been largely destroyed by construction or buried beneath reservoirs. The Friends of the Columbia River Gorge (see Getting There and Getting Around in the Essentials chapter) occasionally feature jaunts highlighting native heritage sites in a respectful way.

Finally, such events as the Celilo salmon bake and the Native American guides described in the Getting There and Getting Around section of the Essentials chapter present opportunities to reflect on the profound legacy of the first Oregonians.

EARLY EURO-AMERICAN EXPLORERS

Most published accounts credit the discovery of the Columbia River to an American, **Captain Robert Gray.** He crossed over the treacherous bar of the river's estuary (later described by Lewis and Clark as a "seven-shouldered horror") in 1792, claiming the waterway for the United States and naming after his ship, the *Columbia Rediviva,* in the process. His accomplishment would not have been possible without the maps and charts of Spanish mariners who had been plying Pacific waters near the Columbia's mouth for almost 200 years. Gray's 14-mile foray into Columbia waters left him about 100 miles shy of the Columbia River Gorge.

Later that same year, English explorer George Vancouver dispatched **Lt. William Broughton** upstream from present-day Astoria at the river's mouth. He reached an area five miles east of the Sandy and Washougal Rivers. Along the way, he named some of the Cascade Range volcanoes after members of the British naval command (Hood and Rainier). He also threw down the gauntlet for British claims to the region that persisted well into the next century. David Thompson canoed to the confluence of the Columbia and the Snake Rivers in 1811, reinforcing British dominion over the region. Today, westbound travelers on I-84 can gaze upon the area of islands where the HMS *Chatham* crew under Broughton went ashore in the Gorge. A scenic turnout off I-84 (two miles east of the Corbett exit and four miles west of the Bridal Veil exit) at the Viewpoint sign offers this scene annotated by a heritage marker describing the first European incursion into the Gorge.

LEWIS AND CLARK'S EXPEDITION

Alarmed by crown presence here and eager to learn more about the land encompassed in the recently completed Louisiana Purchase and the lands to the west, U.S. President Thomas

Jefferson organized the Lewis and Clark Expedition, which departed St. Louis in 1804. The 31-person Corps of Discovery journeyed 8,000 miles, following the drainages of the Missouri and Columbia Rivers.

What compelled the path along these waterways was the lingering myth of a Northwest Passage— a mythical waterway connecting the Atlantic and Pacific Oceans and a major impetus to sea and land exploration in the Pacific Northwest. While Lewis and Clark failed to find such a waterway, their journey paved the way for the United States to become a two-ocean power.

Lewis and Clark

The explorers also documented previously unknown plant (see the sidebar Lewis and Clark's Botanical Legacy in the Oregon Gorge chapter) and animal species and mapped concentrations of such economically exploitable resources as beaver, salmon, and timber. Their discoveries were chronicled in a journal with such vividness that it still captivates readers today.

The explorers' ability to establish relations with native populations, aided by the presence of the Shoshone Indian woman, **Sacajawea,** contributed greatly to the expedition's success. Her translation and survival skills also aided the Corps of Discovery, who were at times hungry enough to eat their dogs and candles. Sacajawea also purportedly saved the expedition's journals from Columbia River waters after they had fallen out of a canoe. The references in this work to the great gathering of the tribes along the banks of the Columbia and the immensity of the salmon population had important implications for future trading opportunities.

With the approach of The Lewis and Clark Bicentennial (2003–2006), interest in this seminal voyage of discovery mandates special coverage of the expedition in the Columbia River Gorge. The Oregon Gorge chapter of this book features two sidebars aimed at those who intend to walk in these explorers' footsteps. **The Columbia River Gorge in the *Journals of Lewis and Clark*** in the Troutdale section helps readers tour the western Gorge annotated by this classic work. In like measure, **Lewis and Clark's Botanical Legacy,** in The Dalles section, lays out a species-filled trail of discoveries made by the expedition. Site-specific references to time spent by the Corps of Discovery in the region have been also included throughout the book. The Gorge was where expedition members first realized that they were on the last leg of their march to the sea. After reading journal entries describing ocean currents and marine mammals in the middle of the Gorge as well as Natives wearing British military uniforms obtained in trade 200 miles downstream, it's hard to put the book down. At the western portal to the Gorge, the sight of the Sandy River and Mt. Hood told them they had entered the first area in thousands of miles where white men had come before. This topography had been described and mapped by the British Navy, who had charted the course of the Columbia between here and the Pacific in 1792. Thus, the Columbia River Gorge was the first place where the U.S. could be mapped from sea to shining sea.

MISSIONARIES AND OREGON TRAIL EMIGRANTS

During the next several decades, other American and English explorers came here specifically to exploit trading commerce. However, another event had far greater implications for Euro-American presence in the Gorge. When a contingent of tribes from the region came to St. Louis in 1825 to ask explorer William Clark to send emissaries to teach them The Book of Heaven, he responded by dispatching Protestant evangelists to the Northwest. The Gorge's first mission (Methodist) was established in The Dalles in 1838.

BOB RACE

Five years later, missionaries **Marcus and Narcissa Whitman** came with about a thousand people during **The Great Migration,** the first major pioneer influx along the Oregon Trail, a 2,000-mile overland route from the Midwest. When the Whitmans were murdered and their mission on the upper Columbia destroyed in 1847, the federal government felt the settlers needed military protection and established the first army fort between the Gorge and the Rockies at The Dalles in 1850.

The arrival of the military here was immediately followed by the largest incursion of Oregon Trail emigrants since the frontier thoroughfare began around 1840. The majority that came West on the trail in the mid-19th century were drawn by stories that "West of The Cascades, the crops never failed." To Midwestern farmers facing drought, a cholera epidemic and a currency panic resulting in property foreclosures, Oregon's verdant Willamette Valley just west of the Gorge eventually became known as "the land at eden's gate." Traveling 15 miles a day from Missouri, it generally took six months to reach Oregon. During this, the greatest peacetime migration in American history, over 30,000 people died with the majority consigned to unmarked graves. Contrary to popular misconception, a lot more people died from cholera than anything else, including encounters with hostile Indians along the trail.

OREGON TERRITORY

In 1848 Congress established the Oregon Territory, the first formal territory west of the Rockies. The territory included the present states of Washington (Washington became a separate territory in 1853), Oregon, and Idaho, plus parts of Wyoming and Montana. The year before the Whitman massacre, a boundary with British-owned Canada was adjudicated, effectively removing crown presence from the region. To further cement the U.S. claim to the Northwest, The Land Donation Act of 1850 offered 640 free acres to pioneer couples settling in the Oregon Territory. This caused tensions with Gorge tribes. In the mid-19th century, a series of skirmishes resulted in more troops coming here. Despite the growing population and military presence, the road to Oregon was still fraught with danger for the emigrants.

After braving the deserts of the Snake River Plain and the steep passes of the Blue Mountains, the beleaguered Oregon Trail migrants had to choose between two precarious entryways to the fertile Willamette Valley. At first, continuing overland west from The Dalles was complicated by the precipitous grade of the Cascades Range. Wagons simply could not make it up and over the steep Gorge cliffs. The initial solution involved a wild ride downriver on makeshift but expensive rafts to the Great Cascades of the Columbia near present-day Cascade Locks. After loss of life and property suffered by pioneers attempting to shoot the rapids here, a portage route around this hazard became the preferred route west.

The other alternative, the Barlow Trail, also expensive and fraught with danger, became available in 1846. This toll road went south from the Dalles veering west to Oregon City over the lower slopes of Mt. Hood. It was so steep in parts that pioneer wagons had to be hitched to trees to prevent runaways as they were lowered down the mountain. It's still possible today to see rope marks created by these wagons on trees along the Barlow Trail on Laurel Hill off ORE 26 near Government Camp.

Today's Gorge travelers will appreciate heritage markers denoting both Lewis and Clark Trail and Oregon Trail landmarks. This is the only area in the country where both trails come together.

TRANSPORTATION AND INDUSTRIALIZATION

People and commerce have been traveling the Columbia River Gorge for eons in search of resources, markets, or land. The torch of commerce that was passed from Chinook traders to the French voyageurs and English merchants of Fort Vancouver fell to the Oregon Trail settlers in mid-19th century. The demand for Gorge foodstuffs and timber in such population centers as post–Gold Rush California and Portland spurred the development of technologies to get these goods to market. Steamships fueled by Gorge cordwood in the 1850s were eventually supplanted by the iron horse. The region's first tracks were laid for portage trains along the banks of the Gorge's north shoreline to bypass rapids in the 1850s, with the first transcontinental railroad traveling along Oregon's Gorge shoreline in 1883. Soon products such as canned Columbia River salmon, Wasco County wool and grain, and Hood River pears and apples could successfully be marketed nationwide. The advent of the automobile and large-scale container shipping in the next century continued this legacy. In addition to the flow of commerce, the Gorge has played another important role in transportation history.

COLUMBIA RIVER HIGHWAY

Oregon's Columbia River Highway began in 1911 with **Samuel Hill,** a wealthy, eccentric railroad lawyer. His idea gained acolytes in the Portland business community, who were swept up in the fervor stirred by the national Good Roads campaign of the time. This movement supported the construction of paved highways with scenic qualities to foment tourism. In 1909, Hill had constructed the Maryhill Loops in Washington but failed to get that state's legislature to foot the cost of connecting this macadam thoroughfare to a 75-mile Gorge-wide scenic highway. Several years after this false start, the development of automobile tourism at home and abroad created fertile ground for his dreams to take root on the Oregon side of the Gorge.

When the first Model T rolled off Henry Ford's assembly line in 1913, Hill's dream began to take form. Convict and volunteer labor joined European artisans in crews recruited for this revolutionary effort. Timber magnate and hotelier Simon Benson coordinated the project's fiscal management (in addition to buying up a lot of scenic areas to donate as roadside parks) and promotion and mill-owner John Yeon volunteered as roadmaster of the work crews. **Samuel Lancaster,** a visionary Tennessee engineer recruited by Hill, added the artistic inspiration for what came to be known as "a poem in stone."

This was not only the Northwest's first paved public road but one of the defining events in the growth of modern American tourism. Scores of middle-class Portland families in their Model Ts took to the hills above the Columbia on this architecturally aesthetic thoroughfare following the 1915 completion of this highway's first section. After the mileage between Troutdale and The Dalles was completed in 1922, it was dubbed "king of roads" by *The Illustrated London News.* Tourists of the time referred to themselves as "Thoreaus at 29 cents a gallon."

Replete with such ornate flourishes as rock-windowed tunnels and dozens of beautiful bridges (of which no two were identical), this route echoed the source of its designers' inspiration—the mountain roads of Europe. Dry masonry (without mortar) techniques employed by Charlemagne in stone walls built during the 9th century along the Rhine also influenced architecture on the Oregon road. Terraced vineyards and roadside perspectives from Bingen-on-Rhine were so evocative of the Gorge terrain that Hill was moved to announce that the Columbia River Highway would exceed the grandeur of Europe's alpine switchbacks by "highlighting a view on every turn." Lancaster began work in 1913 with the words, "Our first order of business was to find the beauty spots, or those points where the most beautiful things along the line might be seen in the best advantage, and if possible to locate the road in such a way as to reach them." Throughout construction, Lancaster exhorted his crew to minimize environmental impact "so as not to mar what God had put there." To reassure the business community, many of whom were donating land in the Gorge, and state legislators who were voting on construction costs, Hill explained, "We will cash in, year after year, on our crop of scenic beauty without depleting it in any way."

In any case, service stations, roadside rest stops, motor courts (later called "motels"), and resort hotels that catered to the motorized carriage trade developed here, contributing substantially to economic growth within the Gorge. Of the several dozen roadhouses that lined this highway 1915–1960, only a few structures remain today. Plans for a modern freeway built closer to the river were made in 1931 but languished during wartime and the Depression. The call for a river-level highway regained impetus in 1946 however, when cars became too wide to pass one another in the Mosier Tunnels (see the Hood River section of the Oregon Gorge chapter). For a few years, the state used a signal to regulate one-way traffic through the tunnels. Work on the roadbed for the new interstate began a few years later. The completion of the interstate in the 1950s and '60s made Gorge travel faster, but the charm of the earlier era was lost. Today Interstate 84 provides scenic vistas but it's hard to get the big picture at sea level, especially when the speed limit is 65 mph.

Fortunately, the "king of roads" experienced a resurgence in the 1980s. Political activists, volunteers, government agencies, and federal legislation provided the spadework for the reborn Historic Columbia River Highway. Thanks to its inclusion on the National Register of Historic Places (the only road on the list) as well as listings as an All-American Road, National Scenic

Byway, National Heritage Road, and National Historic Landmark, the rebirth and protection of Lancaster's dream are becoming realities.

Plans are afoot to restore most of the route between Troutdale and The Dalles by 2010. Currently, the old highway's Troutdale-to-Ainsworth State Park and Mosier-to-The Dalles segments attract millions of motorists annually. Other sections of the old road are being rebuilt with attention to architectural nuance and potential recreational and interpretive uses. The reconstructed Mosier Twin Tunnels east of Hood River as well as the restored Columbia River Highway sections between Cascade Locks and Eagle Creek and in the Bonneville-to-Tanner Creek corridor exemplify how parts of the historic highway have broken new ground as hiking and biking trails.

HYDROPOWER

The introduction of the car wasn't the only 20th century technological breakthrough here with profound implications for tourism, commerce,

construction on the Columbia River Highway

ecology, and quality of life. Beginning with Bonneville in 1938, the construction of the great dams on the Columbia changed the course of one of the world's mightiest rivers. Some historians believe the concept of damming the Columbia for power dates back to a time when President Herbert Hoover was riding a train through the region during the early years of the Great Depression. The idea of harnessing the river to spin turbines and create electricity might have occurred to this former engineer (who spent most of the summers of his youth in Oregon) but it took the public works programs of his suc-

cessor, Franklin D. Roosevelt, to make it reality. Bonneville and Grand Coulee Dams supplied power for the war effort with regional beneficiaries such as Kaiser shipyards and Boeing. Today, Northwest businesses and residents still benefit from abundant hydropower but at the possible cost of the greatest salmon runs ever known. Besides billions of dollars worth of pollution-free renewable energy at what is usually the lowest cost in the western United States, other Bonneville byproducts include 370-miles of lucrative inland shipping, irrigation water for agriculture, and perfect windsurfing conditions.

Economy

Despite the $200 million (and growing) annual impact of tourism and recreation, agriculture is still the leading source of revenue here. Among the latter, orchard crops are nationally renowned—The Dalles is the country's leading maraschino cherry processor and Hood River the leader in winter pears. Just beyond The Dalles, two skyscraper-sized grain elevators at Biggs Junction mark the 2nd largest grain port in the nation. More evidence of this can be seen from Maryhill Museum, at the eastern extremity of Washington's Gorge, where the view across the river offers a look at the endless wheat fields of Moro and The Dalles.

The aluminum industry, with plants in The Dalles and Goldendale, is the other large private sector employer. These plants had their genesis with Henry Kaiser's World War II shipbuilding factories downriver in the '30s. Just as cheap hydropower from Bonneville Dam helped foster the latter developments, the construction of other hydroelectric dams farther east and north (notably The Dalles Dam in 1957) encouraged the building of aluminum smelters in this area.

Tourism's economic role is best appreciated by such distinctions as Multnomah Falls, continually rated Oregon's single most visited natural attraction (averaging 2.5 million visitors annually), and Hood River, the world's leading des-

© OREGON DEPT. OF TRANSPORTATION

Multnomah Falls is the most visited natural site in Oregon.

tination for windsurfers. Outdoor recreationists in the Gorge can windsurf when the wind comes up with the sun, ski in the afternoon on Mt. Hood, and bike or hike to a picture-perfect viewpoint at sunset. And with the Lewis and Clark Bicentennial, the already flourishing packaged tour and cruise industries should continue to grow.

Essentials

Outdoor Activities

While site-specific recommendations about all outdoor activities are included in the travel chapters, the paragraphs below detail some tips on the most high-profile Gorge activities—hiking, camping, and windsurfing. For biking coverage, see the Getting There and Getting Around section of this chapter as well as specific travel chapters. Aquatic activities other than windsurfing (canoeing, kayaking, rafting, swimming, and more) are also profiled in the travel chapters. The few rock climbing and horseback riding venues offered in the Gorge are noted in site-specific chapters.

The **Subaru Gorge Games,** 541/386-7774, www.gorgegames.com, is headquartered in Hood River, with events held Gorge-wide during the second week of July. This nationally televised event draws competitors from all over the world and includes windsurfing, mountain biking, kayaking, snowboarding, kitesailing, a 10K run, rock-climbing, and other activities. Whether it's kayaking a Class IV rapid on the Klickitat River or inching up a 5.9 climbing route on Beacon Rock, certain events here leave little doubt as to the meaning of the term "extreme sports."

WINDSURFING AND KITEBOARDING

Two decades ago, the sport of windsurfing had most of its serious enthusiasts in San Francisco and Hawaii, with a few

Victorian-era rowers at Beacon Rock, Washington

hardy souls breaking ground for a new mecca in the Gorge. With stunning scenery and predictably stiff winds on a daily basis for much of the year, the sport grew rapidly here and today is synonymous with the region.

Other than the San Francisco Bay Area, there's no other place in the continental U.S. boasting summertime air flows as consistently strong as those in the Columbia River Gorge. Wind currents that can occasionally range 20–40 mph are complemented by water temperatures 55–65°F. Since the great river of the West frequently runs in the opposite direction of summertime air flows, windsurfers can maintain their positions relative to the shore.

If we had to single out one tenet for happy sailing in the Gorge, it would be "never leave wind to find wind." A good way to "catch a blow" is to go where the clouds end and the sun begins. In summer, the cool coastal winds blown by the prevailing westerlies are generally at their strongest at the eastern edge of the Gorge.

As for costs, expect to rent a full rig for $30–40 per day. Many sites on the Oregon side level a $3 day-use fee. A two-day beginner's class at the well-known **Rhonda Smith Windsurfing School,** 541/386-9463, costs $125 including equipment. Rentals here are $25 half day, $30–40

for a full day and $150–200 per week, depending on the equipment and location. Lessons, including equipment, start at $20 per hour. A private launch area and rescue service round out the package. To get there, go to Exit 64 off I-84, then follow the signs to the Hood River Marina.

An easier-to-learn but potentially more risky activity is kiteboarding. Imagine hanging onto a bar attached to an airborne kite that pulls you atop a 5- to 6-foot fiberglass board through the water. Every so often, you take flight to perform aerial maneuvers before being gently lowered back down to the river. Lessons run $55 per hour at **Gorge Animal,** 541/386-5524. Expect to be ready in three or four lessons to ride the winds on your own. A good equipment source is **Sail World,** 800/492-6309, in Hood River. While a training kite can run $100–140, an on-water kite, control bar, lines, and harness costs $1,500–2,000.

HIKING AND CAMPING

You can do your part in protecting a national treasure by observing the land ethic in the Columbia Gorge Scenic Area:

• Stay on the trails so you do not increase the rate of erosion or destroy such fragile vegetation as alpine wildflowers.

Hood River, windsurfing mecca

© BRIAN LITT

- Use established campsites, and avoid digging tent trenches or cutting vegetation.
- Camp 75 steps (200 feet) from water sources.
- As for trash, if you pack it in, pack it out. Leave nothing but footprints.
- Avoid feeding wild animals so you do not inhibit their natural instinct to fend for themselves.

State Parks, National Forest Service, and Private Campgrounds

Despite charging the highest camping fees in the West, Oregon's 224 state parks are still the most heavily used (per state park acre) in the country—a tribute to their excellence. Of Oregon's 20 state park sites in the Gorge, Viento, Ainsworth, Deschutes, and Memaloose State Parks offer overnight camping. Across the river, Washington State Parks has three overnight camping sites at Beacon Rock, Horsethief Lake, and Maryhill, all near leading sightseeing attractions. To help manage the influx, the states have created information phones: in Oregon, dial 800/551-6949; in Washington, call 800/233-0321. A toll-free reservation line, 800/452-5687, serves both states. Peak season (spring and summer) hours are Mon.–Fri. 8 A.M.–8 P.M. Otherwise, winter and fall service hours are 8 A.M.–5 P.M. Reservations may be made up to 11 months in advance. The reservation fee is $6. State park campground entries included in this book will specify fees which vary with state or camping style (RV, tent, hookups).

The Reservations Northwest center is located on the ground floor of the **Oregon Department of Fish and Wildlife,** 2501 SW 1st Ave., Portland. Visitors can get an Oregon hunting or fishing license, or purchase an Oregon state park day-use permit (no camping reservations are accepted in person). There's usually a 14-day limit on overnight stays. At more popular parks like Rooster Rock, there's a $5 day-use fee.

The National Forest Service provides several first-come, first-served Gorge campsites, mostly in Oregon. They are generally less expensive and less elaborate than their state park counterparts. It's worth noting that Eagle Creek (see Cascade Locks in the Oregon Gorge chapter) was the first NFS campground anywhere in the country, established in the 1930s.

Finally, private RV park campsites, such as KOA and others of that ilk, as well as county campgrounds, are mentioned in the travel chapters where appropriate.

Stay in a Fire Lookout

A relatively new and romantic option for campers in the Northwest are out-of-service or out-of-season fire lookouts. This option is most like camping, given such conditions as wood heat, no electricity, and pit toilets. Bring matches, water, a lantern or flashlight, garbage bags, and a first-aid kit. Since lookouts usually sleep four, bring an air mattress if your party exceeds that. Although furnishings may exist, you have to bring your own bedding, and getting to the lookout can involve an uphill hike of several miles. In some cases, snowshoes are required to get to your hideaway. To reserve one of these ultimate rooms with a view, contact the Forest Service ranger districts that maintain these facilities. Rents typically run in the $25–40 range. Weekends are usually booked up well in advance, but weekdays are often available.

About 25 miles south of the Gorge, Five Mile and Flag Point lookouts in the Cascade foothills, c/o Barlow Ranger District, P.O. Box 67, Dufur, OR 970214, 541/276-3814, present convenient opportunities to sample the lifestyle that inspired such Beat-era writers as Gary Snyder and Jack Kerouac. In contrast to the summertime availability of most of their counterparts, the Barlow District lookouts are available November through May for overnight stays. If the skies are clear here, you can see north to Mt. Adams, Mt. St. Helens, and Mt. Rainier, with Mt. Hood to the west.

> *Whether it's kayaking a Class IV rapid on the Klickitat River or inching up an intense climbing route on Beacon Rock, certain events of the Gorge Games leave little doubt as to the meaning of the term "extreme sports."*

ESSENTIALS

ESSENTIALS

Trail Fees

Recently instituted park trail fees—$5 a day or $30 for an annual Northwest Forest Pass per vehicle to park at all national forest trailheads in the Gorge—comes in response to major reductions in timber harvests and cutbacks in federal money. The resulting revenue shortfall has made it hard to keep up trails and campgrounds at a time when the region's population has put more demand on these facilities. Signs in the Gorge indicate which venues charge, but it's always a good idea to contact the Forest Service at central locations such as Skamania Lodge or at Multnomah Falls, where you can also purchase passes. In the humble opinion of this author, if you can afford this book you probably can pay the fee. Nonetheless, in deference to the fact that family budgets sometimes preclude such extras, free "alternative" parking venues will be indicated from time to time.

For information on fees and trail closures in national forests (most national forest trailheads require a $5 day pass for parking), call 541/386-2333 in Oregon and 509/427-2528 in Washington. A few high-use Oregon state parksalso level day-use fees of $3–5. Beginning in 2002, it will cost $2–7 to hike or picnic in Washington state parks. Fees are collected at kiosks or dispensed by machine. They can also be paid in advance at ranger stations, NFS information outlets, and outdoor equipment stores in Portland and Hood River. Consult **www.fs.fed.us/r6/columbia/trail-park.htm** for a complete list of Trail-Park pass outlets.

In contrast to the old fee system, these passes are good all over the Northwest, eliminating the necessity to purchase a separate pass with each entrance to another national forest.

What to Take

Without belaboring commonsense considerations, a few comments are in order regarding outfitting your camping trip as well as the proper apparel for the Gorge's rainforest-to-desert diversity.

To begin, remember that this region places a premium on practical and informal dress. A predilection for the outdoors as well as a lack of pretense explain the relative dearth of ties and haute couture even in somewhat formal urban settings. The wise Gorge-bound visitor travels light, without encumbering a suitcase with much more than could be put in a backpack.

The Old West is still alive and well east of the Cascades. In the Oregon desert regions, hiking boots are like a second skin. This isn't so much tradition as good sense. It's always advisable to wear hiking boots around horses and when walking in areas east of the Cascades. Boots also make sense on the other side of the Cascades for ankle support on steep trails. **Danner boots,** made right in Oregon, are tailored specifically to the state's rainforest, alpine, and desert regions. Get discount prices at the factory outlet, 12722 NE Airport Way, Portland, 503/251-1111. Whatever brand of hiking boot you buy, it's a safe bet that waterproofing will be useful in the Gorge. Quality athletic shoes at bargain prices are available at the **Nike Outlet Store,** 2650 NE Martin Luther King Blvd., Portland, 503/281-5901, and at the **Adidas Outlet Store,** located in the Columbia Gorge Outlet Mall. The latter can be accessed by getting off I-84 at Troutdale's Exit 17 and following the frontage road a quarter-mile to 257th Ave., making a right, then a quick left into the mall.

Another concern throughout the Gorge is keeping cool. Carry water and wear a shade hat in summer. Cowboy hats work exceptionally well and are in vogue in this region. To avoid dehydration, Gatorade, 7-Up, or good old water might be your best recourse; it's even better than salt tablets or beer for restoring evaporated sodium rates because alcohol depletes the body's water by accelerating perspiration and elimination.

In addition to the assault of desert summer temperatures and the effects of direct sun on the Washington Gorge shoreline, be prepared for western Oregon's and Washington's winter mist cutting through your clothes. Despite goose down's superior insulating qualities when dry, it's almost useless when wet because it clumps up and no longer traps air. The synthetic down imitators insulate well and do much better than real down when wet, but have a stiffness that bothers active wearers. Nonetheless, given the pervasiveness of moisture here, coats with Thinsulate and/or synthetic fleece are becoming more popular than down. A good test of the garment's suitability for vigorous movement is to put it on and quickly raise your fist to your shoulder in an arm-flexing motion. In a better-quality parka, you shouldn't feel insulation material restricting motion at your elbow. These days Eddie Bauer, a well-known Northwest outfitter, has married Gore-Tex to down, so you have a waterproof shell covering a warm insulation layer. Recommended down care for diehards is nothing more than throwing the garment in the washing machine with powdered detergent, then drying it with sneakers to beat the pockets of down into shape. Do this twice a year to maintain the loft. Rather than the aforementioned apparel alternatives, most people layer their clothing with polypropylene, wool, and Gore-Tex. Lightweight down vests are always appreciated for their warmth, and they make great pillows. Those camping in the Columbia Gorge during early spring might bring along rain pants.

Lightness, durability, and water-resistance are also the predominant criteria in choosing tents and sleeping bags. Neophyte hikers are reminded that tents and bags should be as compact as possible. These considerations compel the selection of down as the preferable fill material for sleeping bags for many people, even though these bags can be faulted for becoming useless when wet. By contrast, many of the synthetic bags can retain up to 85 percent of your body heat, even when soaked. The best synthetic fill is Quallofil by Du Pont.

Spring, summer, and fall campers in the Gorge are advised to purchase sleeping bags designed for 20° nights. While Gorge evening temperatures seldom get that cold during peak hiking season, it cools down enough at night from June to October that you'll appreciate the protection in a variety of microclimates (e.g., cold desert nights; moist, sunless conditions below the cliffs of Oregon's western Gorge; and alpine dawns). Unlike the U.S. East Coast, daytime heat and humidity seldom persist into the evening hours, even on the most sweltering days. Regardless of the kind of bag you choose, it should have a waterproof cover—especially for spring forays here.

Dome tents are the best choice, given their ease of setup and lightweight construction; waterproof ones go for a little over $120. Probably the best selection in the state is available at the **REI Co-op,** in Portland's Jantzen Beach Mall, 1798 Jantzen Beach Center, Portland 97217, 503/283-1301, just off I-5 near the Columbia River. For equipment rentals and good prices on new equipment it's hard to beat **Oregon Mountain Community,** 60 NW Davis St., Portland, 503/283-1300. All over Portland, a five-store chain of **GI Joe's** outlets provide competitive prices on outdoor equipment and have sale prices that often undercut everyone.

However, the lowest prices of all are available at **Andy and Bax,** 324 SE Grand, Portland, 503/234-7538. Everything from U.S. Army reissue coolers and other G.I. surplus to a wide variety of camping equipment is available here. Specialty items such as Metsker Oregon County maps and white-water guidebooks will also be appreciated by the outdoors enthusiast.

As long as we're on the subject of camping-gear outfitters, it's worth mentioning that Oregon is one of the best places in the world to purchase equipment. Since these purchases tend to run into higher figures wherever you shop, Oregon's comparatively low overhead and lack of sales tax help keep costs down. Look for markdowns on items with "blems" or cosmetic defects, as well as "annex" stores selling the same or closeout items. If you need a high level of sophistication in your gear, chances are you'll find state-of-the-art hardware within the Beaver State.

One item many travelers might have to purchase on-site is fuel for cookstoves, since its transport is prohibited on commercial airlines. White gas is the best, but for flexibility, bring a stove that uses a variety of fuels. Propane rates highly with many campers because of its low cost and compatibility with other camping implements. Nonetheless, its volatility makes it potentially hazardous. Stoves are very important to have on many treks in the western Gorge because of the shortage of dry firewood.

Flashlights or lanterns are essential for comfort and safety. Common sense items like water-purification tablets, sunscreen, a canteen, a Swiss army knife, cooking and eating utensils, freeze-dried food, maps and compasses, plastic bags, and nylon twine will also ensure a comfortable journey. Certain trips will also require mosquito repellent and wooden matches dipped in nail polish or wax (for waterproofing). Finally, a safety kit containing iodine, lip balm or Chapstick, diarrhea medication, aloe vera, aspirin, antibiotics, and bandages or Band-Aids is also a good idea; add eye drops and antihistamines and/or allergy medicine if you're camping near Hood River in June. Fruit pollen in years of heavy rainfall can be murderous on the afflicted, varying in intensity with wind and elevation. Carry some baking soda in a film canister for bee and yellow jacket stings. It helps to pull out the poison, and it can also double as toothpaste in a pinch. The Red Cross recommends first-aid kits containing tweezers, cotton, adhesive-bandage tape, hydrogen peroxide, antiseptic, ipecac syrup (or something to induce vomiting), elastic bandages, scissors, sterile gauze pads, two rolls of gauze, tongue depressors, and a cold compress. Premade kits are available at drugstores if you don't want to put these items together yourself.

Camping and Hiking Information

Below find some more resources for those interested in sleeping under the stars and hitting the trails.

The **Northwest Interpretive Association,** 83 King St., Suite 212, Seattle, WA 98104, 206/553-7958, produces a free catalog of their interpretive publications. Their *Campground Information Guide* is especially recommended.

In northeast Portland the state-sponsored **Nature of The Northwest Information Center,** 800 NE Oregon St., Suite 177, Portland 97232, 503/731-4444, makes available the gamut of publications having to do with Oregon outdoors. Much of this is free thanks to the Departments of Forestry, Agriculture, Wildlife, Tourism, State Parks, and other agencies; U.S. Geological Survey, Forest Service, and BLM maps, as well as reprints of research papers done by various agencies, are on sale also. The popular NFS map, *Trails of the Columbia River Gorge* is available here. Hours are Mon.–Fri. 10 A.M.–5

P.M. Locating this important information resource isn't easy for those unfamiliar with Portland. At the end of an obscure street, the center sits a few blocks due east from the Oregon Convention Center and south of Lloyd Center on the bottom floor of a nine-floor state office building. To get there from I-5 driving north, take Exit 302A (Coliseum/Broadway/Weidler), go right on Weidler, right on Martin Luther King Boulevard, and then left on Oregon Street. Driving south on I-5, take the Coliseum/City Center exit and veer left toward Vancouver. Turn left on Weidler, right on Martin Luther King Boulevard, and then left on Oregon Street.

Oregon Parks and Recreation, 1115 Commercial St. NE, Suite 1, Salem, OR 97301, www.prd.state.or.us, and their Washington counterpart at P.O. Box 42650, Olympia, WA 98504-2650, www.parks.wa.gov, are also places to find information about your trip. Call 800/551-6949 for information on both states.

The **Northwest Recreation Page,** www.halcyon.com/richardc, not only allows you link up with a plethora of other websites, but also provides a listing of outdoor recreation Usenet newsgroups. Here you can tap into the expertise of the Northwest's online community, who seem to be able to answer any question.

The Mazamas, 909 NW 19th Ave., Portland 97209, 503/227-2345, is a hiking and climbing club that has been around for most of this century. Knowledgeable, safety-oriented, and always eager for new members, this outfit has scheduled outings in the Gorge. Difficult Gorge hikes like Dog Mountain and Mt. Defiance are used as training hikes by this group to prepare members for ascents of Mt. Hood.

Friends of the Columbia Gorge, 319 SW Washington St., Suite 301, Portland 97204, 503/241-3762, is an advocacy group that offers guided hikes available to the public the third weekend of June. Guides are usually exceptionally knowledgeable folks who offer both human and natural history

The **Skamania Lodge Forest Service Information Center,** two miles east of the Bridge of the Gods off Hwy. 14 in Stevenson, WA, 509/427-2528, maintains a website with all the answers—www.fs.fed.us/r6/columbia/camp.htm. The Forest Service bookstore and information desk is located just across from the Skamania Lodge front desk.

Mountain bikers and hikers on Northwest trails will appreciate the maps published by the United States Geological Survey (USGS). These can be purchased in bookstores and outdoor stores for about $3 each. A few hints might help first-time users. First, the fine squiggly lines covering the map are called contour lines. When you see them close together, expect steep slopes. Conversely, kinder, gentler terrain is indicated by larger spaces between contour lines. By molding a pipe cleaner in the pattern of a trail, then straightening it out and superimposing it on the mileage scale at the bottom of the map, you can find out the distance you'll be covering.

Another good series of maps for the Gorge is put out by **Green Trails.** Unlike USGS, these maps show trail mileage and campsites. Look for them at outdoor stores and ranger stations. Similarly, DeLorme puts out both an Oregon and Washington *Atlas & Gazeteer* that is unsurpassed in delineating trailheads. It can be purchased in mass market bookstores and outdoor stores. The best all-in-one collection of topo maps is available from **DeLorme Mapping,** P.O. Box 298, Freeport ME 04032.

A four-color, shaded relief map details natural, cultural, scenic, and recreational opportunities in the Columbia River Gorge. It includes major travel routes, recreational sites, and visitor information. Send $3 to Scenic Area Headquarters, 902 Wasco Ave., Hood River 97031, to obtain this resource.

Another Northwest mapmaker, **Raven Maps,** 34 N. Central, Medford, OR 97501, 541/773-1436 or 800/237-0798, is esteemed among the cartographic cognoscenti. Based on USGS maps, these computer-enhanced topographic projections depict vertical relief (by shading) and three-dimensionality. Many of Raven's offerings are large enough to cover a dining room table, with costs in the $15–20 range. All Raven maps are printed in fade-resistant inks on fine-quality 70-pound paper and are also available in vinyl-laminated versions suitable for framing.

FISHING AND HUNTING

If you are interested in fishing and hunting, contact the **Oregon Department of Fish and Wildlife,** 2501 SW 1st Ave., Portland, 503/872-5275 or 800/233-3306. Anglers can dial 800/ASK-FISH to keep up-to-date on Beaver State fishing conditions. Callers with touch-tone phones can choose from a varied menu of recorded information, including data on campgrounds, wheelchair access, and important state regulations. A user-friendly website, www.dfw.state.or.us, is highly recommended.

The most efficient way to get a fishing or hunting license is to use the state computers available in many sporting goods stores. The agent then asks for all the essential information (age, address, etc.) and enters this along with the requests for licenses, tags, and stamps. Your new forms are then issued by the computer. All the necessary documents come out on a single sheet of paper. Tags and stamps that you need to attach to the kill are also issued. The information is kept in the system to facilitate renewal the following year.

Washington Department of Fish and Wildlife, 600 Capitol Way North, Olympia, WA 98501-1091 or 360/902-2200 or 360/696-6211, issues licenses for that state. For freshwater fishing information, call the agency's hotline, 206/976-3200. The travel chapters will pass along site-specific tips for the Gorge's famed steelhead runs as well as other species. Mature winter-run steelhead, a fighting fish coveted by anglers in the Columbia drainage, are found here from November through April. They spawn December through June. Call the **Northwest Steelheaders,** 503/653-4176, for more information.

Fishing Guides

Oregon Guides and Packers, P.O. 673, Springfield 97477, 541/937-3192, publishes a free catalog of outfitter offerings including fishing guides who specialize in catching salmon, steelhead, walleye, and sturgeon on the Columbia and its tributaries.

Accommodations

Overnight lodgings in the Gorge run the gamut from basic bunkhouses to such four-star digs as Skamania Lodge and The Columbia Gorge Hotel. Just outside the Gorge in West Trout-dale, OR, a concentration of chain motels offer dollar value a short drive from spectacular scenery. Some of the latter, however, come at the cost of sleeping in a parking lot by the interstate. Hostel type accommodations are available in Bingen, WA, and Troutdale, OR, for under $25 if you don't mind a bathroom down the hall. State park and national forest campgrounds offer low-cost overnight lodgings in attractive settings. Most Oregon state parks sites usually run around $16–20 a night (less for tent camping). Washington parks charge $10–16. The majority of these have showers. State parks and private RV parks often come with such amenities as firewood, laundromats, and showers. All you need is a tent. However, private RV campgrounds and their expensive Kampgrounds of America (KOA) counterparts sometimes are crowded with people and vehicles, inhibiting the enjoyment of nature—although new **kabin** options can mitigate these problems. Government campgrounds charge less and often feature more aesthetic surroundings.

To understand the other end of the scale, consider the **Columbia Gorge Hotel,** an eight-decades-old palace of poshness that was originally billed as "The Waldorf of the West." As you might expect, peak season prices at this neo-Moorish castle atop a waterfall on a bluff fronting the Columbia River begin at $175. Close to this price range is **Skamania Lodge,** a cedar-and-stone art-filled clifftop lodge with incomparable views of the river. In between these extremes are bed-and-breakfasts as well as motels of all description that do not charge an inordinate amount of money compared to similar accommodations elsewhere in the country in comparable environments.

We chose the majority of restaurant and lodging recommendations in this book mindful of the traveler who would prefer to have some cash

left over at the end of a meal to take advantage of a raft trip or a museum. At the same time, we recognize that one of the most pleasurable ways to get to know a locale is by staying at a place that showcases the kind of scenery, cuisine, and decor that define a regional identity. In the Gorge that might mean dining on Columbia River salmon garnished by local huckleberries or bedding down under a skylight with a view of Mt. Hood. When bed-and-breakfasts reflect what writer Lawrence Durrell calls "spirit of place," high-end lodging listings will occasionally supplant dollar-value orientation.

Finally, a word of warning. With at least several trains passing through each shoreline of the Gorge during hours when most people are in bed, a set of earplugs might be necessary for light sleepers to have a restful night. Noise-prone lodgings and campsites have been noted in the travel chapters that follow.

Bed-and-Breakfasts

If a turn-of-the-century Victorian or an old farm-house doesn't give a bed-and-breakfast an extra measure of warmth, the camaraderie of the guests and the host family usually will. Many B&B guests describe their innkeepers, often filled with travel advice, as like having a private concierge.

Nonetheless, these lodgings are not for everyone. Most bed-and-breakfasts restrict children, pets, and smoking in deference to what are often close quarters. Private baths are also sometimes in short supply. And not everybody feels comfortable talking to strangers over breakfast in the morning.

The included full or continental breakfast, sometimes in bed, offsets any potential intrusions on privacy. Homemade jams and breads as well as a complimentary glass of a local wine for a nightcap might also be included to put more warmth into the welcome. In addition to the listings in this book, a free directory of 350 bed-and-breakfasts covering Oregon and Washington can be procured by calling **Border-to-Border B&B Directory** at 800/841-5448. Their website, www.bbexplorer.com, contains lots of color photos of properties. A more concentrated focus is provided by **Roomfinder,** 541/386-

6767, www.moriah.com/hoodriverbba, a lodging locator service provided by the Gorge's largest B&B association.

Food and Drink

The restaurant scene in the Columbia River Gorge is a microcosm of the entire Pacific Northwest as it captures the different ecosystems west and east of the Cascades as well as the ambience and food philosophies of those regions.

PACIFIC NORTHWEST/ COLUMBIA RIVER GORGE RESTAURANTS: KNOW BEFORE YOU GO

Consider the following practical considerations regarding dining in the establishments covered by this book. First, many restaurants are closed on Monday. Hours at full service restaurants vary, but typically breakfast runs 7–11 A.M., lunch 11:30 A.M.–2 P.M., and dinner 5–9 P.M. Formal dress is seldom seen, even in the Northwest's fanciest eateries. This is especially the case in the Gorge. Reservations are usually a good idea for dinner, however don't be surprised to find they are sometimes only accepted for parties of six or more. Gratuities of 15 percent are customary here.

In addition to locally procured fresh fish, wild game, blackberries, huckleberries, fiddlehead ferns, and mushrooms, diners might enjoy cultivated ingredients such as Walla Walla Sweets (a sweet onion from Washington's Columbia Basin), marionberries (a hybrid blackberry), and hazelnuts (Oregon grows the world's largest).

NORTHWEST CUISINE

The Northwest's abundance of fresh produce, seafood, and other indigenous ingredients prompted America's apostle of haute cuisine, James Beard, to extol the larder provided by the region of his birth. In his autobiography, ***Delights and Prejudices,*** he says that Pacific salmon, Oregon strawberries, Dungeness crab, and other local fare became his standards by which to judge the culinary staples of the world. This horn of plenty

is the basis of a regional cuisine emphasizing fresh natural foods cooked lightly to preserve color, flavor, and texture. Since the Gorge is a transition zone between wet and dry ecosystems, diners here can enjoy game dishes from the Cascade Mountains, produce from local orchards, beef from herds in the eastern Gorge, and such delicacies as Columbia River salmon and sturgeon.

In addition to locally procured fresh fish, wild game, blackberries, huckleberries, fiddlehead ferns, and mushrooms, cultivated ingredients such as Walla Walla Sweets (a sweet onion from Washington's Columbia Basin), marionberries (a larger hybrid blackberry grown only here and in the Willamette Valley), and hazelnuts (Oregon grows the world's largest) might garnish your plate. While the relative youth of this region has not allowed it to develop the signature dishes of a longstanding culinary center like New Orleans, the Northwest pantry has proved adaptable to a variety of cooking styles. The small towns along the Columbia River however, are still, for the most part, characterized by what may be described as greasy spoons without the grease—unpretentious and inexpensive cafés serving simple, wholesome food. The exception is Hood River, where the array of restaurants and culinary sophistication would usually be found only in locales many times larger. Not many towns with populations of 5,000 people boast their own coffee roaster, a fresh pasta company, several wineries, a microbrewery, and orchard products famous around the world. The best

ESSENTIALS

restaurants here would be right at home in a sophisticated urban setting, with the possible differences being more down-home friendliness, lower prices, and a higher probability of produce from a local purveyor. By contrast, east of the bridge connecting Bingen-White Salmon, WA with Hood River you leave the land of brie and chablis to enter a realm where good old American food classics like chicken-fried steak and biscuits and gravy abound.

LIQUOR LAWS, WINE, AND MICROBREWERIES

Note Northwest liquor laws: liquor is sold by the bottle in state liquor stores open Monday through Saturday. Beer and wine are also sold in grocery stores and retail outlets. Liquor is sold by the drink in licensed establishments 7 A.M.–2:30 A.M. The minimum drinking age is 21. Prices tend to be somewhat higher in Washington than in Oregon.

Throughout the Northwest, you'll hear the words "tavern" and "lounge." Taverns sell beer, often cheaply, and are mostly frequented by locals. Hard liquor, beer, wine, and live music characterize the lounges which usually adjoin a hotel or restaurant. In the latter establishments, happy hour prices are usually higher than in taverns (though the bar food is generally better), and when the bartenders pour, they seem to miss the glass. Nonetheless, a picture window on the Columbia or a waterfall can make up for a multitude of sins.

Another related development throughout the Northwest is the popularity of microbreweries and pubs serving their own custom-made beers. Technically, the term "microbrewery" refers to an establishment that sells beer on the premises in limited quantities—less than 20,000 barrels a year. However, this term connotes more than mere quantitative distinctions. Microbrews are handcrafted beers minus preservatives or chemical additives to enhance head or color. Instead of the rice or corn used by the big outfits, the mi-

crobreweries just use barley, malt, hops, yeast, and water. The end result is a more full-bodied, tastier brew with a distinct personality. The trend is so pervasive in Portland that this metropolis touted as "Munich on the Willamette" and "the city that made Milwaukee nervous." The reason the Northwest is awash in gourmet suds owes much to the availability of top-notch ingredients—hops, barley, and clear water. Almost a third of the world's hops is produced here. Add Cascade Mountain water, malt barley from Washington's Palouse and Oregon's Klamath basin, and Hood River-grown yeast cultures and you can figure out why there are more brewpubs per capita in the Northwest than any region in the country. Such Gorge brewpubs as McMenamin's Edgefield in Troutdale and Full Sail in Hood River are covered in detail in this book. In late July or early August in Portland's Tom McCall Waterfront Park, the **Oregon Brewer's Festival** brings together the largest collection of craft suds-makers anywhere. Contact the Portland Oregon Visitors Authority (POVA) (see Portland—Gateway to the Gorge chapter) for details on this low-cost opportunity to sample the pick of the hops.

Oregon and Washington rank just behind California in the production of wine. Oregon has an international reputation for early-ripening grapes from the northwest Willamette Valley (pinot noir, riesling, and chardonnay) and Washington is known for hot-weather grapes that thrive east of the Cascades such as cabernet, merlot, semillon, and syrah, the upcoming variety of the region. Gorge vineyards feature all of the above and then some due to a polyglot of microclimates. Dessert berry wines, zinfandel, and soft, dry, white wines like gewürztraminer and pinot gris exemplify some of the other offerings found here. Whether it's the multiple vintages found at Hood River vineyards and Flerchinger in the Gorge's transitional climate or the hearty reds from Cascade Cliffs in Maryhill, WA farther east, oenophiles will appreciate the Gorge's half-dozen tasting rooms.

Getting There and Getting Around

For most of the previous century, when people went to the Gorge, it usually meant a day trip by car from Portland to Multnomah Falls. This was perhaps the prototype of that venerable American institution, the Sunday drive with the family. While a Portland-to-Multnomah Falls day trip is still popular, the scope of the typical excursion has increased dramatically. Travelers with a historical and cultural bent are joining hikers and bikers to explore the region in-depth. These land excursions are augmented by the emergence of the Columbia River as the fastest growing domestic cruise destination in the 48 states.

In addition to the modes of travel delineated below, consult the Portland—Gateway to the Gorge chapter for information on Gorge-bound trains and buses. The Gorge travel chapters immediately following also have some information on transportation as well as flightseeing and where to rent rafts and other modes of conveyance.

BY CAR

While the Gorge may be traversed by trains, sternwheelers, cruise ships, planes, and on foot, the automobile remains the mode of choice for exploring the Gorge. Both Oregon and Washington are blessed with good roadbeds despite extreme winter conditions. The following paragraphs profile the major east-west Gorge-bound thoroughfares in Oregon and Washington, I-84 and Hwy. 14.

Interstate 84 through the Gorge is the most scenic stretch of interstate in the country. On this river-level drive you pass waterfalls, windsurfers, sagebrush, native fishing platforms, Oregon Trail wagon ruts, and topographic features named by Lewis and Clark. However, you'll share the roadway with enough trucks to lend credence to Portland's status as a freight hauling capital of the West Coast and vehicles loaded with windsurfing and camping equipment. To avoid this traffic, you have the option of several points of entry onto the Historic Columbia River Highway (an extension of U.S. 30). Technically,

you can only open up to 65 mph on sections of I-84. The rest of the roads in the Gorge have a 55 mph maximum speed limit. Note: Speeding fines in Oregon are among the highest in the nation.

The **Evergreen Highway** in Washington (Hwy. 14) was constructed in the 1920s. Originally called the Lewis and Clark Highway, it's slower than I-84 due to a reduced speed limit as well as winding, narrow roadbeds. Nonetheless, it's a scenic drive with high-rise views from Cape Horn 400 feet above the Columbia, the stark beauty of Washington's eastern desert, and the almost surreal sight of snowcapped Mt. Hood backdropping the Oregon shoreline across the river. The easiest access from Portland is by heading east on I-84, then taking the I-205 bridge across the Columbia River to Camas, WA and Hwy. 14.

Obtain statewide road conditions, 24 hours a day, from anywhere in Oregon by calling 503/889-3999; in Washington call 206/434-7277.

Gas is readily available on the Gorge's main routes, but finding it can be a trickier proposition on the more remote eastern side of the Cascades, especially after 5 P.M. Fuel is especially hard to come by in Washington's Klickitat County in the eastern Gorge after you leave Hwy. 14. Oregon's small-town gas stations are disappearing all over the state due to legislation mandating costly replacements of old gas tanks, which are prone to seepage. Another thing to remember is that Oregon is one of the few states that does not have self-service gasoline outlets, one reason why the state has some of the highest gas prices in the country. Other reasons include the gas tax levied to help pay for Oregon's roads and the lack of competition from local franchises. In Washington, the price is often a little lower but you'll pump your own.

Enterprise Rent-A-Car, 800/736-8222, offers special rates that work out better than most of the competition; however, it's contingent upon the return of a vehicle to its point of origin. With many Gorge-bound visitors using Portland as a gateway and point of departure, going down one

ESSENTIALS

state's shoreline and looping back on the other, this nationwide chain is a good choice for travel here. The company's well-maintained vehicles and competitive prices compound their good reputation. Moreover, Enterprise is the only company offering pickup and drop-off service (e.g. they offer a ride to their lot from your hotel and back) from wherever you may be.

If you only have a day to tour the Gorge by car, we suggest a five-hour itinerary looping the Oregon and Washington shorelines. Such a trip might include a visit to Vista House, photo-ops at several waterfalls on the Historic Columbia River Highway, as well as a museum stop (Maryhill Museum or one of the interpretive centers in Stevenson and The Dalles as well as the Bonneville Dam fish-viewing windows/sturgeon hatchery). The travel chapters have everything needed to plan your trip. Another popular one-day excursion from Portland is the Mt. Hood Loop, which goes through the Columbia River Gorge after circumnavigating an 11,235-foot perpetually snow-clad volcano.

If you have to choose one time of year for a Gorge road trip, choose April. Flowers start blooming at low elevations in the eastern Gorge at that time. The bloom accelerates into May (peak time for the best-known venues), working its way westward and into higher elevations during summer. Gorge waterfalls are usually at their peak in April when late rain keeps lower slopes wet to augment snowmelt.

BY BIKE

The prospect of biking Troutdale to The Dalles on the Historic Columbia River Highway by the end of this decade has bicyclists excited. Currently, the several hiker/biker-only sections of this highway, detailed in the chapters to come, are increasing this anticipation.

It's possible to take bikes on Portland's Tri-Met (503/238-RIDE) out to the Gorge, eliminating 17 miles through traffic-filled suburbs. Bike racks on the front of the bus make this easy. Buses 80, 24, and 81 go to Troutdale (the beginning of the Gorge) from Gresham, a town reachable from downtown Portland on bike-friendly Metropolitan Area Express (MAX) light rail. The buses drop you at the Columbia Gorge Outlet Mall just north of the Historic Highway (pedal a quarter-mile south on 257th Avenue and turn left at the stoplight). To get a bike pass, you must watch a video at Tri-Met headquarters (behind Powell's Travel Bookstore in the southeast corner of Pioneer Square), demonstrate that you can lift a bike onto the rack, and pay $5.

Bicyclists seeking the best the Gorge has to offer within a day's ride on a paved surface can take advantage of the first or last sections of the Historic Columbia River Highway using a two-car shuttle. The beauty of these sections of road feed the soul while local interpretive center exhibits sate your curiosity about the history, geology, botany, and local color of the region. Your two-pedal maiden voyage into this realm should begin at Crown Point's Vista House and end about 10 miles later at the Multnomah Falls visitor center. Along the way, a half-dozen waterfalls coming off the huge basalt cliffs let you experience the kind of vistas inadequately enshrined in calendar art and coffee-table books.

Farther east, another bike-and-car shuttle showcases more of the Historic Highway between Hood River and The Dalles. Shortly after leaving Hood River, the reconstructed Mosier Twin Tunnels highlight the beginning of your journey. Access the tunnels from the east end of downtown Hood River where you turn at China Gorge Restaurant at the junction of I-84 and Hwy. 35. The Columbia River Highway sign then guides bicyclists one and a half miles farther east to a parking lot at the beginning of a five-mile, bike-only section of Historic Highway leading through the Twin Tunnels.

The Gorge has become a mountain biking mecca, due to great rides and a pool of riders who take to the trails when windless days on the Columbia make windsurfing impossible. Hood River serves as the center of the scene, given a resident population of windsurfers and proximity to Mt. Hood skiing. Many fat-tire enthusiasts head over to **Mt. Hood SkiBowl** (during summer they run their lifts for mountain bikers) or Surveyor's Ridge and other trails off Hwy. 35. Mountain bikers in search of a guide should contact Hood River's **Gorge Mountain Velo,** 541/337-2222, ext. 275. Wherever you ride in Oregon, you won't have to share mountain bike trails with motorcycles as is sometimes the case in Washington.

BY TRAIL

As the only place where both the Lewis and Clark and Oregon Trails come together, "doing" the Gorge on foot suggests itself. Whole volumes have been devoted to the marvelous trails in the Gorge. This book mostly concentrates on those that combine exceptional scenery and a level of exertion within the scope of a day hike. In addition to short but sweet jaunts such as Wahclella falls and Beacon Rock, more difficult excursions like Dog Mountain will be included for die-hard hikers.

In addition to the level of exertion and scenery, another consideration in picking a trail is exposure to sunlight. For instance, a stiflingly hot summer day is usually more bearable under cliffs and trees in Oregon's western Gorge than conditions encountered near The Dalles or on the Washington Gorge's sunlit south-facing slopes.

For an expert introduction to hiking in the Gorge, we recommend participation in the Gorge Hiking Weekend, a mid-June affair guided by *Friends of the Columbia Gorge,* 522 SW 5th Ave., Suite 820, Portland 97240, 503/241-3762. Contact them for information on this event as well as the **Wildflower Hiking Weekends** held throughout most of the spring. In the Gorge, their field office is located at 416 Oak Street, Hood River.

BY WATER

As a result of the coming Lewis and Clark Bicentennial (and the interest evoked by a PBS special and several recent best-sellers on these explorers) cruising the Columbia is more popular than ever before. Most cruise ship companies embark from Portland to ply the Columbia, taking in the mouth of the river, the Gorge, and the Snake River. In addition to the latter, several lines also cruise the Willamette River or make an ocean voyage up into Canada. Most of these small cruise ships carry 150–180 people and guarantee view rooms. Itineraries range 4–14 nights. Shore excursions might include the coastal cities of Astoria and Cannon Beach, Multnomah Falls, Mt. St. Helens, several dams, the Whitman Mission, Oregon Trail ruts, and the Maryhill Museum or other Gorge exposition halls. Jetboats or Zodiacs on the Snake River, a Columbia

ESSENTIALS

© BRIAN LITT

Horsethief Butte, on the Washington side of the eastern Gorge

tributary, into Hells Canyon are another highlight. These high-end packages are a good dollar value if an all-inclusive several thousand dollars-a-week trip (double occupancy) is within your budget. The ships come well-appointed with gourmet food and ideal sightlines on the shipping locks and dam facilities. Add expert commentary by qualified interpreters and you have a trip to remember. A spring and fall touring season avoids the summer heat east of the Cascades in Hells Canyon.

Cruise West, 800/888-9378, offers a 1,000-mile itinerary with three small cruise ships, departing Portland in April, May, September, and October. This company is part of Alaska Sightseeing–Cruise West, a company started by Chuck West, architect of the highly regarded Holland America–Westours programs in Alaska, in response to client desires for a more intimate group travel experience. Their 80-passenger ship featuring decor evocative of a national park lodge reflects this orientation.

Special Expeditions, 800/762-0003, has become synonymous with quality in cruise travel. Sven Lindblad packages trips with groups small enough to guarantee individualized attention from an expert crew on state-of-the-art craft. In addition to luxury, these cruises offer an in-depth dunk into the human and natural history of the region thanks to staff historians, naturalists, and professors in a 70-passenger vessel.

American West Steamboat, 800/234-1232, is currently the most popular company on the river. Their paddlewheelers generally don't go faster than 10–15 miles an hour, a pace more conducive to appreciating the scenery. In addition, the 163-passenger *Queen of the West* has the most extensive on-board entertainment and longest-running schedule (slated to sail most of the year). With four- and seven-day cruises, you have a choice of cruise products.

The **Columbia Queen,** 800/457-3619, has one of the more ambitious shore excursion schedules of the ships on the river, as well as the shipboard amenities that made its parent company, Delta Queen, famous. These sternwheeler cruises run spring through fall on eight-night, 1,000-mile cruises.

For day trips on a sternwheeler, October through mid-June, call **Sternwheeler Columbia Gorge,** in Cascade Locks, 541/374-8427. Each cruise concentrates on a different aspect of Gorge heritage (Lewis and Clark, Oregon Trail, and more) with brunch/dinner packages on weekends at prices comparable to their Portland offerings (see Portland—Gateway to the Gorge chapter). Old-time pictures of the sternwheelers that plied the Columbia at the turn of the century decorate the ship and excellent commentary enhance the mood set by seeing the river in the kind of vessel that enjoyed its heyday in the late 19th century.

Finally, **Lewis & Clark Columbia River Cruises,** 888/464-1805 or 503/247-3800, specializes in narrated day trips in a high-speed catamaran along the route followed by the Corps of Discovery. Their five-hour **Highlights of The Gorge** itinerary can be enjoyed as a **Champagne Lunch** cruise ($39) or as a **Sunset Dinner** excursion ($54), offering a scenic sweep of the western Gorge up to and including Bonneville Dam. Two other trips are 12-hour affairs including shore excursions by motor coach. **Gorge Extravaganza,** ($62) highlights Lewis and Clark Trail sights and includes a shore excursion into Hood River and the Hood River Valley. **Discovery Day at The Dalles** ($79) focuses on the sights described in the region's most historic city (including excursions to downtown murals, The Gorge Discovery Center, and The Dalles Dam) as well as Lewis & Clark expedition landmarks encountered. Add $10 to all prices June through September. The vessel is equipped with an onboard snack bar and inside seating with huge picture windows complemented by outside viewing decks. The company also offers tours of the lower river to its mouth, the last leg of the Lewis and Clark Trail. Call for the departure dates, May–October; trips depart from the Jantzen Beach Doubletree off I-5 (Exit 307) in Portland.

TOURS

Native American perspectives come courtesy of two well-known guides who grew up with the old traditions. **Ed Edmo,** 503/256-2257, a noted poet who was raised in The Dalles, shares personal memories of tribal life before The Dalles Dam flooded Celilo Falls in 1957, plus other topics germane to an understanding of a native worldview. Indian hunting and gathering practices on the Washington side of the Gorge are explained by **James Selam.** He has written definitive works on the subject based on childhood experiences with tribal salmon fisheries and yearly pilgrimages to Huckleberry Heaven. He shares the latter and other lore on guided excursions as well as around the Flying L's fireplace in the evening. Contact him care of The North Cascades Institute, 2105 Hwy. 20, Sedro-Woolley, WA 98284, 360/856-5700.

You'll get another up close and personal perspective on the region from **Julee's Gorgetours,** 541/506-2897, www.julee@gorgetours.com. Customize your itinerary from a list of 40 interests and activities including Native American culture, berry picking, ice cave visits, kayaking, windsurfing, waterfalls, and geology. Stay at local hotels and bed-and-breakfasts along the way.

Health and Safety

A Word about Safety

While visitors need to be as wary in Portland as in other large urban areas, the Gorge has a negligible incidence of crime, especially those of a life-threatening nature. Rather than armed robbery, "car clouting" at trailheads typifies the kind of crime a traveler might fall prey to here. Every year, dozens of break-ins are reported, so keep all valuables locked in your trunk. Even crowded areas such as the Multnomah Falls parking lot are not exempt from such transgressions, although more likely venues are such isolated parking lots as John Yeon State Park (near the Elowah Falls Trailhead) and Wahclella Falls.

Another potential danger might befall those who stumble upon a marijuana patch (the leading cash crop on the West Coast) planted on national forest land or in county parks. Growers sometimes choose this option to escape surveillance, guarding their crop at gunpoint during the October harvest season and/or booby-trapping it other times of year. This gives picnickers and hikers another reason to stay on established pathways, not to mention avoiding off-trail erosion.

Finally, racial intolerance or discrimination based upon sexual orientation can sometimes be endemic to small-town environments. While the Gorge hasn't traditionally been a hotbed for these sorts of problems, remember that some rural burgs moving east from Portland aren't used to visitors in general.

HEALTH HAZARDS

Hypothermia

Eighty-five percent of hiking-related fatalities are due to hypothermia. This condition occurs when your body loses more heat than can be recovered and shock ensues.

Hikers should be especially alert to such problems west of the Cascades. Here, the damp chilly maritime fronts pose more of a hypothermia threat than the dry continental climate of the eastern gorge because a wet human body loses heat 23 times faster than a dry one. Even runners who neglect to dress in layers in the cold fog characteristic of the area west of the Cascades often contract low-level symptoms during the accelerated cooling-off period following a workout.

The affliction sets in when your core body temperature drops to 95°F or below. One of the first signs is a diminished ability to think and act rationally. Speech can become slurred, and uncontrollable shivering usually takes place. Stumbling, memory lapses, and drowsiness also tend to characterize the afflicted. Unless the body temperature can be raised several degrees by a knowledgeable helper, cardiac arrhythmia and/or cardiac arrest may occur. Getting out of the wind and rain into a dry, warm environment is essential for survival. This might mean placing the victim into a prewarmed sleeping bag, which can be prepared by having a healthy hiker strip and climb into the bag with his or her endangered companion. Ideally, a ground cloth should be used to insulate the sleeping bag from cold surface temperatures. Internal heat can be generated by feeding the victim high-carbohydrate snacks and hot liquids. Placing wrapped heated objects against the victim's body is also a good way to restore body heat. Be careful not to raise body heat too quickly, which could also cause heart problems. If body temperature doesn't drop below 90°F, chances for complete recovery are good; with body temperatures between 80° and 90°F, victims are more likely to suffer some sort of lasting damage. Most victims won't survive a body temperature below 80°F.

Measures you can take to prevent hypothermia include eating a nutritious diet, avoiding overexertion followed by exposure to wet and cold, and dressing warmly in layers of wool and polypropylene. Wool insulates even when wet, and because polypropylene tends to wick moisture away from your skin, it makes a good first layer. Gore-Tex and its counterparts like Helly-Tech or other new "miracle" fabrics make for more comfortable rain gear than nylon because they don't become cumbersome and hot in a steady rain. Finally, wear a hat—more radiated heat leaves from the head than from any other part of the body.

Frostbite

This is not generally a major problem until the combined air and windchill temperature falls below 20°F. Outer appendages like fingers and toes are the most susceptible, with the ears and nose running a close second. Frostbite occurs when blood is redirected out of the limbs to warm vital organs in cold weather, and the exposed parts of the face and peripherals cool very rapidly. Mild frostbite is characterized by extremely pale skin with random splotchiness; in more severe cases, the skin will take on a gray, ashen look and feel numb. At the first signs of suspected frostbite, gently warm the afflicted area. In more aggravated cases, immerse hands and feet in warm water between 108–113°F. Do not massage or risk further skin damage. Warming frostbitten areas against the skin of another person is suitable for less serious frostbite. The

warmth of a campfire cannot help once the skin is discolored. As with hypothermia, it's important to avoid exposing the hands and feet to wind and wetness by dressing properly.

Poison Oak

Neither the best intentions nor knowledge from a lifetime in the woods can spare the Northwest hiker at least one brush with poison oak. In this writer's experience, 90 percent of the afflicted campers knew to look out for the three shiny leaves, but still woke up the next morning looking like a pepperoni pizza.

Since the plant seems to thrive in hardwood forests (particularly in the central Gorge's oak savanna), it's always a good idea to wear long pants, shirts, and other coverings on excursions to this ecosystem. In the fall, poison oak leaves are tinged with red, giving the appearance of Christmas decorations. Unfortunately, this is one gift that keeps on giving long after the holidays. Even when the plant is totally denuded in winter, the toxicity still remains a threat. Whatever the season, fair-skinned people tend to be more prone to severe symptoms. Direct contact is not the only way to get the rash. Someone else's clothing or a pet can transmit the oils; you can even get it by inhaling smoke if the shrub is in a burning pile of brush.

When you know that you've been exposed, try to get your clothes off before the toxic resin permeates your garments. Follow up as soon as possible with a cold bath treated with liberal amounts of baking soda or bleach, or a shower with lots of abrasive soap (Fels Naptha or Boraxo). Conventional wisdom counsels against the use of hot water because it opens up the pores and can aggravate the condition. Nonetheless, there are people who will tell you to apply hot water first to draw out the itch, followed by cold water to seal up the pores. If this doesn't stop the symptoms, cooling the inflamed area with copious applications of aloe vera or calamine lotion, which draws out the contaminants, is another recourse. Clay is also considered effective in expelling the poison. In emergency situations, cortisone cream might kill a poison oak rash but can take lots of healthy cells along with it, too. Some tree-planters build up their immunity by eating poison-oak honey and drinking milk from goats who graze on the weed. Health-food stores now sell a poison oak extract that, if taken over time prior to exposure, is said to mollify the symptoms.

Scientists in Oregon might have come up with the best answer of all. **Tech Laboratories,** P.O. Box 1958, Albany, OR 97321, 541/926-4577, has developed a cleanser to remove toxic plant oils from the skin and a chemical agent to deal with the itch, marketed under the name Technu. All products are sold at Wal-Mart outlets throughout the state (in the Gorge, there's an outlet at Hood River).

Allergies

Even if you come out of the forests unscathed, Willamette Valley and Gorge-bound travelers during springtime might have to confront another pernicious health hazard: perennial allergic rhinitis. With the world's highest volume of grass seed produced south of Portland, allergy-susceptible visitors should expect some sneezing and wheezing as well as itchy eyes during the June–July pollination season. In addition to grass seed, the earlier bloom of various ornamentals and trees throughout western Oregon might occasion such discomfort. Hood River and the adjoining Hood River Valley are the Gorge's number one trouble spots in June, particularly in wet years. Here, the intensity of the symptoms can vary dramatically with elevation. Throughout the Gorge, the ubiquitous presence of alders might also pose a problem for those sensitive to springtime tree pollen. These trees are frequently found in stream-disturbed loamy soils and growing in the wake of Douglas fir clear-cuts. Unlike conifer pollen which is too large and heavy to travel far on wind, tiny alder pollen granules can travel for miles.

As long-term immunotherapy allergy shots are not always practical, antihistamines can be effective as a short-term remedy for those just visiting. Unfortunately, such side effects as depression and sleepiness have been attributed to these drugs. Lately, many doctors have been prescribing Allegra, an asthma medicine, for allergies. This prescription drug (available over the counter in Canada) combats allergic reactions without side effects. Regular chiropractic and acupuncture adjustments have helped some residents build their own natural resistance to the pollens. Many health-food stores offer herbal and homeopathic remedies, but these both usually fall short of the quick-fix relief demanded by travelers. Finally, honey from the area of the offending allergen taken regularly several months prior to the allergy season is often mentioned as a folk remedy.

Beaver Fever

Folk remedies just won't do it for that other hiker headache, beaver fever. Medically known as **giardiasis,** this syndrome afflicts those who drink water contaminated by *Giardia lamblia* parasites. Even water from cold, clear streams can be infested by this microorganism, which is spread throughout the backcountry by beavers, muskrats, livestock, and other hikers. **Boiling water** for 20 minutes is the most common prevention to spare you endless hours as king or queen of the throne during and after your trip. (At higher elevations, it's a good idea to boil water longer than 20 minutes.) Should that prove inconvenient, try better living through chemistry: apply five drops of chlorine, or preferably iodine, to every quart of water and let it sit for a half hour. Also available are water pumps that filter out *Giardia* and other organisms, but these cost $35–140. First-Need Deluxe is a filter/pump device that runs about $70 and offers effectiveness and dollar value. Potable water is also achieved by purification pills like Potable Aqua, iodine-based tablets that cost about a nickel each. However, these chemical approaches are less reliable than boiling. Whatever method you choose, try to avoid major rivers or any creek that runs through a meadow as your source of water.

Bites

Mosquito bites in the Gorge are becoming commonplace. Thanks to a wet climatic regime expected to last two decades if past precedent is any indication, the creation of stagnant pools hospitable to mosquito larvae should create a serious problem for some time to come. Meteorologists claim that the Northwest alternates 20-year cycles of lower rainfall with higher totals; we appear to be several years into the latter. Nowhere, perhaps, was this more apparent than in the small towns of the western Gorge during the summer of 1999. That year, Washington's Skamania County experienced an infestation large enough to make the front pages of the Northwest's largest newspaper, *The Oregonian.* Travelers to the Gorge in previous years probably would not have received enough bites to notice anything out of the ordinary, but that year standing water was increased by cooler than normal summer temperatures and more cloud cover, slowing the rate of evaporation. While repellents abound, only those that contain DEET, a far from benign substance (it "can peel paint, melt nylon, destroy plastic, wreck wood finishes and destroy fishing line," according to *Foghorn Outdoors: Oregon Camping* by Tom Stienstra, Avalon Travel Publishing, Emeryville, CA 2002), generally have success. Cutter is a popular brand. While citronella-based products, natural repellents, are not toxic, they only work for a few hours before a reapplication is necessary Beyond that, just remember that mosquitoes sense human presence from the carbon dioxide we exhale, and, from this author's experience, seem to gravitate to the smell of banana and bright colors. When all is said and done, perhaps government plans to spray afflicted areas with biological agents harmless to humans that prey on mosquito larvae might mitigate this problem.

While **tick** bites have not produced the dreaded symptoms of Lyme disease in the Gorge, the discomfort and the potential for the spread of tick-borne diseases mandate caution in such areas as The Mosier Twin Tunnels and Rowena Crest in Oregon and Horsethief Lake State Park and Catherine Creek in Washington. Ticks tend to prefer the hotter, drier, eastern parts of the Gorge. If one area and season had to be singled out for tick trepidation (along with poison oak precautions), however, it would be springtime in the central Gorge's oak savanna. The chief thing to remember about tick removal is to extract the whole insect from beneath the surface of the skin. Too often, extraction with a lit match (a folk remedy) leaves the head in, causing lingering discomfort and possible infection.

Gorge residents complain about brown **recluse**

spider bites more than visitors passing through because these pests tend to hang out in the family woodpile. As their bite is considered to be more venomous than the black widow, seek medical attention if you are bitten. Although rarely fatal, problems occur because the bite is commonly ignored until symptoms of nausea manifest several days later.

Finally, a word about **rattlesnakes,** which maintian a frequent presence on the lower reaches of Washington's popular Dog Mountain Trail as well as at Oregon's Rowena Plateau. While the incidence of bites is low enough (you have to literally step on or corner a rattlesnake to get bit) to make a snake-bite kit unnecessary for hikers, do exercise caution in hot, dry areas. Remember, too, that dead rattlers are still capable of biting due to a reflex action.

Trail Safety

Finally, any discussion of outdoor safety would not be complete without heeding the advice of the Portland hiking group, the Mazamas. This group advocates hiking in groups of at least three people, so that if one person is incapacitated, it's possible for one of the group to seek help while another stays with the afflicted. Despite the multitude of manicured trails here and proximity to highways and health care, Gorge hiking should not be viewed as a totally benign experience. Every year, people sustain serious or fatal injuries. Trouble spots include the most popular trails, Oregon's Multnomah Falls and Eagle Creek. At each place, rockfalls come down on hikers, such as the Greyhound bus-sized boulders that fell from the top of Multnomah Falls in 1995. At Eagle Creek, a trail with steep dropoffs on one side and a high, overhanging cliff on the other side of a narrow track provide an added element of danger for hikers with metal frame packs. In these instances, it takes concentrated effort to avoid the possibility of being jostled into a disastrous fall, as evidenced by the several serious accidents that have taken place here in some years. Farther up the trail on the Benson Plateau, snow frequently lingers into July, often resulting in obscured trail markers—a factor in the disappearance of a hiker for four days here in 1999.

Information and Services

The **The Columbia River Gorge Visitors Association,** 800/98-GORGE, maintains a website, www.gorge.net, offering listings that run the gamut of Gorge-bound travelers' concerns. Over the phone, the association personnel will also answer your questions about the region.

If you're going to the Gorge with youngsters, a well-done audio tape is *Columbia Gorge Driving Tours,* sold at Powell's Books and the Oregon History Center in Portland—or you can order by calling 503/730-7495. For $15, you get a breezy, informative run-down of history, geology, and local color spiced up with dramatic (sometimes overly so) readings of native legends. The entertaining narration is kept simple enough for kids, but will satisfy older travelers as well. Another tape put out by Friends of the Columbia Gorge is a more complete treatment of the region, but apt to be appreciated only by adults. Buy it at Powell's or by contacting Friends of the Columbia Gorge at 522 SW 5th Ave., Suite 820, Portland 97240, 503/241-3762, www.gorgefriends.org. The latter group also runs hiking and wildflower weekends where experts accompany public tours.

For information on trail and road closures, contact the **Columbia River Gorge Scenic Area,** 902 Wasco Ave., Suite 200, Hood River 97031, 541/386-2333.

Each year, the *Gorge Guide* comes out with news, reviews, and other perspectives on the region. The magazine is an excellent publication to which this book owes a debt of gratitude. Available throughout the Gorge, it can also be purchased at many media outlets in Portland and Vancouver. It is also sometimes distributed free at visitor information centers.

Procure free state highway maps at visitor information centers or get one mailed directly from the Oregon State Tourism Commission, 800/547-7842.

EMERGENCY SERVICES

Throughout the region, dial 911 for medical, police, or fire emergencies. Isolated rural areas often have separate numbers for all three, and these are listed under the Information and Services sections for each part of the book. You can also always be connected with an operator by dialing 0. Most hospitals offer a 24-hour emergency room. The Portland-Vancouver area maintains switchboard referral services as well as hospital-sponsored free advice lines. Remember that medical costs are high here, as in the rest of the U.S.; emergency rooms are the most expensive. Low-cost inoculation and testing for certain infectious diseases is available through the county health departments in major cities.

Information about **trail closures** in the Gorge can be obtained by calling these numbers: in Oregon, 541/386-2333, and in Washington, 509/427-2528.

RECREATION INFORMATION FOR TRAVELERS WITH DISABILITIES

The following numbers will serve outdoor recreationists with disabilities by providing specific information on the many options in Oregon: the **U.S. Forest Service,** 503/872-2750; the **Bureau of Land Management,** 503/375-5646; the **U.S. Fish and Wildlife Department,** 503/231-6214; and the **Oregon Department of Fish and Wildlife,** 503/229-5403.

Region-wide, consult **Access-Able Travel Source,** P.O. Box 1796, Wheat Ridge, CO 80034, 303/232-2979. Their informative website is www.access-able.com.

MEDIA

The Oregonian has gained a bevy of Pulitzers and other awards and has several special sections of interest to the traveler. Terry Richard's Sunday travel column frequently offers tips for the active traveler—be it a hiking trail or news about a natural history museum. In like measure, the Wednesday Science section might have a geology article explaining part of the Gorge's landscape or perhaps the latest research on Columbia River salmon runs. On Friday, Arts and Entertainment outlines a full cultural calendar with news and reviews of movies, plays, concerts, literary readings, gallery openings, and restaurants. Though the focus is on Portland, major Gorge festivals and events are often given space. Gorge lodging listings can be found in the Sunday Travel section. *The Oregonian* is distributed statewide and in western Washington. The editorial content of the paper is mostly middle of the road but can be left-activist on environmental issues. While this last assessment would be challenged by residents of different parts of this politically diverse region, an equal number of letters to the editor from the extreme right and the extreme left each day indicates a measure of balance.

The **Portland Tribune** and **Willamette Week** are both free and have a citywide focus. The *Portland Tribune* has a group of longtime Portland columnists who make this Tuesday and Friday publication a valued voice in the community. *Willamette Week* hits the streets on Wednesday. It contains excellent cultural listings (foodies will especially enjoy the restaurant reviews of Roger Porter) and investigative journalism stories sometimes ignored by the dailies. Its classifieds always feature a few Gorge lodging ads.

The Vancouver Columbian is worth a gander for occasional news and travel articles of interest to Gorge-bound travelers. The Gorge Life section of the weekend edition of the *Hood River News* is another resource for the traveler, given its articles on regional attractions.

Portland dominates the broadcast media of both states in the Gorge, serving far-flung rural communities by means of electronic translators. Public radio on the Washington side of the Gorge comes out of Portland via a White Salmon, WA translator, for example. Similarly, television in Klickitat County on the far eastern periphery of Washington's Gorge is dominated by the Portland media.

MONEY

Although the prices listed for hotels, meals, and attractions were current at press time, they will undoubtedly increase due to inflation. But while the rates are not absolute, they will prove useful in comparing prices between establishments.

In any case, you'll need cash or credit cards to make your transactions in Oregon; foreign currency can be exchanged at most major banks throughout the state. Canadian coins, in particular, are considered by many merchants as the bane of existence, and they will not accept them. Banks also turn up their noses at Canadian silver, because it costs them more in shipping and handling than it's worth. The major exception to this are the Hood River businesses that cater to Canadian windsurfers.

However, the presidents on your dollar bills aren't the only ones smiling, because Oregon is one of three states in the country that has **no sales tax.** Many visitors take advantage of Oregon's generally low prices and lack of sales tax to purchase big-ticket items to take home. On the other hand, expect to pay a "bed" tax for any expense incurred that involves lodging. It usually runs 5–12 percent, depending on the locale.

Be aware that Washington *does* have a state sales tax—6.5 percent—and counties and cities can assess an additional few percentage points on top of this, so the actual rate of tax varies with the location. While not levied in grocery stores, the tax does appy to other forms of exchange and in restaurants.

MEASUREMENTS

The Northwest—like the rest of the U.S.—has been slow to join the world community and adopt the metric system. You may see some exceptions now and then, like a bank sign displaying the temperature in degrees Celsius or perhaps liter-sized containers at the supermarket, but basically Oregon clings to the English system. To aid the traveler not familiar with the English system, we have included a conversion chart in the back of the book.

COMMUNICATIONS
Mail

Most post offices open 7–9 A.M., and close 5–6 P.M. In some of the larger cities, you will find main branches open on Saturday. Sometimes drugstores or card shops have a postal substation open on weekends and holidays when the government operations are closed. If it happens to be Sunday and the post office is closed, you can also get stamps from grocery stores and hotels, with little or no markup. Oregon also has many Federal Express, UPS, and other private shipping companies operating across the state to complement government mail services.

Telephone

Oregon has three area codes: **503, 971,** and **541.** The first two cover the greater Portland metropolitan area including Mt. Hood and the western Columbia River Gorge; the region east of the Bonneville Dam uses the 541 code. For long-distance calls within the state, dial 1 before the correct area code and then the seven-digit telephone number. For directory assistance dial 1, the appropriate area code for the locale you are searching, then 555-1212. For areas served by both 503 and 971 area codes, it is necessary to dial ten digits (area code plus number) for local calls. The 971 prefix has been assigned to newer numbers (necessitated by numbers being used up by the profusion of faxes, computers, cell phones) that would have previously fallen under the 503 area code, making it necessary to differentiate between the two.

On the Washington side of the Gorge, the area code east of the Bonneville Dam is 509. To the west, the prefix is 360, although at press time, it was announced that another area code would be assigned to new numbers there; this will eventually require 10-digit dialing in southwest Washington as well.

ESSENTIALS

The Oregon Gorge

Troutdale and the Historic Highway

Troutdale, where Oregon's western portal of the Columbia River Gorge meets the northern Willamette Valley, has taken advantage of its auspicious location since pioneer days. Even before the town site was established in 1854, the area was an important crossroads en route to hundreds of free acres of tillable paradise—each pioneer's reward for a 2,000-mile walk. To this end, Oregon Trail emigrants either resumed their raft trip down the Columbia here after portaging the white water in the Gorge's midsection, or turned inland (south from the Columbia) at the mouth of the Sandy River. Two heritage markers—one at the main entrance to the Columbia Gorge Factory Stores and one at the Harlow House—detail the town's history as the gateway to the eastern Willamette Valley.

In the next century, oil was discovered, and Troutdale's agricultural bounty gave overland and steamship transport a short-lived high profile here. While incarnations as a railway hub, smelt-fishing mecca, and as the self-proclaimed "celery capital of the world" have also come and gone, this town has plied the Columbia River Highway tourist trade since the second decade of the 20th century. The construction of the Columbia River Highway in 1913 was accompanied by the

west of Hood River

appearance of tea rooms, hot dog and produce stands, and dance halls in town and along the Sandy River. Such ambitions are still evident in downtown Troutdale's four blocks of nouveau pioneer-style storefronts housing galleries and boutiques. The western edge of town is marked by an outlet mall, a cut-rate motel colony, and a popular 38-acre resort and recreation complex, McMenamin's Edgefield. Much of the latter has been completed in the last decade, enabling Troutdale to reclaim some of the Gorge gateway status it temporarily lost after a section of the new freeway bypassed the town in the 1960s. If Troutdale's creature comforts and shopping can wait, drive four miles on I-84 past Troutdale to what Gray Line tour drivers call the "Corbett curves" (Exit 22 off I-84) and more quickly access the prettiest part of the Historic Columbia River Highway between Portland Women's Forum State Park and the waterfalls.

SIGHTS

Troutdale and Historic Highway Access Routes

Travelers interested in delving into the region's history should take Exit 18 heading east on I-84 (the second Troutdale exit) to **Lewis and Clark State Park.** On November 3, 1805, the Pacific-bound explorers described the Sandy River riverbed as "a very bad quicksand." Murky as the mouth of the Sandy might have seemed to Lewis and Clark, the Mt. Hood Glacier runoff that sources this waterway has supplied Portland with some of the purest tap water in the country (from the Bull Run Reservoir near the headwaters of this 102-mile river) for nearly a century.

Besides Lewis and Clark, the Sandy River had other illustrious visitors. A heritage marker just past the Sandy River Bridge a short distance south and east on the Historic Highway describes the Vancouver Expedition's exploration of the Sandy's mouth in 1792 by the first Europeans to visit the Gorge. President Herbert Hoover, who spent much of his boyhood in Oregon, is said to have come to the Sandy to enjoy the now sporadic smelt runs as well as the still thriving steelhead fishery.

Smelt were also important to native peoples. Lewis and Clark referred to them as anchovies, a fish harvested by Indians and used for food, oil, and when dried, as candles. The latter practices were endemic to native cultures between Oregon and Alaska. The smelt's decline in the Sandy is likely a byproduct of the altered ecosystem of the Columbia and its tributaries. Dams and other human activities have changed flow, water temperature, and the makeup of riparian plant and animal species here; siltation and pollution have also been suggested as culprits. Be that as it may, the smelt returned to the river in March 2001.

In town, the turn-of-the-century **Harlow House,** 726 E. Historic Columbia River Hwy., 503/661-2164, deserves mention not only as the home of the Troutdale's founding family, but as the place where a death blow was inflicted on what remained of the Gorge native culture. Along with the trout ponds town father Capt. John Harlow kept here that inspired the town's name, he also had a pond stocked with carp. The latter escaped during an 1880s Sandy River flood and bred enough to destroy the wapato growing in the shallows of the Columbia River throughout most of the Gorge. The wapato, a starchy tuber, along with camas bulbs, was a staple for the Chinook peoples of the region. It is not surprising that after the decimation of this vital food source, the already beleaguered population dwindled to extinction.

Today, the turn-of-the-century white clapboard farmhouse shows off period furniture and other artifacts. It's open weekends Oct.–May 1–4 P.M.; $3 pp. The **Rail Depot Museum,** 473 E. Columbia River Hwy., 503/661-2164, has the same hours, featuring exhibits that go back to the Union Pacific's 1907 establishment of this terminal site. Call for June–September hours at both Troutdale museums.

If you don't take Exit 18 off I-84 heading east from Portland, another way to get on the Highway is to take Exit 17 off the Interstate followed by a right on 257th Avenue. Just past the outlet mall on your left pick up the Historic Highway by heading east (left) at the light and follow the highway through town. A more circuitous but interesting route is to bypass the turn onto the Historic Highway through town and take a left at the next light onto Cherry Park Lane. After a mile make a right turn a quarter mile past the Troutdale post office and travel 1.6 miles down the hill to Stark Street. After a left on Stark, the sight of subdivisions gobbling up orchard country is supplanted by the forested foothills of the Cascades Range and the stone retaining walls built by Historic Highway artisans. While this part of Stark Street was one of the original entries to the old road from Portland, it lost popularity when more direct routes became available with the completion of I-84 in the 1960s. Nonetheless, connoisseurs of the Historic Highway's masonry have always enjoyed this alternate access. The next display of such craftsmanship can be found 10 miles east at the arched railings near Crown Point on the Historic Highway itself.

At the end of Stark Street just before a bridge over the Sandy River, you'll come to the site of the 1912 headquarters of the Portland Auto Club on the east side of the highway. After crossing the bridge you enter the only **National Scenic Area** currently in existence. The 85 miles between here and the Deschutes River (and Washougal and Maryhill on the Washington side) define the scenic area boundaries in Oregon. This jurisdiction was established to balance the rights to property as well as to help establish an economic base for residents of the Gorge's 13 towns by accenting the region's aesthetic, ecological, recreational, cultural, and historical resources (see the "Columbia River Gorge Scenic Area" sidebar in the Introduction chapter). In about a half mile, just before **Dabney State Park** ($3 day-use fee), where there is restrooms, swimming, and prime picnic spots under big old maples, you'll find restored mile marker posts from the old highway. The first one you see is marked 17, reflecting the mileage from Portland on the old route. Because these mileposts no longer apply to the different access routes to the Historic Highway, readers should use the reference system in the sections following.

Whether it's antique and decorative arts stores in Troutdale's downtown or a nearby outlet mall featuring discounted merchandise from such brands as Adidas and Harry and David, this is one town that makes it easy to shop till you drop.

To take back a special souvenir home from the Gorge, visit **Boston Antiques,** 248 E. Historic Columbia River Hwy. (in Troutdale's downtown), 503/492-4462, a store purveying vintage photos and hand-painted postcards portraying the Gorge when steamships and Model Ts were popular modes of conveyance here. Many of the latter show the Columbia River Highway as the "poem in stone" Samuel Lancaster had envisioned. Scenes of waterfalls and rock formations also abound. These bits of vintage Americana sometimes go back as far as 1915, before the Historic Highway was paved.

HISTORIC HIGHWAY—SANDY RIVER BRIDGE (MILE 0) TO MULTNOMAH FALLS (MILE 19)

We've designated the Sandy River bridge as "ground zero" in this book's mile-by-mile delineation of the first section of the Historic Highway. Located a couple of miles west of the Stark Street bridge, the road is most directly accessed by Exit 18 off I-84. After crossing the bridge, the forested foothills of the Sandy River Gorge replace downtown boutiques; the whooshing river and Broughton's Bluff mute the drone of interstate traffic. The next 20 miles traverse historic bridges and stonework, lush orchard country, rainforested slot canyons, more than a half-dozen large waterfalls, and cliffside views of the Columbia River Gorge. The attractions between Corbett and Horsetail Falls make an especially good argument for the Historic Columbia River Highway (the nation's first federally designated scenic highway) being rated by both the American Automobile Association and Rand McNally as one of the top-10 scenic roads in the country.

Roadside Observations

After the highway climbs uphill east out of the Sandy River Gorge, it pulls away from the river and goes through **Springdale** and **Corbett,** where area residents stage an old-fashioned July 4th parade with whimsical homemade floats and classic cars, bake-offs, cakewalks, and spelling bees along with the inevitable fireworks.

For those interested in the most direct route to Historic Highway sightseeing highlights, turn right at Springdale (mile 3.8), and follow Crown Point signs thereafter; two-tenths of a mile later, take a left at the intersection with Hurlbut Road. A food convenience stop is located several miles up the road at the **Corbett Country Market** (mile 7.5), where you can enjoy everything from chicken strips and microwave burritos to locally made jams and smoked salmon. The market also has the only gas pump until Cascades Locks, 13 miles east. During the era of Columbia River steamboats (late 1850s to the 1920s), potatoes were grown here in the bluffs above the Columbia and transported down to Corbett Landing's docks below.

Portland Women's Forum State Park (Mile 8.5)

The view east from Chanticleer Point in Portland Woman's Forum State Park is the first cliffside panorama of the Columbia and its gorge that most travelers experience on the highway. It also graces many thematic postcards and calendar photos. This classic tableau features Crown Point's domed Vista House jutting out on an escarpment about a mile to the east, giving human scale to the cleft in the Cascades 725 feet below. This same perspective on the Columbia (minus the domed observatory) from the now-defunct Chanticleer Hotel in 1913 inspired Sam Hill, Sam Lancaster, John Yeon, and other prominent men to cast the final vote to build the Columbia River Highway.

Behind a barrier on the western side of the Portland Women's Forum parking lot is a short remnant of a 1912 access road that brought Chanticleer Hotel visitors here on a hair-raising ride from the Rooster Rock train station near the shoreline. After a fire destroyed the hotel in 1930, the point was annexed to the holdings of Julius Meier, a prominent Portland department store owner who also became governor of Oregon. Travelers pass his former estate, **Menucha** (Hebrew for "waters of life"), now a retreat center, on the highway west of here. In 1956, the Portland Women's Forum purchased Chanticleer Point and donated it to the state park system six years later. Another notable purchase by the

Women's Forum during this decade includes land bordering waterfalls that had been slated for logging. The state park here was named for the group to honor such activism.

If the highway from Troutdale is too slow or too removed from views of the Columbia, quicker access to Portland Women's Forum State Park and the spectacular Historic Highway views thereafter is provided by Exit 22 (Corbett) off I-84. After passing Corbett Station, a boarded up roadhouse, make a right to climb the hill. You'll follow a steep curvy mile-long rise (not recommended for large RVs or vehicles with trailers) and bear left at the top of the hill in Corbett. You'll have two occasions to veer right off this road, but keep left. The expanses of agricultural land eventually give way to river views beginning with Portland Woman's Forum. This state park also is a prime place to experience the Gorge winds at their gustiest.

If you wish to get even more intimate with the river prior to climbing the hill onto the Historic Highway, take Exit 22 off I-84 for one of the few chances to drive down to the water's edge in this part of the Gorge. Just make a left turn instead of a right as you reach the top of the exit ramp.

From Women's Forum to Multnomah Falls, readers should note mile references carefully, because geographical features and state parks don't have street addresses, making some of them easy to bypass.

Larch Mountain Turnoff (Mile 9.1)

If you veer right at the Y intersection on the road marked Larch Mountain (mile 9.1), you'll go 14 miles to an overlook featuring views of the snowcapped Cascades as well as views of the Columbia all the way west to Portland. There are also picnic tables and trailheads to the Gorge below, with gorgeous bear grass blossoms in June. Later in the year, huckleberries in August and mushrooms after the first rains await foragers. Also of interest are old-growth firs in the area. Despite this botanical bounty and the area's moniker, there's not a larch tree in sight as this species grows east of the Cascades Range. The misnomer is due to old-time loggers referring to noble firs as "larch" trees.

THE COLUMBIA GORGE IN THE
JOURNALS OF LEWIS AND CLARK

The accessibility and scenery of the Columbia River Gorge make it an excellent place to get introduced to *The Journals of Lewis and Clark*. In the course of a day, you can visit all the landmarks noted by the Corps of Discovery during 17 days in the winter of 1805 and 12 days in the spring of 1806. However, using the explorers' own words to add a historical dimension to your sense of place here is sometimes complicated by the vernacular of the times. *Journals* entries frequently contain archaic sentence structure, odd punctuation, and the misspellings typifing such works. The navigation and scientific data that so fascinated Thomas Jefferson can also occasionally make the *Journals* difficult reading.

The following entries are presented shorn of such extraneous detail but with enough historical context to add to your understanding of the expedition in the western Gorge.

The Sandy River

On November 3, 1805, the Corps of Discovery's march to the sea temporarily halted at the mouth of the Sandy River at present-day Lewis and Clark State Park in Troutdale. It was in this approximate location that Meriwether Lewis noted that the river's current threw out "emence quantities of sand and is very shallow." Clark attempted to wade across but "found the bed was a very bad quicksand."

While this incident inspired the name of the Sandy River, there is no quicksand here. The icy water of this Columbia River tributary emanates from a glacier on the west side of Mt. Hood, carrying with it viscous silt and particulate matter. The mudflow triggered by the volcanic eruption here less than a decade before Lewis and Clark's arrival (a time period confirmed by 4–6 inches of carbon-dated volcanic ash) also probably washed mucky debris down into the riverbed, impeding their crossing.

They traveled upstream 1.5 miles on the Sandy before returning to make camp on Diamond Island in the Columbia River, now known as Government Island. Having previously noted the presence of more game and timber for fuel in the western Gorge than east of the Cascades, Lewis and Clark considered this region a "good wintering place" before their eventual choice of Fort Clatsop on the coast. Their arrival in the Gorge's western portal in early November 1805 marked the first time in thousands of miles that the Corps of Discovery were in an area documented by previous explorers (the 1792 Vancouver Expedition). The sighting of Mt. Hood compounded this impression, according to a November 3, 1805 entry in the journal of Sergeant Patrick Gass.

Our commanding officers are of the opinion that it is Mt. Hood discovered by a Lieutenant of Vancoover who was up this river 75 miles.

On the same day, Private Joseph Whitehouse observed that this juncture of the expedition's journey was auspicious for other reasons.

Towards evening we met Several Indians in a canoe who were going up the River. they Signed to us that in two Sleeps we Should See the Ocean vessels and white people.

Heading east on their homeward journey in April 1806 the expedition camped the better part of a week on a "handsome prairie" opposite the Sandy to make some "selestial observations, to examine the Quicksand River and kill some meat."

Several captains had determined from local natives that they bypassed a major Columbia tributary en route to their present location at the western portal of the Gorge. According to the *Journals,* the natives also communicated that the river drained an "open plain of great extent." Accompanied by seven men and an Indian guide, Clark backtracked to explore the lower Willamette River, making landfall in the northern part of present-day Portland. Called the "Multnomah River" by Clark, the discovery of this tributary planted seeds for future exploration and settlement in the Willamette Valley. This valley is 120 miles long and 40–60 miles wide, possessing fertile soil deposited by prehistoric Columbia River floods that took a southerly turn thousands of years ago. Previous to Clark's foray, the explorers had assumed the Sandy River drained the Willamette Valley.

Beacon Rock

This 848-foot core of an ancient volcano first becomes visible to eastbound Historic Highway travelers at Portland Women's Forum State Park. While I-84 motorists also get an especially good perspective on Beacon Rock between Exit 35 (Ainsworth) and Exit 40 (Bonneville Dam), Portland Women's Forum offers a more panoramic view. Looking northeast from the Forum's cliffside aerie, this belljar-shaped mound of basalt appears on the distant Washington shoreline across a 20-mile sweep of river. Beacon Rock's name is commonly thought to have been derived from its visibility. However, the following *Journals* entry implies the rock's weatherbeaten appearance may have been the original inspiration. On October 31, 1805 Clark observed from the perspective of Strawberry Island in the center of the Gorge:

a remarkable high detached rock stands in a bottom on the starboard side near the lower part of this island about 800 feet high and 400 paces around we call the Beaten rock.

Not until the homeward journey in April 1806 did the *Journals* refer to it by its current name. On April 6, Lewis observed that

it is only in the fall of the year when the river is low that the tides are persceptable as high at the beacon rock.

Tidal fluctuations were also observed near Beacon Rock in the fall of the previous year. At that time, the presence of what the *Journals* mistakenly referred to as "sea otters" (in actuality, seals) also gave strong indications that the Pacific was close enough to exert influences on the Gorge's ecosystem.

Multnomah Falls

Other *Journals* landmarks that Historic Highway and I-84 travelers can enjoy are **Mist Falls** and Multnomah Falls, noted but not named in April 1806 entries. Mist Falls is best seen from I-84's Exit 30 turnoff across Benson Lake. This gossamer cascade wafts down a rock face 500 feet high until it's obscured from view by the trees.

On the Columbia River Highway itself, the turnout on the south side of the road at the eastern end of Benson Lake (look for a yellow sign reading 25 mph) lines up well enough with Mist Falls to offer a closer, but not better vantage point. Multnomah Falls can be seen from interstate Exit 31 and the Historic Highway about a mile east of Mist Falls. The superlatives used to describe Multnomah Falls in the following April 9, 1806 *Journals* entry echo the adjectives in guidebooks today.

We passed several beautifull casscades which fell from a great height over the Stupendous rocks which closes the river on both sides nearly, except for a small bottom on the South side in which our hunters were encamped. The most remarkable of these casscades falls about 300 feet perpendicularly over a solid rock into a narrow bottom of the river on the south side. it is a large creek situated about 5 miles above our encampment of the last evening. Several smaller streams fall from a much greater hight, and in their decent become a perfect mist which collecting on the rocks below again become visible and decend a second time in the same manner before they reach the base of the rocks.

Lewis and Clark's *Journals* are almost devoid of reflection on the many dramatic environmental changes the Corps of Discovery experienced here. If the explorers on their way west in 1805 were struck by the contrast of entering the rainforested western Gorge after leaving the semiarid desert a short distance upstream, it is lost in the descriptions of shooting at a California condor, running the rapids on the Columbia River, and buying dogs from the natives for food. Only the following sentence written on October 31, 1805 in the area of Beacon Rock refers to the explorers' reactions to the transition from a continental to a heavily timbered maritime ecosystem.

After being so long accustomed to the dreary nakedness of the country above,

(continued)

THE OREGON GORGE

THE COLUMBIA GORGE IN THE
JOURNALS OF LEWIS AND CLARK (cont'd)

the change is as grateful to the eye as it is useful in supplying us with fuel.

Whatever their feelings about environmental matters, it's clear that one of the first sightings of the Cascades from east of the range signaled to the explorers that they might be approaching the homestretch of their westward journey. On October 19, 1805, Clark had speculated that a snowy Cascades peak on the distant horizon "must be one of the mountains laid down by Vancouver, as Seen from the mouth of the Columbia River."

Two centuries after Lewis and Clark, the flow of the river has been altered, the air is occasionally clouded by smog, and the sleep of riverside campers is sometimes disturbed by train whistles and the roar of motorized vehicles. And while windsurfers, rafters, and kayakers perform impressive stunts on the Columbia and its tributaries, there will never be anything to equal the sight of expedition members navigating Class V rapids near The Dalles in a dugout canoe before hundreds of amazed native onlookers. Nevertheless, the dramatic topography the explorers described in *The Journals of Lewis and Clark* as well as accounts of their own undaunted courage remain to inspire modern-day Gorge travelers.

To enjoy one of Oregon's classic sunset experiences, head to the northeast corner of the Larch Mountain parking lot around sunset and follow a gently rolling quarter-mile paved path through forests of old-growth noble fir. The trail's last 100 yards involve a steep climb up to an elevated outcropping—**Sherrard Point,** one of the country's preeminent alpine views. To the east, across miles of treetops, is Mt. Hood. To the south is Mt. Jefferson's symmetrical cone. To the north, you can see Mounts St. Helens, Rainier, and Adams. Also to the east, the Columbia River burns with a reddish glow as the sun sets. With nightfall, the lights of Portland become accentuated in the darkness.

The full moon rising over Mt. Hood is also spectacular from this vantage point. However, keep in mind that for several months in winter, the road to the Sherrard Point trailhead is sometimes blocked four miles away due to concern over snowy, icy conditions in the sloping parking lot. Call 541/386-2333 for updates.

An ambitious hike here involving a car shuttle between trailheads lets you trek from Larch Mountain down to Multnomah Falls Lodge. The trail drops 4,000 feet in 6.8 miles. To reach the descent route from Larch Mountain viewpoint, retrace your steps along the path back toward the parking lot. At about halfway, veer right up the spur trail that crests on a hill. From this hill-top head west a short distance toward a picnic area where the trail down to the Gorge begins.

After visiting Larch Mountain and returning to the turnoff onto the Historic Highway, the pick-your-own blueberry farm near the junction makes a good summertime snacking stop.

Crown Point and Vista House (Mile 9.9)

Driving the interstate, you might notice the distinctive outline of an octagonal structure on a high bluff in the western Gorge. This is the **Vista House Visitor Center at Crown Point** (mile 9.9), 733 feet above the Columbia. Construction began on the center in 1916 when the Columbia River Highway was formally dedicated. The occasion was marked by Woodrow Wilson touching a button in the White House, electronically unfurling the U.S. flag at the flat circular dirt area that was to become the visitor center. In deference to Prohibition, the event was toasted with loganberry juice as black sedans chugged along the highway to just east of Eagle Creek, the highway's easternmost spur until the 1922 completion of the entire route to The Dalles.

Vista House was completed two years after work began on it. The outside observation deck up the steps from the main rotunda showcases 30 miles of the Columbia River Gorge. Samuel Lancaster is paid homage with a plaque outside Vista House aptly describing his route as possessed of "poetry and drama." Photos of the various stages of the road's construction are displayed in the main rotunda, as are wildflower cuttings of the region's endemic plants. Downstairs you'll find the visitor center's bookshop and wallboard of printed materials about the Gorge, both past and present. Vista House hours are 9 A.M.–6 P.M. daily, April–October. Upstairs, the information desk is staffed by friendly and knowledgeable volunteer Friends of Vista House, 503/695-2230, www .vistahouse.com.

Predating the visitor center was the **Crown Point Chalet** (1915–1927) where such luminaries as Charlie Chaplin and Henry Ford spent the night. Crown Point was originally called Thor's Crown by Edgar Lazarus, architect of Vista House. This promontory began as a basalt flow between 14 and 25 million years ago when lava filled a canyon of the ancestral Columbia River.

Figure Eight Loops

The highway between Crown Point and Latourell Falls drops 600 feet in elevation in several miles; the vertical grade of the roadbed was reduced by a series of figure eight loops. As you wend your way downhill from Vista House, it becomes apparent that Lancaster softened the grade of the road here by means of switchbacks. With a grade never exceeding 5 percent and a curve radius of not less than 100 feet, this section presents little problem for modern vehicles, but it challenged period cars and trucks during the highway's first decades. During construction, Scottish stonecutters and Italian masons sometimes hung suspended on ropes, singing songs from their native lands while they worked on the precipitous, circuitous roadbed.

Latourell Falls (Mile 12)

Latourell Falls is the first of a half-dozen roadside waterfalls that can be seen by motorists. When the highway was built, special care was taken that the bridge crossing Latourell Creek provided a good view of the falls. Nonetheless, be sure to take the paved, 150-yard trail from the parking lot to base of this 249-foot cataract. Here, the shade and cooling spray create a microclimate for fleabane, a delicate bluish member of the aster family, and other flowers normally common to alpine biomes. The filmy tendrils of water against the columnar basalt formations on the cliffs make Latourell a favorite with photographers. Foragers appreciate maidenhair fern and thimbleberries, but hopefully not enough to ever denude the slope.

Another trailhead begins in the middle of the

THE OREGON GORGE

Vista House

© WEISTER CO.

parking lot and climbs around and above the falls, though bushes obscure the overhang from which the water descends when you're looking down from the top. You'll probably be more inclined to stop after 50 yards and take in the distant perspective of Latourell from across the canyon. Latourell Creek flows from the falls underneath the highway bridge toward Guy Talbot State Park with picnic tables shaded by an ancient forest.

Close by is the town of Latourell, the erstwhile social hub for loggers and Joseph Latourell's mill workers who would kick up their heels at the community dance hall during the 1880s. By the turn of the century, saloons, a house of negotiable affection, and a billiard hall were also serving sternwheeler and train passengers. In 1915, Latourell Villa carried on the tradition, serving lunches, dinner, and locally distilled spirits. Tourism here grew with the highway and the town also prospered during the heyday of postwar Oregon's resource-based economy. The decline of lumber and fishing, along with the coming of I-84, brought about Latourell's current incarnation as a peaceful small town with turn-of-the-century structures. You can drive into this bucolic postcard from the past by turning left (north) a quarter mile west of the ornate highway bridge leading to Latourell Falls parking lot.

Shepperd's Dell (Mile 13.3)

Shepperd's Dell is named for a settler who retreated here for spiritual renewal because of the lack of good roads to a nearby church. This lush forested canyon cut by a waterfall is one of the visual highlights of the Gorge, despite the fact that little of this splendor is apparent from the road. An 80-yard, paved sloping walkway descends from a bridge (and the parking lot east of it) with intricate architecture; to best appreciate it, glance over your shoulder. Chances are, however, your gaze will be riveted on Shepperd's Dell Fall coursing down out of the forest to plummet sharply over a precipice. This cascade emanates from tiny Young Creek, which comes into focus at trail's end.

Some historians speculate that Lewis and Clark's journals made reference to the area between Shepperd's Dell and Rooster Rock in April 4 and April 6, 1806 entries describing the Corps of Discovery's hunting grounds.

Bishop's Cap (Mile 13.4)

Bishop's Cap embodies the highway engineering art of Sam Lancaster. Here, the base of a basalt outcropping was undercut as little as possible to accommodate traffic. Locals call this altered formation "mushroom rock" since it looks

Latourell Bridge

like a stem connecting to a mushroom cap. The same motif is repeated around the bend. More highway artisanship is evident here in the dry masonry walls and stone guard rails.

Bridal Veil Falls State Park (Mile 14)

Another legacy from the past, the 1926-era Bridal Veil Lodge, lies across from the state park. This establishment, along with the Columbia Gorge Hotel west of Hood River, are the only operating lodgings from the heyday of the Columbia River Highway. See the Accommodations section under Practicalities in this chapter for more information.

Across from Bridal Veil Lodge, the falls for which the state park is named are accessed by a trailhead at the east end of the parking lot. A short two-thirds of a mile round-trip hike takes you to the observation platform at the base of this gushing bi-level cascade.

In addition to tree-shaded picnic tables and bathrooms that are open all year, the park features the **largest camas patch** in the Columbia River Gorge. Camas, together with the wapato, were the leading Native American food staples. If you're here in April, just look for patches of blue along the short **Overlook Trail,** which is about 20 yards west of the Bridal Veil Falls trailhead. The camas bulb looks like an onion and tastes very sweet after it is slowly baked. Please leave the camas here alone, out of respect for a traditional food source as well as for your own safety. Camas with white flowers are poisonous, a fact that is not always established when the bulb is being harvested.

Following Overlook Trail leads you to the **Pillars of Hercules,** a pair of giant basalt monoliths below the railing backdropped by I-84 and the Columbia River. These formations are also called Spilyai's children, after the Native American coyote demi-god. According to legend, Spilyai transformed his wife into Latourell Falls and his children into these volcanic formations to prevent them from leaving him.

Bridal Veil Falls State Park is also the trailhead for the 33.5-mile **Gorge Trail 400.** Between here and Wyeth, this largely level trail takes in the Gorge's highest waterfalls as well as newly opened sections of the Historic Columbia River Highway that are closed to vehicular traffic.

© ALBERT BARNES/MARYHILL MUSEUM OF ART

Shepperd's Dell Bridge, on the Columbia River Highway

Bridal Veil Post Office

The Bridal Veil Falls area is where industrial logging began in the Gorge. A town was named for the Bridal Veil Lumber Company, one of several in the area. With implements like the "misery whip" (the two-man crosscut saw) and horse teams for transporting fallen logs over steep slopes, the hardiness of early timber workers was the stuff of legend. Eventually, a log flume was built that brought Douglas fir, hemlock, noble fir, and cedar down from Larch Mountain first to a paper mill, then to a sawmill. The nearby mill town of Palmer grew up in the 1880s and thrived well into the next century.

In 1940, several hundred people lived in the Bridal Veil area, thanks largely to the timber economy. A fire touched off by a spark from a train caused a population decline two years later. However, the mill's legacy extended four more decades providing lumber for Hood River's fruit boxes and Kraft cheese boxes as well as construction materials for the postwar housing boom.

While this era is no more, the Bridal Veil Post Office shack (97010), the country's second smallest, still survives. To reach it, drive down the hill from the state park and make a left turn heading west, bypassing the freeway entrance ramp (if

THE OREGON GORGE

you're heading east from Portland on I-84 look for Exit 28). The post office sits on a bluff overlooking I-84 and the Columbia River; the building has also enjoyed incarnations as a first-aid station, a saw filer's workshop, and a rock collector's storage shed. The original post office had been located close by in a general store near the railroad tracks until 1942. Reportedly, more than 80,000 people have been coming here yearly over the last decade to send out mail. Given the remoteness of this postal station, it's a safe bet that many visit solely to imprint their letters and wedding invitations with Bridal Veil's unique and romantic postmark. Visitors also enjoy coming here to gab with the locals and pick up travel tips. It's open Mon.–Sat. 8 A.M.–2 P.M.

Wahkeena Falls (Mile 18.4)

The name means "most beautiful," and this 242-foot series of cascades that descend in staircase fashion to the parking lot is certainly a contender. To the right of the small footbridge abutting the road is a trailhead to upper Wahkeenah Falls. Follow this largely paved trail to a bench just beyond the falls that affords views of both upper and lower cascades. Higher up enjoy panoramic vistas of the Columbia River and Gorge and the ridgeline pathway connecting Wahkeenah to Multnomah. This trail is especially striking in October, when the cottonwoods and the bigleaf and vine maples sport colorful fall foliage. A picnic area lies north of the Historic Highway across from the falls.

Note: At this writing, the wooden staircase to Perdition Trail, a spur trail to high elevations, had not been replaced after the fires of October 1991 and the mudslides that followed.

Multnomah Falls (Mile 19)

This 620-foot high waterfall is among the most beautiful in the country, as well as the nation's second highest continuously running waterfall. You can get here from I-84 by tunnel access from the parking area or by following the Historic Highway eastbound from Exit 28 or westbound from Exit 35. The short-but-steep trail to the bridge should be attempted by anyone capable of a small amount of exertion. Here you can bathe in the

© ALBERT BARNES/MARYHILL MUSEUM OF ART

Multnomah Falls and bridges, on the Columbia River Highway

cool mists of the upper falls and appreciate the power of Multnomah's billowy flumes. The more intrepid can reach the top of the falls and beyond, but the view from the parking lot is also satisfying. Placards detailing forest canopies and their understories at different elevations, and other aspects of the ecosystem, are on display the first 100 yards of the trail. On the way up keep an eye out for such indigenous species as the Larch Mountain salamander and Howell's daisy. If you hear a whistle at higher elevations, it might be a pika.

Look too for the image of an Indian maiden's face on the rock behind the falls. Legend (disavowed by Native American sources) has it that she threw herself over the falls as a sacrifice to head off an epidemic. Now, when the breeze blows through the water, a silvery stream separates from the upper falls, framing the maiden's form as a token of the spirits' acceptance of her gesture.

While some of the falls in the surrounding area emanate from creeks fed by melting snows on Larch Mountain, Multnomah is primarily spring-fed, enabling it to run year-round. Over two million visitors yearly make Multnomah

Falls the most visited natural attraction in the state. It attained this status even before the construction of the Columbia River Highway thanks to the late 19th-century steamboat excursions of Oregon Steamship and Navigation Company. The name Multnomah is of Chinookan origin and is thought to have originally been used as a Sauvie Island tribal name. It first surfaced in print in the *Journals of Lewis and Clark,* who used this term to refer to the Willamette River. In 1915, Simon Benson bought much of the area around Multnomah and Wahkeenah Falls from the Union Pacific railroad and donated it to Portland City Parks. Today it is administered by the U.S. Forest Service.

The falls area features an outdoor snack bar as well as **Multnomah Falls Lodge Restaurant,** 503/695-2376. A magnificent structure, the lodge was built eight decades ago by the city of Portland and is operated today by a private concessionaire under the supervision of the U.S. Forest Service. The lodge architect was A.E. Doyle, whose handiwork can also be admired at the central branch of the Portland Public Library.

OUTDOOR RECREATION

Hikes

Wonderful hikes abound here. In addition to those described below, we recommend the U.S Forest Service map, *Short Hiking Loops Near Multnomah Falls,* available free at the Multnomah Falls Visitor Center. Particularly recommended is the complex of cascades accessible between Horsetail Falls and upper Oneonta Creek.

Up from the Ashes—Angel's Rest Hike

In early October 1991, massive fires engulfed portions of the Mt. Hood National Forest off the Historic Highway. At the time, it was feared that massive erosion from the devastation of the trees and the understory would spell the end of the network of trails in and around the route of the waterfalls. But as you will see, this cloud had a silver lining.

For a good perspective on the fire as well as a great view of the Gorge, Angel's Rest Trail #415 is recommended. To get there off I-84 take east-

bound Exit 28 and follow the exit road a quarter mile to its junction with the Historic Highway. At this point, hang a sharp right as if you were going to head up the hill (west) toward Crown Point, but pull over into the parking area on the north side of the highway instead. The trailhead is on the south side of the road. The steep, 2.3-mile path to the top of this rocky outcropping gains 1,600 feet and takes you from an unburned forest through vigorous new brush growth beneath live evergreens with singed bark. The latter gives way to charred conifers as you near the summit. Scientists hope these snags and new openings in the forest can breed more biodiversity in the ecosystem. At any rate, the lack of foliage on the branches of burnt trees has opened new vistas of the Columbia Gorge below.

From the top, enjoy a balcony seat overlooking a large swathe of the Columbia River Gorge. Late October foliage highlights the Washington Cascades across the river and clear winter days show off snowcapped peaks backdropping the northeast Gorge. On the return trip, the waters of 117-foot Coopey Falls, about a half-mile from the parking lot, let footsore hikers cool their heels.

The Wahkeena-Multnomah Loop

Spanning about five miles with panoramic river views, this hike offers perspectives on four waterfalls and ancient forests. Though the first mile of the trail is very steep, it is easily negotiable thereafter.

To get to Wahkeena Falls, drive I-84 to Exit 28. Several miles east of this exit you'll come to the Wahkeena Falls parking area and trailhead. If you take the trail to the right of the bridge over the Wahkeena Falls runoff stream (a few steps from the parking area), you'll begin a steep climb up a paved walkway. In about a quarter-mile you'll reach an overlook between upper and lower Wahkeena Falls. The pavement ends shortly thereafter but the steep ascent continues another .3 miles to Fairy Falls, so named for its ethereal quality.

Once you get past the first 1.5 miles of this trail's initial steep ascent, the rest of the route is of moderate difficulty. As you begin your descent, you might become confused by a lack of signs at the junction of Trail #420 and the Larch

Mountain Trail. Hang a sharp left on #441 to head west and down along Multnomah Creek. At this point, you have hiked several miles. At the rear of this gorge is pretty **Ecola Falls.** Several other cascades can be seen along the route. When you hit the blacktopped section of #441, you can either hang a left to enjoy views from the top of the falls a short distance away or make a direct ascent. In any case, at the end of the hike, we recommend dinner at the Multnomah Falls Lodge Restaurant. After dinner, hike back on trail #442 above the Historic Highway to the Wahkeena Falls parking area.

The USDA Forest Service Scenic Area Office has good trail maps of the Gorge. Their office is in Hood River; call 541/308-1700. Or try the Multnomah Falls Lodge Forest Service Information Center, which offers a free map.

Horsetail Falls and Triple Falls

Several miles past Multnomah Falls and just east of Oneonta Gorge is a hike custom-made for waterfall lovers. This several-mile excursion starts at a spectral 176-foot plume, ascends to a basalt overhang where you can walk behind a waterfall, and ends up at a three-pronged cascade plunging 120 feet into a scenic canyon. The trail begins next to the pool of stunning Horsetail Falls by a big wooden sign depicting the trail map. The trailhead sits 5.7 miles past Exit 28 and 1.4 miles west of Exit 35.

Hikers with limited time will enjoy the 1.5-mile round-trip to 80-foot **Ponytail Falls** which can be viewed from a cirque behind it. A few old growth trees also highlight the route. A nearly six-mile round-trip to Triple Falls from Horsetail Falls (taking in Ponytail Falls) will take several hours. The elevated view of water at Triple Falls descending in a pitchfork pattern is such a highlight, however, that you might want to factor in more time for repose. It's possible to go to Triple Falls directly via a trailhead off the highway a half-mile west of Horsetail Falls; this hike is a round-trip of less than four miles.

Elowah Falls/McCord Creek Trails

To avoid the crowds while taking in spectacularly varied Gorge landscapes, try Elowah Falls/Upper McCord Creek trails, also the location of the northwest's oldest pulp mill.

From Portland, take I-84 five miles past Multnomah Falls east to Exit 35 (Ainsworth State Park). As you come off the access road you'll have a choice of left turns. Take the frontage road with signs for Dodson. (Dodson may also be accessed via the Historic Highway five miles east of Multnomah Falls.) Drive about two miles to the small parking lot of John Yeon State Park, named for one of the major benefactors of the Columbia River Highway. In the western corner of the lot is the trailhead. Follow it a half mile up the hill. When you reach a junction of two trails, turn right for Upper McCord Creek and left for Elowah Falls.

The 1.1-mile Upper McCord Creek Trail leads to a mossy glade framing a creek at the top of a waterfall just under a mile from the junction. En route, the trail narrows to a ledge blasted out of a cliff. From behind a railing, gaze hundreds of feet down at the Columbia in the foreground of 12,306-foot Mt. Adams. Across the gully, layered basalt strata indicate successive lava flows. This is a good place to look for osprey riding the thermals before they dive down to the Columbia for a fish. The trail is also one of the better places to see endemic wildflowers. The trail continues to a view of dual cascades descending the rock face. These are the feeder streams of Elowah Falls. A short while later, recline on the shady banks of Upper McCord Creek where a babbling brook makes the drone of the interstate seem worlds away.

Retrace your steps to where the trail forks and descend a half mile from the junction to Elowah Falls. This several-hundred-foot-high feathery cascade is set in a steep rock amphitheater amid hues of green that conjure the verdant lushness of Hawaii. Elowah Falls was chosen to grace the cover of *Oregon III,* a famous coffee-table book of Ray Atkeson photos (Portland: Graphic Arts, 1983).

Day-trippers interested in accessing I-84 westbound back to Portland may do so in the nearby town of Warrendale, the sight of 19th-century salmon wheels and canneries.

Other Recreation

Swimming at **Glen Otto Park** on the Sandy River on the west side of the Sandy River Bridge can be precarious due to cold water and swift currents. In the last decade, more than a dozen drownings have occurred in the glacial water (below 50° in May) here, where currents attain 11 mph in spring. Look for lifeguards here in late spring through summer before diving in. The city government is contemplating requiring swimmers to wear lifejackets. You can borrow one from Jack's Snack and Tackle. They mostly fit infants and children up to 90 pounds.

Swimming is safe at historic and scenic **Rooster Rock State Park,** Exit 25 off of I-84 near Troutdale. A $3 parking charge is levied on each car. West of the parking area you'll see the monolith for which the park is named. According to some sources, Lewis and Clark labeled the cucumber-shaped promontory on November 2, 1805. Geologists theorize that Rooster Rock is a portion of the lava flow that created Crown Point which then broke off and slid down to the canyon floor. In the late 19th and early 20th centuries, steamers would deposit tourists here as well as cordwood for fuel and lumber from the Northwest's oldest commercial timber companies. Today, playing fields and a gazebo front a sandy beach on the banks of the Columbia here. The water in the roped-in swimming area is shallow but refreshing.

A mile or so east is one of the only **nude beaches** officially sanctioned by the state (the other one, near downtown Portland, is Collins Beach on Sauvie Island). Scenes from the 1994 movie *Maverick* starring Mel Gibson, Jody Foster, and James Garner were shot near here. Picnic tables and boating facilities still attract visitors even when the river is low. The water tends to be shallowest on weekends when water demand by industry is low and during the dry days of late summer. On spring and fall "east wind days" here, it's possible to watch windsurfers enjoying their sport's westernmost Gorge venue.

Benson Park at Exit 31 off I-84 (accessible only from eastbound lanes) offers a boat ramp and swimming. A $3 day-use fee is assessed. Across the freeway, nearby Dalton Point offers Columbia River access.

River Trails Rentals, 336 East Columbia River Hwy., Troutdale, 503/667-1964, rents rafts, kayaks, and canoes. For a safe, scenic, and sedate float, call Ken Barker at **Northwest Discoveries,** 503/624-4829. On this trip, you paddle yourself in a four-person raft and watch abundant wildlife on the Sandy. A guide-naturalist will instruct you how to control the raft through mild rapids and where to look for critters. June is an optimum time for this experience. The entire cost including shuttle is only $40.

PRACTICALITIES

Accommodations

With abundant budget options available in nearby Portland, we've listed one rock-bottom budget choice (there are no shortage of cut-rate motels in Troutdale) and two special lodgings more apropos of the setting.

Motel 6, 1610 NW Frontage Rd., Troutdale, 503/665-2254, covers the basics with rooms around $40. As you're easing onto the exit ramp off I-84's Exit 17, just look up to your right to find it. There is a pool and easy access to downtown Portland (15 miles west) as well as an outlet mall and fast food restaurants a mile or two east. Best of all, you're near the Troutdale access to the Historic Columbia River Highway.

For a special escape we recommend **Bridal Veil Lodge,** P.O. Box 10, Bridal Veil, 503/695-2333. The lodge, across the road from Bridal Veil Falls State Park, is the last surviving accommodation from the "roadhouse" era on this part of the Historic Highway. The knotty pine walls, antique quilts, and historic photos set the mood. Several generations of the same family have been serving travelers here since 1926, so hospitality is second nature to the innkeepers. You can stay in the main lodge, where you share a bath, or in the cottage rooms. The guest cottage is a self-contained unit with open-beam ceilings, skylights, and private baths. Included breakfasts feature French toast (or waffles with fruit and whipped cream) made from thick, homemade bread topped with fruit and accompanied by bacon or sausage. This is a great place to stay with kids if you are visiting Portland because you're only a half-hour drive from the city but surrounded by the grandeur of the Gorge. Rooms run $75 double.

Imagine a lovingly landscaped 38-acre estate featuring several restaurants, a hotel, a brewery, a winery and tasting room, a movie theater, and a pitch-and-putt golf course and you have **McMenamin's Edgefield,** 2126 SW Halsey, Troutdale, 503/669-8610 or 800/669-8610. Oregon's preeminent brewpub owners have transformed what had been in previous incarnations the County Poor Farm and later a convalescent home into a good base from which to explore the Gorge or Portland. This is truly the best of the country near the best of the city. Set amid lavish gardens with antiques and artwork at every turn, guests choose from charmingly decorated hotel rooms for $85 (with shared bath) or $125 (with private bath), or hostel beds for $20. Rates include a full breakfast. Seasonal packages are available.

Hikers coming to Edgefield after a day on one of the many Gorge "thigh burner" trails are advised to enjoy a dinner at the excellent Black Rabbit Restaurant ($13 –20) and a massage from an on-site therapist.

Camping

Just outside the Gorge, Oxbow County Park (see Portland—Gateway to the Gorge chapter) is probably your best bet for camping here.

In the Gorge itself, there's a campground 35 miles east of Portland (17 miles east of Troutdale) off I-84 Exit 35, at the end of the first section of the Historic Highway. **Ainsworth State Park,** 800/452-5687, is named for a famous steamboat operator. Picnic tables, fire rings, flush toilets, and an RV camp with full hookups enhance the prime location near the trails and waterfalls of the Columbia River Gorge. The nightly rate is $14–19 on a first-come, first served basis. Noise from trains, cars (especially), and airplanes here might make you forget you're surrounded by the Gorge's spectacular waterfalls and cliffs, so light sleepers should bring earplugs. Otherwise, the 47 sites provide everything for your comfort. A laundry room and firewood are also available. Open spring through fall.

Food

Restrictions on development in this part of the National Scenic Area translate into limited dining choices. Assuming you forego dining in nearby Portland or one of Edgefield's excellent eateries (see Accommodations above), a few places do offer local color and decent food.

Tad's Chicken 'n' Dumplins, 1325 E. Columbia River Hwy., 503/666-5337, is one of the first places you'll pass after crossing the bridge to leave downtown Troutdale. Its classic weather-beaten roadhouse facade has graced this highway since the 1930s. If you decide to forego the restaurant's namesake dish, there's decent fried oysters and fried chicken as well as steak and salmon. It's good old American food that'll taste even better with drinks on the porch overlooking the Sandy River. Dinner entrées run $11–22.

In Springdale, coffee and a pastry at **Mom's Garden Bakery at the Blue House,** 32030 Historic Columbia River Hwy., 503/695-3285, is highly recommended. Quiche of the day with soup and salad, breakfast specials, and turkey or roast beef sandwiches for lunch (all in the $6–7 range) are complemented by first-rate cinnamon buns ($1.40) and other home-baked goods and espresso. Closed Sunday and Monday.

Multnomah Falls Lodge, 503/695-2376, has a second floor dining room that dates back to the early decades of the 20th century. While service can sometimes be uneven here due to the crush of visitors, the food can be surprisingly good when the kitchen isn't overwhelmed. A cheery solarium, adjacent to the high-ceilinged dining room and built from native wood and stone, makes a casually elegant setting to begin or end a day of hiking. If it's cold however, stay in the main dining room near the fireplace, where you can enjoy the paintings and vintage photos of Columbia Gorge scenes. On warm days the outside patio is delightful and if you crane your neck you can see the falls. The menu—with such indigenous fare as Caesar salad with Columbia River smoked salmon, $11—also effectively articulates the surroundings. In this vein, grilled salmon or trout with eggs makes a good breakfast ($8.75). Particularly recommended is the mini loaf of homemade wheat bread and soup for lunch, $6.50. Dinner is a more elaborate affair with steak, seafood, and chicken main courses averaging $12–20. To help forestall hunger pangs along the trail, consider ordering a microbrew or a huckleberry tart. Friday night seafood buffets and Sunday brunches round out the offerings. The Lodge operates daily, between 8 A.M. and 9 P.M.

Information and Services

The **Multnomah Falls Visitor Information Center,** P.O. Box 68, Bridal Veil 97019, 503/695-2372, has a ranger and volunteers on duty year-round to recommend campgrounds and hikes. Ask here about nearby jaunts to Horsetail Falls, Triple Falls, and Oneonta Gorge among others. The latter trail is where a stream cuts through hundreds of feet of basalt a mile east of Multnomah Falls. A slide at Oneonta Gorge in 2000 transformed what had been a popular half-mile, creek-bed trail to a waterfall into an at-your-own-risk scramble over logs. Nonetheless, the scenery is evocative of Utah's Canyonlands and the cool temperatures provide respite on hot days. Be sure to request the *Short Hiking Loops Near Multnomah Falls* map for a visual depiction of this network of trails. The center is open until 8 P.M. in summer, until 5 P.M. in winter.

Cascade Locks

The sleepy appearance of modern-day Cascade Locks belies its historical significance. The town is perched on a small bluff between the river and I-84, and its services and creature comforts are mostly confined to the main drag, Wa Na Pa Street, which was part of the original Columbia River Highway. Before the shipping locks that inspired the burg's utilitarian name were constructed in 1896 to help steamboats navigate around hazardous rapids, most cargo had to be portaged around the Great Cascades of the Columbia. These waters had been viewed as the greatest obstacle facing Willamette Valley-bound Oregon Trail emigrants.

But this town of nearly 1,000 people has had other claims to fame. The first of these may not have existed at all, but many reputable scientists now believe that an ancient natural bridge once spanned the Columbia's mile-wide channel. According to Native American legends, this rock formation, connecting north and south shorelines, was destroyed by the Great Spirit to punish warring tribes. The conflict was due to a brotherly brouhaha over a beautiful woman The story gained widespread popularity after the publication of an 1890 romantic novel by a Hood River clergyman—*Bridge of the Gods,* by Frederic Homer Balch. The book recounts the idyllic life of Columbia River tribes before outside settlers arrived. In any case, what are believed to be subterranean remnants of a 700-year-old rockslide large enough to have facilitated a river crossing (and inspire the Native story) lie just upstream from a modern structure called the **Bridge of the Gods** ($.75 toll to cross into Washington) in honor of the Indian landmark. Originally built in 1926, the span was raised to its present height in 1938 to compensate for a heightened river level caused by Bonneville Dam. An old bridge-tender supposedly witnessed aviator Charles Lindbergh flying under the bridge after altering his trajectory to avoid high tension wires.

Civil War legend **Phil Sheridan** is also part of the town's history. He helped thwart an Indian attack on an area fort across the river in March 1856 during which his nose was grazed by a hostile round and the man beside him was killed. Sheridan arrived at Fort Vancouver the year before to take part in a series of skirmishes (see Fort Cascades under Washougal to Dog Mountain in the Washington Gorge chapter) against the natives in the wake of an 1855 treaty that usurped Gorge tribal lands. These incidents lead to the transport of military and arms here by steamship and stimulated the growth of commercial river traffic. The steamer *Bailey-Gatzert* (1890-1918), which made regular runs with passengers and freight between Portland and Cascades Locks (as well as other Gorge ports of call), created such a large wake on the river that smaller boat pilots took to calling it the "daily bastard."

The third event, the construction of the Bonneville Dam in the 1930s, created boom times in the area. Dam construction resulted in 48-mile Lake Bonneville, which submerged the shipping locks. Today you can see Native American fishermen by the 1896 locks site in the town's riverfront Marine Park. Look for natives selling whole fresh salmon and other species from late August into September, weekends 10 A.M.–dusk. Bring waxed paper and or a cooler with ice to help keep the fish fresh till you're back in camp. Call 888/BUY-1855 for more information. Cash only.

Boom times are gone now, but this little town with a dazzling river view and down-to-earth people is a refreshing change of pace from the big city to the west as well as the burgeoning tourist scene of its neighbors to the east. Reasonably priced food and lodging, a historical museum, the Bonneville Dam, and sternwheeler tours together with superlative hiking trails nearby also make it a nice stopover, as long as you don't come during winter. Most of the 75-inch annual precipitation falls at that time, along with ice storms and gale-force winds. Two funnel clouds were even sighted outside of town during the Columbus Day storm of 1962. Such violent weather is not completely devoid of benefits, however. The rains fostered the growth of massive Douglas fir trees near here, which led to a once-thriving timber industry. Nowadays, the winds account for the Columbia Gorge's status as the windsurfing capital of the world, and the tourist economy's ripple effects are starting to be felt in Cascade Locks.

SIGHTS

Bonneville Dam

The Bonneville Dam (write to Public Information, U.S. Army Corps of Engineers, P.O. Box 2946, Portland 97208) can be reached via Exit 40 off I-84. The signs lead you under the interstate through a tunnel to the site of the complex, **Bradford Island.** En route to the visitor center you drive over a retractable bridge above the modern shipping locks. On the other side are the powerhouse and turbine room. Downriver is the second-largest exposed monolith in the world (Gibraltar is first). Abutting the shoreline, this

848-foot lava promontory is known as **Beacon Rock,** a moniker bestowed by Lewis and Clark, who camped in the area. Beyond the generating facilities is a bridge, underneath which is the fish-diversion canal. These fishways cause back eddies and guide the salmon, shad, steelhead, and other species past turbine blades. You'll want to stop for a brief look at the spillways of the 500-foot-wide Bonneville Dam, especially if they're open.

While Bonneville isn't anywhere near the largest or the most powerful dam on the river, it was the first project on the leading hydroelectric waterway in the world. Along with its potential for generating 40 percent of America's power needs, the Columbia's storage of irrigation water and its dam-related recreation sites make the river the most valuable resource in the Northwest—too valuable to be diverted for drinking water in southern California, despite pleas from Los Angeles politicians In 2001, however, Bonneville power helped forestall rolling blackouts in parts of northern California.

Benefits notwithstanding, the downside of damming is graphically illustrated by the sight of Native American fishermen enacting a weary pantomime of their forefathers by the Bonneville spillways. The **visitor center,** 503/374-8820, is open 9 A.M.–5 P.M. year-round. Ask the Army Corps of Engineers personnel at the reception desk about tours of the power-generating facilities and about public campgrounds, boat ramps, swimming, and picnicking areas. The reception area has exhibits on dam operations, pioneer and navigation history on the Columbia, and fish migration. A long elevator ride takes you down to the fish-viewing windows, where the sight of lamprey eels—which accompany the mid-May and mid-September salmon runs—and the fish-counting procedures are particularly fascinating. The fish-counting practice helps determine catch limits on the popular species. Outside the facility there's access to an overlook above the fish ladders. A walkway back to the parking lot is decorated with gorgeous roses from spring into fall.

Retrace your route back to the mainland from Bradford Island (an old Native American burial ground) and turn right, following the signs to the fish hatchery. This facility is open every day 7:30 A.M.–5 P.M. Visit during spawning season (May and September) to see the salmon making their way upriver. At this time head to the west end of the hatchery, where steps lead you down to a series of canals and holding pens. So great is the zeal of these fish to spawn that they occasionally leap more than a foot out of the water. Inside the building you can see the beginnings of a process that produces the largest number of salmon fry in the state. Here fish culturists sort the fish and extract the bright red salmon roe from the females. These eggs are taken to the windowed incubation building, where you can view trays holding millions of eggs that will eventually hatch into salmon. Once these fry grow into fingerlings, they are moved to outdoor pools where they live until being released into the Columbia River by way of the Tanner Creek canal. The whole process is annotated by placards above the windows inside the incubation building.

The salmon and trout ponds and the floral displays are worth your attention at certain times of the year, but the **sturgeon pools** to the rear of the visitor center are always something to see. Bonneville is the nation's only white sturgeon hatchery and the government has made this facility user-friendly. In addition to the pool housing several sturgeon, the glass-enclosed home of "Herman the Sturgeon" offers a window on a 60-year-old eight-foot-long 500-pound fish. The largest Columbia sturgeon ever recorded was 12.5 feet long and weighed 1,287 pounds. Along with this exceptional visual perspective, statistics on size, age, and habits of sturgeon as well as on the evolution of the Columbia's sturgeon fishery are provided. Biologists say the Columbia River white sturgeon, with bony plates instead of scales, has remained unchanged for 200 million years. The expression "living fossil" takes on more meaning when you consider the sturgeon, catfish-like creatures, can attain ages of 150–200 years of age.

Despite being the largest freshwater species in North America, this river-bottom scavenger was largely ignored until the gourmet feeding frenzy of the last two decades put a premium on domestic sources of caviar. When *New York Times*

food columnist Craig Claiborne pronounced the Columbia's product superior to that of the Caspian Sea several decades ago, its notoriety was established and catch limits were reestablished. It is currently illegal to sell sturgeon eggs. Fishermen pulling in sturgeon under 40 inches or over 6 feet long (large enough to produce roe) are subject to catch-and-release limits.

The Bonneville Dam visitor center and fish hatchery are both free of charge.

Cascade Locks Marine Park

Down by the river is the Marine Park (Exit 44 off I-84 eastbound). Look for it on your left going east on Wa Na Pa Street; just follow the signs. Here the sternwheeler *Columbia Gorge,* 503/223-3928 and 541/374-8427, makes it possible to ride up the river in the style of a century ago. River legends and scenic splendor accompany you on a two-hour narrated cruise. There are several interesting packages of varying themes and duration. The boat, a 145-foot, 330-ton replica, carries 599 passengers on three decks. Sightseeing cruises depart June 13–October 10 for these excursions; the Lewis and Clark Expedition runs 10 A.M.–12 P.M., the Oregon Trail Adventure 12:30–2:30 P.M., and Steamboatin' U.S.A. 3–5 P.M. The fare is $12.95 for adults, $7.95 for kids 4–12. An outdoor deck, an inside galley (brunch cruises offered), and entertaining narration have made these trips popular for years. Such photo opportunities as Mt. Hood and Indian fishing platforms together with the sternwheeler's own photo collection of some of the first passenger vessels here will further enhance your Columbia River reverie.

Port of Cascade Locks, 541/374-6427, houses the ticket office as well as an information center and gift shop, which sells an excellent local hiking trails map for $2. The facility also offers historical photos of early sternwheelers and $1 showers for hikers.

About a quarter mile west of the visitor center, **Cascade Locks Historical Museum,** P.O. Box 307, Cascade Locks 97014, 503/374-8535, is housed in an old lockkeeper's residence and exhibits Native American artifacts alongside pioneer, logging, and steamboat memorabilia.

THE OREGON GORGE

Information about the fish wheel, a paddle-wheel-like contraption that hauled salmon out of the river and into a pen via conveyor belt is especially fascinating. This diabolical device was perfected in Oregon in the early 20th century and was so successful at denuding the Columbia of fish that it was outlawed. From June through September, the museum is open Mon.–Wed. noon–5 P.M., THURS.–SUN. 10 a.m.–5 P.M. In May it's open weekends 10 A.M.–5 P.M.

Outside the museum is the diminutive *Oregon Pony*, the first steam locomotive on the Pacific coast. Its maiden voyage dates back to 1862 when it replaced the 4.5-mile portage with a rail route around the Cascades.

Before leaving, take a walk over to the old Cascade shipping locks. Built in 1878 to circumnavigate the steep gradient of the river, they were completed in 1896. By the time the locks were finished, however, river traffic had unfortunately decreased due to cargo being sent by train, so the effects of altering the river flow here were negligible.

HIKES

The following hikes require the annual Northwest Forest Pass ($30) or a $5 day pass (see Hiking section in Essentials chapter).

Wahclella Falls and Old Highway Hiker-Biker Trail

The best short hike in the Gorge that doesn't involve significant elevation gain is the walk along Tanner Creek to Wahclella Falls. After a mile of walking you've reached the terminus of the canyon framing the creek below thundering Wahclella Falls. En route, the gently hilly pathway shows off this pretty steep-walled arroyo to great advantage, but the destination is better than the journey. In a scene evocative of a Japanese brush stroke painting, a two-tiered waterfall pours down dramatically at canyon's end, seen to best advantage from a bridge over the creek. Look for water ouzels here, birds that dive underwater and flaps their wings, enabling them to run along the bottom looking for insect larvae. While the trail on the other side of the river is worthwhile—fea-

turing a lava cavern and bus-sized boulders from a 1973 slide—it doesn't loop all the way back to the parking lot so you'll have to retrace your steps. From I-84 eastbound, the trailhead is reached by taking Exit 40 (Bonneville Dam) and making a right at the bottom of the exit ramp into a small parking lot instead of a left under the tunnel to Bonneville Dam. To avoid missing the exit, look for the Fish Hatchery sign preceding it.

From this same parking lot you may access a resuscitated portion of the Columbia River Highway by heading east. However, with lanes barely wide enough to accommodate a golf cart you'll have to leave the car behind. The state decided to repave this 2.5-mile section of the old road for hikers and bikers, re-creating the arched guardrails, bridges, viaducts, and tunnels between here and Cascades Locks to join the surviving ones. In addition to the ornate stonework, the curving, undulating roadbed blasted out of the mountainside before 1920 offers unsurpassed views. While the Historic Highway parallels the interstate, its elevated perspective on the river and surrounding architectural artistry are a refreshing change of pace from the modern thoroughfare. The highlight of the route is a reproduction of the **Toothrock Viaduct** annotated by plaques and heritage markers. It was within view of this area that Oregon Trail migrants portaged on a primitive trail around the Great Cascades of the Columbia during the 1840s. Those pioneers that tried to raft over this part of the river (where the "Great Shute" dropped 20 feet in 400 yards) lost their possessions and/or their lives. By the mid-1850s, a portage tramway, and thereafter a Military Portage Road, eased the way considerably. In the 1860s, Oregon's first locomotive steamed around Toothrock to connect with steamboats on the Columbia River.

After exiting this one-mile section of the highway via a stairway into the parking lot of the Eagle Creek Fish Hatchery, head east a short distance to the second leg of the hiker-biker trail. While most of the 2.5-mile trek doesn't offer the architectural nuances and river views of the Historic Highway sections to the west, the Eagle Creek-to-Cascades Locks section is highlighted by

THE OREGON GORGE

© WEISTER CO.

Punchbowl Falls, Eagle Creek

a pretty waterfall at the beginning and a well-rendered tunnel a quarter mile from its terminus below the Bridge of the Gods. From the Bridge of the Gods in Cascade Locks, you can look west and see how a centuries-old rockslide rendered this section of the Columbia narrower than the rest of the river.

Eagle Creek Trail

Because the Eagle Creek Trail is highly recommended by a lot of people, try to avoid peak-use times such as summer weekends. This trail begins at Eagle Creek Campground (see Camping under Practicalities, below) and runs 14 miles to Wahtum Lake, where it intersects the Pacific Crest Trail. Along the way are seven waterfalls, one of which features a perspective from behind the cascade itself. Ideally, this is a two-day backpacking trip, but if you prefer a day trip, consider Eagle Creek Trail #440 about two miles to a short spur trail leading down to picturesque **Punchbowl Falls.** It can be reached from the Eagle Creek Campground via Exit 41 off I-84. The four-mile round-trip to the falls is an easy hike. If you can, come in February when tourists are scarce and stream flow is high.

From Punchbowl Falls you can continue 1.5 miles to High Bridge. Tall trees, spring wild-flowers, basalt outcroppings, and nice views into Eagle Creek's white-water cleft make the journey almost as compelling as the destination. High Bridge is 80 feet above this particularly beautiful section of the creek. The trail continues on the other side of the gorge several more miles to 100-foot-high **Tunnel Falls,** where you can walk under an overhang blasted behind the cataract by the 1915 trail crew.

Wildflowers spring up in April and linger on into August in the higher elevations. To identify such Columbia Gorge endemics as Oregon flea-bane and Howell's daisy, bring along Russ Jolley's *Wildflowers of the Columbia.* Many of these one-of-a-kind species are left over from a previous glacial period and have adapted because of the shade and moistness on the south side of the Gorge. Almost two dozen varieties of fern, trillium, bear grass, yellow arnica, penstemon, monkeyflower, and devil's club are among the more common species here. This hike is 13 miles round-trip and is best undertaken on a weekday in spring to catch the blooms and avoid the crowds.

As a prelude to hiking Eagle Creek or one of several other trails in the area, you might want to wander an informative interpretive loop of less than a mile. Just cross the footbridge on the approach road to the Eagle Creek Trailhead over to the other side of the river. After crossing the bridge, follow the markers that describe the region's mixed-conifer forest at various elevations. At trail's end, a steep two-mile trail leads to Wauna Point. While this trail isn't as visually arresting as other area jaunts, the view of the Columbia River and its Gorge at the summit makes the effort worthwhile.

PRACTICALITIES

Accommodations

With no shortage of camping and numerous lodging alternatives close by, one place that shows off the river stands out. If the best view of the Columbia from a hotel room is important to you, then you'll book a riverfront unit at the **Best Western Columbia River Inn,** 735 Wa Na Pa St., 503/374-8777 or 800/595-7108. These large, beautifully appointed rooms are well worth the $84–140 rate. But while watching boats go under the Bridge of the Gods might sound restful, trains passing below your window might disturb the sleep of noise-sensitive guests. The few bucks expended on a set of earplugs, however, should make this place the perfect retreat after a day of hiking.

Some high end rooms have hot tubs and all rooms feature microwaves and refrigerators; many rooms also have balconies. There's a health club with a whirlpool (with a view), a pool, and exercise facilities. With the Charburger next door and the Historic Highway hiker-biker trail and Marine Park nearby, this property has an excellent location.

Camping

There's no shortage of options for campers in this area. However, keep in mind the western Gorge is Portland's backyard and can be very crowded, so avoid peak times whenever possible. The following have been chosen on the basis of location (e.g., near attractions or a prime trailhead) or for special amenities.

While the **Eagle Creek Campground,** 541/386-2333, can be noisy and crowded, it's an ideal base camp for hiking as it's close to several trailheads. Reservations are only taken for groups at this first campground ever created by

the National Forest Service (in the 1930s). There are sites for tents and for RVs up to 22 feet long, with picnic tables, fire grills, flush toilets, sanitary services, and firewood available. It's located between Bonneville Dam and Cascade Locks off I-84 and is open mid-May to October. The fee is $8. Traffic noise is a problem here, particularly at site 13, located atop a bluff with a view of the Columbia. Sites 1–5 are farther from panoramic river views but are quieter. At the seven-mile point of the Eagle Creek Trail (see Hikes, above) there's a primitive free campground, but it fills up on summer weekends.

Wyeth Campground, 541/386-2333, a favorite of windsurfers, is a relatively quiet (for the Gorge) overnight spot. RVs and tents can put in here, but there are no hookups. Piped water, flush toilets, and fire pits are provided. Reservations aren't accepted at this Forest Service facility, where the fee is $8. It's located seven miles past Cascade Locks at Exit 51 and operates mid-May–October. Follow a county road from here a half-mile to Wyeth along Gordon Creek.

Cascade Locks Marine Park, P.O. Box 307, Cascade Locks 97014, 503/374-8619, offers campsites close to the center of town. The museum and the sternwheeler are housed in the complex, as are tennis courts. Whatever amenities are not available on-site are within walking distance. It's open all year and the fee is $10.

Finally, two miles east of town near the banks of the Columbia is the Cascade Locks **KOA Kampground,** P.O. Box 660, Cascade Locks 97014, 541/374-8668 (information), 800/KOA-8698 (reservations). Open from March 21–October 20, this private campground features the basics plus a spa (hot tub/sauna), hot showers, and a heated swimming pool for $17 per couple, $3 each extra person. Kamping Kabins that come in one room (queen bed and a bunk bed) or two room (queen bed and two sets of bunks) varieties cost $30 and $35 per night respectively (bring your own linens, pillows, towels, sleeping bag, etc.). Kabins fill up quickly, especially on weekends, so reserve well in advance. To get there, take U.S. 30 east from town, and turn left onto Forest Lane. Proceed 1.2 miles down and you'll see the campground on the left.

Food

Forget health food and haute cuisine until you get to Hood River. In Cascade Locks, you get down-home country cooking—and lots of it—at a decent price.

The Charburger, 714 Wa Na Pa St., 503/374-8477, is near the Bridge of the Gods at the beginning of town. This is a great place if you're on the go and don't want to spend a fortune for a quick bite. In addition to an extensive salad bar and a bakery, there is a cafeteria line specializing in "home-baked" (and it tastes that way) chicken, good burgers, omelettes cooked to order, and other wholesome dishes. Prices for a meal seldom exceed $6. Other options include a take-out window as well as Tex-Mex specialties and a Sunday brunch downstairs. Walls festooned by pioneer gear and photos of the stern-wheeler and Model-T eras as well as a knockout view of the river here instill a sense of place. The restaurant's Hood River outlet, 4100 West-cliff, Hood River, 503/386-3101, is at the west end of that town.

East Wind Ice Cream, located between the Charburger and Marine Park, is a traditional stop for families on a Columbia River Gorge Sunday drive.

The Salmon Row Pub, corner of Wa Na Pa and Regulator Sts., 541/374-9310, is a small, dark brewpub whose smoked salmon chowder, pizza, and sandwiches fill you up for less than $8.

Events

The last weekend in June, the sternwheeler *Columbia Gorge* is welcomed back to Cascade Locks.

Free rides on the boat, dozens of food and craft booths, a salmon bake, and races all bring out the community in force. Call 503/374-8313 for more information.

July 4th fireworks here are ranked among the state's best displays. The multicolored explosions are set off on Thunder Island below the Bridge of the Gods over the Columbia River. Watch from the city park where the Volunteer Fire Department puts on a high-quality salmon bake. Better yet, book Cascade Stern-wheeler's package (including the salmon dinner for around $30) to take in the fireworks from aboard the riverboat. A DJ spins tasteful renditions of patriotic songs amid the rockets' red glare. You can book this excursion from Portland through Gray Line, 503/285-9845 or 800/422-7042.

Horseback Riding

East of town, **Mt. Shadow Ranch,** 541/374-8592, is at Wyeth off Exit 51 (near Herman Horse Camp). Their 23 acres front the Columbia River with the 2,000-foot facade of a mountain behind it. The ranch has a special permit to conduct guided rides in the Mt. Hood National Forest.

Information and Services

In addition to the previously mentioned Marine Park Visitors Center, the **Port of Cascade Locks Tourism Committee,** P.O. Box 355, Cascade Locks 97014, 503/374-8619 (ask for Tahoma), can provide help in planning your visit.

The **state police** can be reached at 800/452-8573.

Hood River and Vicinity

In the past, Hood River was known to the traveling public primarily as the start of a scenic drive through the orchard country beneath the snowcapped backdrop of Mt. Hood, Oregon's highest peak. Since the early '80s, however, well-heeled adherents of windsurfing have transformed this town into an outdoor recreation mecca. Instead of just the traditional dependence on cherries, apples, peaches, and pears, Hood River now rakes in tens of millions of dollars annually from the presence of "boardheads."

The fury of the winds derives from the heat of the eastern desert drawing in the Pacific westerlies. The confining contours of the Gorge dam up these air masses and precipitate their gusty release. Many local business owners are familiar with the "20-knot clause," which permits their workers time off to "catch a blow" when the winds are "nukin'" at this speed.

Bounded by picturesque orchard country and the Columbia River with the snowcapped volcanoes serving as distant backdrops, this town of 4,500 enjoys a magnificent setting. The main thoroughfare, Oak Street (which becomes Cascade Street as you head west), is set on a plateau between the riverfront marine park to the north and streets running up the Cascade foothills to the south. New brick facades dress up old storefronts, and casual attire and sandals predominate.

HISTORY

Dr. Herbert Krieger, curator of the Smithsonian Institution, came here in 1934 to excavate alongside a stream that once ran between 13th, Oak, and State Streets. Arrowheads and artifacts told of Native presence here, but the discovery of 30 ash pits of the type found in Chinook tepees indicated that at one time there had been a village in the area of present-day downtown Hood River. Another dig in Mosier a few miles east of Hood River unearthed an ancient cemetery. Many coins of diverse origins were found here, probably taken by the Natives in trade. Some of the coins were Chinese, possibly from Warrendale cannery workers. There were also Roman coins and a token from the Northwest Fur Trading Company, predating this enterprise's early 19th-century presence in Astoria. Finally, Russian flag standards also pointed to a rich legacy of Columbia River barter.

Pioneers began to build farms in the Hood River Valley after the land giveaways of The Land Donation Act of 1850. The rich volcanic soil, glacier water, and mild climate here provided an impetus for agriculture. In 1855, the Coe family came to establish the first post office and planted orchards in the area of present-day 11th and State Streets. Five years later a sawmill was built in the Hood River Valley. At that time, the first census showed that only 70 people lived in the area. The region's first large-scale commercial orchard was established in 1876 specializing in Newtown pippin apples. In the next decade, rail lines enabled strawberries from the area to gain renown in New York. Similar prominence was soon accorded Hood River pears and apples in other large cities. During this era, the first name given to this area by pioneers, Dog River Valley (denoting the sustenance during times of duress), was dropped in favor of a more respectable name. Pears took over the produce business when a killer frost devastated local apple orchards here in 1919 and the commercial strawberry crop was wiped out forever by a fungus in the 1930s. Today, the valley is considered the nation's leader in winter pears (d'Ajou, comice, and bosc) and ranks first in production of Anjou pears. Today 80 percent of the crop is devoted to pears, with apples, cherries, and peaches marketed in smaller quantities.

While the completion of the Columbia River Highway and the Columbia Gorge Hotel in the 1920s gave birth to tourism here, it wasn't until in the early '80s, with windsurfing's popularity, that the leisure economy became a focal point of the local identity. On days when windsurfers can't "rig up," many take to the hills on mountain bikes or hit the slopes at nearby Mt. Hood, enlarging the appeal of the town as a mecca for outdoor recreationists. By the spring of 1997, an estimated 35 companies with sailboarding ties—board and sail makers, designers of harnesses and clothing—made Hood River their base.

WEATHER

Hood River has average summer daytime highs of 66°F and average winter lows of 33°F. Conditions can vary greatly between parts of town fronting the river and the upper Hood River Valley where the elevation tops 2,000 feet. Even though snow and ice regularly visit all parts of the region each winter, winds off Mt. Hood's glaciers can create especially severe conditions in the upper Hood River Valley.

SIGHTS
Scenic Views

The scenic highlights of Hood River are the orchards during the end of the April Blossom Festival and the leaves during the fall color season in October. For a view of the Hood River Valley that does justice to these events, drive to the east end of town and turn right on ORE 35. Head south till you see the sign for **Panorama Point.** After a left

turn, head south about a mile on East Side Road and make a right on a road that'll take you to the top of a knoll with views to the south and west that do justice to the name Panorama Point. Vistas here afford a distant perspective on the orchards below Mt. Hood, which have forever served as a visual archetype of the Pacific Northwest.

As you look at this America the Beautiful postcard-come-to-life, try to imagine an ancestral Columbia River flowing south through the Hood River Valley passing under the site of what would become Mt. Hood. Geologists tell us that this original channel of the river pre-dated the formation of the Cascades. Tens of millions of years ago this waterway flowed down to the area of present-day Salem, which was then seacoast. In other incarnations, the scene before you was buried beneath glacial debris and volcanic ash that descended the slopes of Mt. Hood. In short, it's important to realize that the present-day Hood River Valley is but an eye blink in geologic time, and that the forces that created it are in temporary remission. The white apple and pear blossoms flower in the lower valley during late April. As this display is waning two weeks later, the upper valley above 2,000 feet starts to bloom.

© OREGON DEPT. OF TRANSPORTATION

Mt Hood and Hood River

THE OREGON GORGE

About 15 miles west of Hood River off I-84 you'll find **Mitchell Point Overlook,** a bluff facing west over a large expanse of the Gorge. This area had been part of the old highway, famous for the five massive windows cut out of solid rock into the Tunnel of Many Vistas. While the tunnel is no more, the parking lot views here can be accessed from Hood River by going west on I-84 and departing the interstate via Exit 56 to loop back on I-84 eastbound a few miles. By the way, the tunnels were the single most expensive piece of construction on the original highway. Here, as at Crown Point and many other places, engineers had to hang 200 feet over cliffs on ropes to blast footing enough to make a survey. Chief highway engineer Lancaster mandated that this tunnel be designed to surpass the three-windowed Axenstrasse Tunnels of Switzerland. The tunnel was destroyed in 1966 and all that remains today is a rock wall fragment visible 50 feet above I-84.

Closer to town, take advantage of another Gorge photo op at **Ruthton Point,** a small picnic area just off I-84 on Exit 62 (Westcliff Drive). This area sits a few miles west of town, a half-mile beyond the Columbia Gorge Hotel, on the river side of the westbound freeway. Across the river are views of Underwood Mountain, a one-time volcano now covered in orchards, vineyards, and expensive "view lots."

Columbia Gorge Hotel

The Columbia Gorge Hotel, 4000 Westcliff Dr., Hood River 97031, 503/386-5566 (local), 800/345-1921 (toll free), www.gorge.net/lodging/cghotel, is a landmark worth visiting even if you have no plans to stay the night. Take Exit 62 off of I-84 and go over the bridge to the north side of the highway and follow Westcliff Drive west. The hotel is a lovingly rendered homage to the Jazz Age of the Roaring Twenties, when it was graced by visits from presidents Coolidge and Roosevelt, Rudolph Valentino, Clara Bow, and the big bands. The hotel was built by lumber magnate Simon Benson (who was also a patron of the Columbia River Highway) in 1921, and the grounds feature a 207-foot waterfall and an eye-catching floral display fronting the inn's neo-

looking west from Ruthton Point, near Hood River, Oregon

© BRIAN UTT

Moorish facade. Glittering chandeliers in the lobby, large wing chairs around the fireplace, and fresh-cut bouquets in the dining room also bespeak the refinement of a hotel they used to call the "Waldorf of the West."

Rates here are high (expect to spend $175–275 a night during peak season, although winter rates are close to half that), but a more romantic retreat would be hard to come by. Spacious rooms with heavy wooden beams, brass beds, fluffed-up pillows, and period furniture clearly demonstrate what was meant by the "good ol' days." The readers of *Condé Nast* travel agree, voting the hotel to a list of the top 500 hotels in the world.

The dining room looks east at the Columbia rolling toward the hotel from out of the mountains and west toward alpenglow. Local mushrooms, fruits, and wild game as well as Columbia River salmon and sturgeon are featured prominently here. There is also the "world famous farm breakfast." Imagine four courses running the gamut of American breakfast food served with such theatrical flourishes as "honey from the sky"—Hood River Valley apple blossom honey poured from a height of several feet above the table onto hot, fresh-baked biscuits. This symbolizes the 207-foot-high Wah Gwin Gwin (Rushing Water) Falls that descend the precipice in back of the hotel. As they say at the hotel, "You don't just get a choice—you get it all."

Downtown Sights

To learn the history of the region, drive back to the junction of State Street and ORE 35, then turn left (north) and cross I-84 toward the river. At the intersection turn left and follow the signs to Marina Park and the **Hood River Museum,** 300 E. Port Marina Dr., 541/386-6772, Hrchm@gorge.net. To get there off I-84, take Exit 64 and follow the signs. Exhibits trace life in the Hood River Valley from prehistoric times to the founding of the first pioneer settlement in 1854. Thereafter, the area's development as a renowned fruit-growing center is emphasized. Native American stone artifacts, beadwork, and basketry, pioneer quilts, and a Victorian parlor set the time machine in motion. The contributions of the local Finnish and Japanese communities (imported to work in the orchards), along with WW I memorabilia, introduce the first half of the 20th century. Photos and implements related to fruit harvesting and packing methods round out the historical collections on the first floor. Antique logging equipment, dolls, and remnants of a presentation by local schoolchildren for the Lewis and Clark Exposition in 1905 are also on display. The museum is open April–Aug. daily 10 A.M.–4 P.M., Sunday noon–4 P.M.; SEPT.–OCT. DAILY NOON–4 p.m. Other months, it's open Monday and Tuesday by appointment. Admission is free but donations are appreciated.

Lovers of antiquity are advised to pick up the self-guided *Hood River Historic District Tour* pamphlet at the chamber of commerce. In addition to 19th-century pioneer homes, the tour includes a National Historic Landmark Train Station at the base of 13th Street.

The **International Museum of Carousel Art,** 304 Oak St., 541/387-4622, www.carouselmuseum.com, boasts the world's largest and most complete collection of antique carousel art. Most examples of this turn-of-century genre have been lost, taken out of circulation, or broken. This is easily forgotten amid the gay–sad strains of a 1917 Wurlitzer organ that welcomes you here, along with a carved wooden giraffe and a jeweled horse. The museum displays upwards of 130 such antiques (some dating back to the 16th century), including the world's biggest carousel tiger. A working carousel will soon be added. Hours are Saturday 10 A.M.–4 P.M., Sunday noon–4 P.M. April through October. Admission costs $5 adults, $4 seniors, $3 children. Call to inquire about hours of guided tours.

The **Mt. Hood Railroad,** 800/872-4661, goes from this historic railroad station up through the Hood River Valley to Parkdale in an enclosed Pullman coach dating back to 1910–20. En route, classic views of the orchards with Mt. Hood behind as well as over-the-shoulder views of Mt. Adams are the draw. While this isn't always a thrill-a-minute experience, it can be memorable during April blossom season or during the October leaf time. No matter when you go, the red caboose will be there to brighten up your photos and the ride is always a winner with children. Fares for the daily train April–October are $23, with discounts for seniors and kids.

South of Town Sights

Most of the following attractions can be accessed by following 13th Street (ORE 281) in Hood River south en route to Dee, Odell, and Parkdale. Driving south on ORE 35 to the Parkdale exits and heading west also takes in the listed attractions. Fruit stands, pick-your-own operations (on the decline due to insurance regulations), wineries, and country stores can be enjoyed with a self-guided *Fruit Loop* tour pamphlet from the chamber of commerce (see Information and Services under Practicalities, below) or by referring to the website www.gorge.net/fruitloop. The April blossom season and October fall color may titillate the eye, but the harvest seasons in June (strawberries and raspberries), July and August (cherries, apricots, peaches) and early fall (apples and pears) give visitors something they can sink their teeth into. Perennial favorites among fruit stands include McCurdy's, 2080 Tucker Rd., 541/386-1628; Rasmussen Farms, 3020 Thomsen Rd., 541/386-4622; and Smiley's Red Barn, ORE 35 and Erck Hill Rd., 541/386-9121. Also, don't miss **Riverbend Country Store,** 2363 Tucker Rd., 541/386-8766. Homemade pies and jams and all manner of prepared foods line the shelves of this antiques-filled place. Gardens and a picnic area round out the welcoming experience.

In Parkdale at the train depot, be sure to visit the **Hutson Museum,** 541/352-6808. Indian artifacts, pioneer hand tools, and one of the better rock collections in the Northwest make it worthwhile. A nominal admission is charged. Afterward, take advantage of the nearby fruit stands between spring and fall. Here (or in town), you can also pick up the Mt. Hood Railroad.

Also near Parkdale is a series of **lava beds.** From ORE 35 south, go right at the Mt. Hood Country Store on Baseline Road en route to Parkdale, then right on Lava Bed Drive. The beds are located a mile west of town. Surprisingly, this lava did not emanate from the slopes of the mountain. Instead it came from a vent more than three miles south and west of town. This flow is thought to be several thousand years old, a fraction of the 30 million year old volcanic legacy of the Gorge.

The picture of Mt. Hood above **Lost Lake** has to be included in any list of classic regional photos. The 25-mile drive to the lake begins on 13th Street, which changes names several more times (ORE 281, Tucker Road, and Dee Highway) on its way up the flanks of Mt. Hood. About 12 miles from downtown, take a right at the Dee Lumber Mill where a green Lost Lake sign points the way. From here, just bear left and follow the signs. The lake offers hiking trails, fishing, rowboat rentals, and a small store. There are also campsites and cabins. The cabins range $45–100, with the high end unit sleeping 6–8. Call 503/386-6366 at least two weeks in advance to reserve campsites and cabins. Come prepared; the closest fuel is in Parkdale. Late August huckleberry season is a highlight here but the weather and diminished crowds in September are preferable. In July and August, the rangers have campfire programs on Saturday night. A half-mile long boardwalk through an old growth cedar grove, part of the Lakeshore Trail, is a highlight. Pick up a map with natural history captions that correspond to numbered posts along the route. The old growth grove begins two miles into Lakeshore Trail, passing eight-foot thick cedars.

The best way to get up close and personal with Mt. Hood is with a visit to **Cloud Cap.** Unfortunately, the beautiful old lodge up here is closed, but the entrance to the Mt. Hood Wilderness lies on the north side of the volcano. To get there, travel 24 miles south of Hood River on ORE 35

© BRIAN LITT

Highway 30 at Rowena

THAR SHE BLOWS!

Although the 1980 eruption of Mt. St. Helens has given her more name recognition and public awareness than her Oregon counterpart, Mt. Hood is nonetheless a slumbering giant that occasionally snores loudly. Consider that local newspapers reported activity in 1853, 1854, 1859, and 1865. In 1835, missionary Samuel Parker wrote that he had heard Indian reports of "smoke and fire" on the mountain. In 1907, there was also some activity. According to a carbon-dated 4–6-inch layer of ash found on the southwest flank of the mountain, Lewis and Clark missed the last eruption by a few years. It has been suggested that their difficulty in crossing the Sandy River in Troutdale on November 3, 1805, might have been caused by mudflows that washed down from this eruption. Sporadic climber reports of sulfur smells up to a mile away from its source at Crater Rock, 700 feet south of the summit, also compound the impression of volcanic potential here. And after 445 quakes (65 of which came within 5 days) recorded in July 1980 following Mt. St. Helens' May 18 eruption, campsites here were evacuated and scientists placed sensitive seismic monitoring equipment to keep tabs on the volcano. Dozens of small quakes around the mountain over several days in both February 1998 and January 1999 (including a flurry of tremors exceeding 3.0 that paralleled similar events in 1989 and 1990) were also cause for trepidation. Finally, the 20th anniversary of Mt. St. Helens' May 18, 1980 eruption was marked by a 2.3 magnitude earthquake on Mt. Hood.

While Old Man Mountain still appears to be sleeping, the Portland Office of Emergency Management has drafted contingency plans for worst-case scenarios. Portland is located far enough away to be out of range of most volcanic debris, but its water source would be cut off. Portland relies upon the bountiful Bull Run watershed located on Mt. Hood; ash and mudflows from a major eruption would have devastating effects upon the city's water supply. Giant mudflows into the Columbia River present another threat—downstream flooding. A report issued in 1997 (see the website vulcan.wr.usgs.gov) says that the several thousand people living in the river valleys within 22 miles of the volcano could be inundated within an hour of an eruption. Landslides of superheated rock called pyroclastic flow moving as fast as 90 mph present another threat.

The federal government has gotten involved by developing complex evacuation plans for the foothill communities of Sandy, Troutdale, and Hood River. The residents may be lucky enough to escape with their hides intact, but the lush fields and well-groomed orchards on the northeastern side of the mountain would very likely be blanketed with enough ash and debris to set Columbia Gorge agriculture back for years. The timber industry would also be hard hit by a major eruption. In addition to thousands of square miles of stumpage destroyed by mud, ash, and lava flows, scientists suggest there would be a high probability of forest fires as well. Like the fruit growers of the Hood River Valley, the region's loggers would be hard-pressed to eke out a living from the charred ground should the mountain ever blow.

The good news is that the aftereffects of a volcanic eruption soften with time. In the wake of the Mt. St. Helens blast, insects, vegetation, and wildlife returned to the area within a year or two. Some farmers in eastern Washington who saw their crops destroyed in 1980 were able to enjoy bumper yields within a decade due to the soil's increased fertility. When ash falls it's a sterile growth medium, but a few years of erosion from Northwest winter precipitation can create a nutrient-rich mix. In fact, volcanic debris can supply such soil-enriching chemicals as calcium, phosphorous, sulfur, and potassium to an ecosystem. Be that as it may, many locals still look to the Cascades Range with dread and wonder if it will soon be Mt. Hood's turn to roar.

to Cooper Spur Road. Drive past the ski area until you come to Cloud Cap at the end of a 10-mile twisting gravel road. The road is passable only in summer months due to snow at that altitude. From here, hardy adventurers can rub elbows with glaciers, walking up Cooper Spur (a side ridge of Mt. Hood) without climbing gear in late summer, to almost 8,600 feet above sea level.

Rowena Crest

The highlight of the continuation of the Historic Columbia River Highway is Rowena Crest. You can get there by going east on I-84 past Hood for River several miles and exiting the freeway at Exit 69 (Mosier), then head east through town. Springtime blossoms and the Mosier Grange's summertime cherry booth on 2nd Street preserve this orchard town's legacy. At the eastern edge of town the Historic Highway takes you past cherry trees and hills dotted with sagebrush toward Rowena Crest. On the way up, Memaloose Overlook (see The Dalles section, below, for background) makes a magnificent photo-op with an informative heritage marker. Your next stop is **Tom McCall Nature Preserve** atop Rowena Dell.

The dry eastern and wetter western faces of the Columbia River Gorge are clearly delineated here if you follow the McCall Preserve's trail to its end and gaze east-to-west along the river. Another interesting perspective is offered directly across the river, where buff-colored terraces were left on the Washington shoreline by the Missoula Floods, 12,000–19,000 years ago. Backdropping the Washington shoreline is the town of Lyle. Farther east across the river is a nice view of the Klickitat River Canyon. Birdwatchers will relish sighting osprey, red-winged blackbirds, horned larks, red-tailed hawks, golden eagles, western meadowlarks, mountain bluebirds, and other species in the skies above. More information on the geology and ecosystem is available from a free pamphlet in the drop box on the north side of the highway, courtesy of the preserve. This 2,300-acre sanctuary was created by the Nature Conservancy and has trails on the hillsides that are open to the public. A short distance east is a circular driveway that leads to Rowena Crest overlook. Below are the Rowena

Loops, one of the more impressive views of Historic Highway architecture, an opinion corroborated by producers of televised car commercials.

Rowena Crest rose up so steeply that Willamette Valley–bound Oregon Trail pioneers had to find another way to proceed west other than by wagon train. Some decided to build rafts and float the then-hazardous rapids on the river. Before 1845 and the establishment of the Barlow Trail around the south flank of Mt. Hood to Oregon City, this was where the westernmost extent of the original overland Oregon Trail ended.

Today, Tom McCall Nature Preserve is the site of a mid-May pilgrimage by wildflower lovers. Because the preserve lies in the transition zone between the Cascades' wet western slope and the dry eastern prairies, several hundred species flourish here (among them four endemics). The fertile volcanic soil left by Mt. St. Helens eruptions (ash one inch deep was noted nearby in The Dalles in 1842) made this floral fantasia possible beginning 6,000 years ago when it dropped up to four feet of ash on the then barren plateau. The showiest blooms in the spring display include yellow wild sunflowers (balsamroot), purple blooms of shooting stars, scarlet Indian paintbrush, and blue-flowered camas. Other eye-catching species include gold star, Thompson's broadleaf lupine (an endemic), and fringecups. While the flowers are enticing, be careful of ticks and poison oak. Finally, don't forget that this area was originally named Hog Canyon due to settlers releasing their pigs in hopes that they'd kill rattlesnakes, an idea that proved unsuccessful.

If you follow the Rowena Loops east, it's possible to get back on the freeway (to go east or west) at the base of the cliffs or continue east toward the Dalles on U.S. 30 (the Columbia River Highway). Civil War buffs will be fascinated to know that Ulysses S. Grant briefly lived near Rowena Crest in one of his first commissions in the region prior to becoming a quartermaster at Fort Vancouver. During the 1850s, Fort Vancouver hosted other prominent names from the conflict including Phil Sheridan, George McClellan, Jeb Stuart, and George Pickett. Many of these military legends were stationed in Oregon and Washington territories to protect settlers

© OREGON DEPARTMENT OF TRANSPORTATION

a windsurfer on the Columbia River

THE OREGON GORGE

from Indians until 1859 when the Civil War beckoned them back to the eastern seaboard.

RECREATION AND ACTIVITIES

Windsurfing

No serious discussion of windsurfing would be complete without mentioning the Gorge's reigning status as a world center of the sport. Hood River is *the center* of the windsurfing scene, in terms of sailing sites, businesses, and the sport's unique subculture. In fact, the meteoric rise of windsurfing in the early and mid-1980s transformed this formerly sleepy rural community into a vibrant, hipster-jock haven. It catapulted Hood River onto the international scene, as evidenced by the whimsical bumper stickers around town bearing the legend "Paris, Tokyo, Rome, Hood River." Blessed by a propitious mix of geography, climate, and river currents, the Gorge was discovered as a place with strong, very reliable summer westerlies (winds going west to east), countered by the strong, westbound Columbia River current.

Actually, three of the top-rated sites for advanced sailors (and for fans) are actually located in Washington. Doug's Beach, the Hatchery, and Swell City are just across the Hood River Bridge.

Three distinct windsurf beaches lie within the Hood River city limits; all three charge a day-use fee—call the Port of Hood River, 541/386-1645, for more information. The **Hood River Marina Sailpark** is the largest and most developed of the three. A series of improvements by the Port of Hood River has given the site more amenities than any other windsurf launch in the Gorge. These include bathrooms with showers, food concessions, picnic area, grassy lawn for rigging, an exercise course, and a great family swim beach area with sheltered, shallow water for tykes. And, as the name implies, here you'll find the largest boat marina with boat launches. Beware of shallow sandbars off the shore, and the boats entering and exiting the marina. Due to the offerings here (including ample, close-by parking), this can be one of the most crowded sites around. The well-known **Rhonda Smith Windsurfing School,** 541/386-9463, provides rentals at $25 a half-day, $30–40 for a full day, and $150–200 per week, depending on the equipment and location. Lessons, including equipment, start at $20 per hour. A private launch area and rescue service round out the package. To get there, go to Exit 64 off I-84, then follow the signs to the Marina.

The Event Site, a newer and somewhat smaller

site, is located to the west of the Hood River's confluence with the Columbia. Major events, including well-known competitions, occur here. It has a lawn for rigging, and a small bleacher for spectators. This, plus its convenient location to downtown, make this an ideal spot for nonparticipants to watch the action. It provides quicker access to deeper water than the Marina, but it can also be quite crowded at times. Portable toilets and water are available, but otherwise not many creature comforts. The Event Site is located off Exit 63, or at the north end of Second Street. The Hook, named for the shape of the artificial berm built some years back that created a protected harbor, is ideal for beginners to get their feet wet. Several schools provide instruction in the gentle basin. Instead of a beach, the shore is largely steep and rocky, and the dirt road in later summer can get a bit dusty. Conditions are quite variable, particularly as some places are in a wind shadow caused by nearby Wells Island (which, by the way, is a sensitive wildlife area vulnerable to prolonged human presence). Once you're out in the main channel, winds can be strong. The views to the west from here (and hence, the sunsets) are just grand. Access to the Hook is at the west end of Portway, the paved road that first takes you to the Event Site.

About eight miles west of town, **Viento State Park** offers good river access for sailing in a beautiful, natural setting. The park has a campground, picnic area, restrooms, and water. Spectators won't have a lot of room, but the wind and wave action can get spicy here at times. Viento is located off Exit 56 from I-84. In the opposite direction, six miles east of Hood River, you'll find the **Rock Creek** launch site in Mosier. Amenities are spare, but there is a portable toilet. The river is wide here, and the chop can get high. You can reach Rock Creek off I-84 at Exit 69. At the top of the ramp, hang a right, then your first left onto Rock Creek Road. The site's on your right just past the dry creek bed.

For information about windsurfing, wind,

Many local business owners are familiar with the "20-knot clause," which permits their workers time off to "catch a blow" when the winds are "nukin'" at this speed.

and weather, call 387-WIND (387-9463), or pick up a copy of *Northwest Sailboard,* P.O. Box 918, Hood River 97031. This magazine is available all over town. In Hood River, the following schools cater to beginners: **Big Winds,** 541/386-6088; **Front St. Sailboards,** 541/386-4044; **Gorge Surf Club,** 541/386-5434; and **Hood River Windsurfing,** 541/386-5787. Most of these academies of aerodynamics offer lessons through mid-October.

Regarding fall windsurfing, pros will tell you it's the best. It's less crowded, the water's warm, and winds are lighter at school sites. Parking and rigging space at launching areas is easier to find, and there's a quality of light upon the water with enough clear days to add aesthetic appeal. Best of all for beginners is the availability of individualized instruction during fall. While conditions are generally good at most locations along the river during the season, the best places are said to be in the east end of the gorge, notably around Three Mile Canyon and other launch sites in the Arlington, Oregon, and Roosevelt, Washington areas.

Other Water Sports

As mentioned above, the Hood River Marina offers an excellent family swim area, boat marina, and also has personal watercraft rentals. **Koberg Beach State Park,** one mile east of town off I-84, but accessible from westbound lanes only, offers a sandy swim beach in a pretty setting. Be warned, however, the drop-off is steep and not safe for small children or weak swimmers. The Hook offers a nice area (when the winds and windsurfers are absent) for some gentle canoeing or kayaking.

Fishing

The area offers two different types of fishing. You can go for trout in several beautiful, small mountain lakes, most of which are west and south of the Hood River Valley. Notable among the latter are **Wahtum, Rainy,** and **North Lakes,** all about 45 minutes west of town on good gravel roads. Then too, there is the previously detailed Lost Lake whose heavy visitation might detract from its desirability during some seasons. Pick up licenses in any Hood River sport shop.

The other option is fishing the Hood River itself, or the Columbia. The Hood also offers good trout fishing and both rivers have good seasonal steelhead/salmon fishing. The Hood River can be accessed from the county parks detailed in the Camping section under Practicalities, below. Call **The Gorge Fly Shop,** 541/386-6977, for information. For a guide, call **Gorge Flyfishing Expeditions,** 541/354-2286. **Phoenix Pharms,** just off ORE 35, 10 miles south of town, 541/386-7770, is a stocked rainbow trout pond where the kids are guaranteed to reel in a big one.

Golf

Offering great views of Mt. Hood is the relatively new and popular **Indian Creek Country Club,** 3605 Brookside Dr., 541/386-3009. The ninth hole offers a photo opportunity of Mt. Hood framed by the branches of a giant pine tree.

A little farther from town is **Hood River Golf,** 1850 Country Club Rd., 541/386-3009. It features 18 holes (a bit hillier than Indian Creek) and beautiful views of Mt. Hood, Mt. Adams, elk, and geese. Open daylight to dark, come in fall if only to see the spectacular foliage. Weekdays it's a bargain at only $20 for 18 holes.

Winetasting

Tasting and tours are offered at the **Hood River Vineyard,** 4693 Westwood Dr., Hood River 97031, 541/386-7772, open daily 11 A.M.–5 P.M. The microclimate of this area is similar to that which produces Germany's Rhine wines. In addition to the rieslings, chardonnays, gewürztraminers, and other white-wine varietals produced here, the area is famous for fruit wines and award-winning pinot noir. Sweet wines, such as Anjou pear, marionberry, and zinfandel are done with great flair.

The cabernet sauvignon from **Flerchinger Vineyard,** 4200 Post Canyon Dr., 800/516-8710, took "best of show" at the prestigious Newport Seafood and Wine competition. The winery also produces chardonnay, riesling, and merlot. Open daily 11 A.M.–5 P.M. Because it's a little obscure, follow these directions to Flerchinger. As with the previous vineyard, take Exit 62 off I-84. Turn right on Country Club Road, which heads west for a brief time right after exiting the freeway. A left onto Post Canyon Drive takes you south to the winery.

Art

The **Columbia Art Gallery,** 207 2nd St., 541/386-4512, has works by local artists in exhibits that change monthly. This community-sponsored nonprofit gallery is open Friday–Monday noon–5 P.M. and weekdays 10 A.M.–5 P.M.

Rail Tour

Train buffs will be delighted to ride the **Mt. Hood Railroad,** 541/386-3556 or 800/872-4661, www.mthoodrr.com, which goes from the old railroad depot behind the Hood River Hotel through the scenic Hood River Valley to its terminus in Parkdale, seemingly at the very base of Mt. Hood (because of the volcano's immensity and proximity). Riders sit in a lovingly restored enclosed Pullman coach. Also featured are an antique concession car and, of course, the obligatory red caboose. The standard ride takes about four hours round-trip, including a stop in Parkdale. The railroad also features dinner and brunch trains, and many special events rides, such as the Fruit Blossom Special in April and Christmas Tree Trains, bedecked with carolers and other holiday trimmings. The main season is April–October. Fares for the regular excursion train are $23 adults, with a discount for seniors, and $15 for kids under 12.

Air Tour

Scenic Flights Northwest, 541/386-1099, offers a 45-minute Gorge flyover for $45 per person. **Air Columbia,** 541/490-1779, features helicopter flights at the Blossom Festival and by appointment. These tours require a two-person minimum and run $125 for a 55-minute trip to Beacon Rock and Portland Airport or Mt. Hood and Timberline Lodge. Call 541/386-1133 for packages in the same price range. For more information on scenic flights, call the Port of Hood River (they operate the airport) at 541/386-1645.

THE OREGON GORGE

Skiing

Off ORE 35 on the east side of Mt. Hood is **Cooper Spur,** 541/352-7803. Day and night skiing and cross-country skiing are offered. Low prices, $8–12, and a laidback atmosphere make this place a favorite with families and beginners.

Historic Columbia River Highway Trail

This five-mile long segment of the Historic Columbia River Highway is a must-see. It provides a great walking and biking experience (car traffic is verboten), with the spectacular engineering feat of the re-opened **Mosier Twin Tunnels** in the middle. Carved out of solid basalt and adorned with artful masonry work, the highway has become famous for the tunnels. They are about a mile from the trail's east end and 600 feet above the river. To start on the east end, take Exit 69 off I-84, turn right off the ramp, then take your first left on Rock Creek Road. Go under the railroad, and continue for less than a mile. The parking area is on your left; the highway segment begins across the road.

This portion of the old road was closed in 1953, after years of serious rockfall problems at the tunnel's west portal and the construction of the river grade highway. The state of Oregon has constructed a special rockfall shelter to protect recreationists from the hazard. The trail also features restored original stone masonry work in several places, besides the tunnels. The trailhead parking areas on either end are both called the Mark O. Hatfield Trailhead, just east and west versions. This reflects the instrumental role the influential ex-Senator had in securing federal funding to make this dream a reality.

Access to the west side parking area is gained from downtown Hood River by going to the State Street and Highway 35 junction, then heading up the hill on Old Columbia River Drive. This road actually is the Historic Columbia River Highway (officially numbered as U.S. 30). The west end has a small visitor contact/information building, with restrooms. Going west to east lets a hiker, in a mere five miles, witness a rapid climate/vegetation transition zone rarely encountered in such a short distance. Starting on the Hood River side, the highway winds its way through lush, towering Douglas fir groves. By the time you reach the east side of the tunnels by Mosier, you're in a dry oak savannah-grassland ecosystem. About halfway down the trail, a small interpretive loop trail has been developed, rewarding hikers with stunning views of this varied and beautiful piece of the Gorge. A dramatic precipice located across the river in Washington, visible from the east end and called Coyote Wall locally, is another reward of the trek.

Hiking and Mountain Biking in the Gorge

While the most famous Gorge hikes tend to cluster around the west end waterfall area, the Hood River environs has its fair share of excellent trails for fat tires and two feet. Several of these trails are right on the Gorge, eight miles west of town, accessible via the Viento Park exit off I-84 (Exit 56). All three are on the south side of the highway.

The **Starvation Creek to Viento Trail** is the shortest and by far the easiest of the three. Actually a restored segment of an abandoned piece of the Historic Columbia River Highway, this path is mostly paved, and runs a little over a mile each way. It offers some decent Gorge views, but will be of more interest to history buffs who want to retrace extant remnants of the old highway. The reference to starvation derives from a snowbound train that fared this fate in 1884. Thanks to supplies aboard and food brought in by packers, death from hunger was less an issue than the discomfort of spending several days here before the train could start moving again.

The other significance of this trail is that it provides access to the other two trails in the area. Both the **Mt. Defiance Trail (Trail 413)** and **Starvation Ridge Trail (Trail 414)** used to be accessible through the Starvation Creek rest stop exit of the highway, but it is now closed. So walk the Starvation to Viento trail, then look for signs for either of the other trails once you get to the west side of the rest stop. Both trails eventually head for the same place, converging high above the Gorge just below the top of Mt. Defiance. Being the highest point in the Gorge at 4,960 feet, Mt. Defiance presents a strenuous workout for even experienced hikers. Either route rewards you with spectacular views of the Gorge, as well as old growth woods and even pristine Warren Lake. Taken in its entirety, the Starvation Ridge Trail is somewhat steeper than the Mt. Defiance Trail. This long loop is about 12 miles round-trip. A short, two-mile loop is also possible, by following Trail 413 for a mile, then heading east (left) onto 414. This eventually takes you back to the highway where you started.

The Wygant Trail is reached off the eastbound-only Exit 58 of I-84, at Mitchell Point. Go right (west) at the top of the ramp, then follow the road heading west. This eventually becomes the trail, and follows the old route of the Historic Highway for a stretch. The trail eventually winds its way for almost four miles to the top of Wygant Peak, at 2,214 feet. Along the way, you'll pass through some native Oregon white oak groves, mixed conifer forests, and some openings with lovely views. In the Wygant Trail parking area look across the river at the remains of the Broughton Log Flume, the last such structure in the Northwest.

For **mountain bikers,** there's a network of old gravel and dirt roads just west of town that local peddlers love. Post Canyon Road starts out as a typical paved rural road, with houses scattered along each side. Shortly after its start at Country Club Road, the pavement ends and the fat-tire fun begins. Several side roads branch off from Post Canyon into the Cascade foothills, and one can ride for a long time without seeing any buildings. You will, no doubt, encounter some clear cuts and other logged areas, so don't expect pristine forests. And be forewarned, the road is at times used by groups of motorbikers, so stay alert. To get there, take Exit 62 off the freeway, go right at the top of the ramp, then take an immediate right onto Country Club Road. Follow this road about a mile as it bends to the south, then right onto the well-signed Post Canyon Road.

Mt. Hood National Forest Trails

There are many beautiful trails in this national forest, which surrounds the Hood River Valley on three sides. Most are to the south, on the way to Mt. Hood. The **East Fork Trail** offers an easy, but very scenic, amble along the swift, glacial-fed East Fork of the Hood River. It can be reached from either the Robin Hood or Sherwood Campgrounds along ORE 35, and is great on foot or mountain bike. It's about four miles between the two campgrounds, and the trail continues beyond (north of) the Sherwood Campground.

Tamanawas Falls Trail takes off from the East Fork Trail, just about a half mile north of Sherwood Campground. A short but steeper hike, this trail is uphill all the way to the reward: the beautiful Tamanawas Falls.

Surveyor's Ridge Trail (#688) traverses the ridgeline on the east side of the upper Hood River Valley for 17 miles. It offers some great Mt. Hood and valley views, and is especially fun for mountain bikers. Between late April when the snow leaves until the busy days of July a 10-mile portion of this trail is as good as it gets for fat tire enthusiasts. Pick the brains of the friendly staff at **Discover Bikes,** 1020 Wasco St., Suite E., 503/386-4820, for equipment and other ideas. The trailhead is off of Forest Service Road 17, which intersects ORE 35 about 11 miles south of Hood River and just past the big lumber mill to the left of the highway. Another popular trail with mountain bikers is the **Dog River Trail.** This 6.2-mile, sometimes steep trail can be reached at either end off ORE 35. The southern (higher) approach is at the Pollallie Campground. The trail parallels the Hood (previously named Dog) River.

Perhaps the best place to experience the transition from western alpine conifer forest to interior high desert is **Lookout Mountain** in the Badger Creek Wilderness. This aptly named 6,525-foot peak is the second highest in the Mt. Hood National Forest. To get there look for Road #44 (the Dufur cutoff). It comes up a bit south of Cooper Spur Road on the east side of the highway, not far from Robin Hood Campground. Follow it to Forest Service Road 4410, marked by a sign after a hilly five mile drive. This route takes you to a parking area opposite the trailhead to High Prairie Trail #493. Remember that there are no signs most of the six miles on Road 4410 to the trailhead, but if you bear left at the outset and ignore all secondary roads, you'll eventually see a sign indicating the final sharp left turn to the trailhead parking area. The 20-minute walk to the top on Trail #493 takes you where there used to be an old fire spotter's cabin. Directly west looms Mt. Hood. Turn 180 degrees and you face the sagebrush and wheat fields of eastern Oregon. To the south, there's the Three Sisters and Broken Top Mountains. West and north of those peaks, Mt. Jefferson's tricorn hat rises up. The body of water to the southwest is Badger Lake. To the north, views of Mts. Adams, St. Helens, and Rainier (on a clear day) will have you reeling with visual intoxication. On most days you can expect cool, windy weather, and there are yellow jackets in August and early September. As with any hike in Oregon, be sure to wear bright colors during hunting season. On the way down, several unsigned spur trails loop back to #493. As long as you keep moving downhill north and west, you'll get back to your car.

The Gorge Route

Windsurfing and vineyard-hopping complement nearby Columbia Gorge hiking and auto touring, as well as Mt. Hood skiing. Regarding the latter, the "gorge route" from Portland (I-84 and ORE 35) to Mt. Hood ski slopes is becoming a popular and scenic alternative to the more direct but traffic-laden U.S. 26. Hood River ski shops offer discounts on rentals to sweeten the deal.

Events

The most popular events in Hood River County highlight windsurfing and the seasons of blossom, harvest, and foliage in the orchards.

The third weekend in April, **Hood River Blossom Festival** celebrates breathtaking views of the valley's orchards in bloom. Arts and crafts, dinners, and the seasonal opening of the Mt. Hood Railroad also can be enjoyed. Contact the Hood River Chamber of Commerce for more details.

The fall counterpart of the Blossom Festival is the **Hood River Harvest Fest.** On the third weekend in October, the valley welcomes visitors for two days of entertainment, crafts, fresh locally grown produce, and colorful foliage. Admission is free and the apples and pears are ripe. Hood River is the winter pear (Anjou) capital of the world and produces Bartletts, comice, bosc, and other varieties at different times of the

year. Cherries, peaches, and apples round out this horn of plenty. Newton pippin apples are another renowned Hood River product. The 15,000 acres of orchards are still the leading economy in the county, with Diamond Packing the leading pear shipper in the United States.

In the second week of July, **The Subaru Gorge Games,** 541/386-7774, www.gorgegames.com, takes place in diverse locales throughout the region. This is an outdoor olympics of extreme sports including windsurfing, mountain biking, kayaking, snowboarding, kitesailing, a l0K run, rockclimbing, and other activities. Top musical acts, street concerts in downtown, special sports clinics, and family events round out this nationally televised event.

In the parking lot between 5th and 6th Streets and Cascade and Columbia is the Saturday **Farmer's Market** featuring local craft and food booths along with live music. Call the chamber of commerce for more information.

PRACTICALITIES

Accommodations

Finding a room in Hood River in the summer isn't easy, and the rates reflect it. All prices herein are summer rates; remember to add an 8 percent room tax within the city of Hood River. Despite this, the area has a surprising variety of good, relatively reasonable (under $80) places to stay.

The west side is as close as Hood River gets to generic strip development, being the newest commercial area in town. Still, there are several decent places to stay here, some with lovely Gorge views. Two motels on the far west end of town and just off Exit 62 of the freeway offer perhaps the nicest Gorge views (not counting the nearby Columbia Gorge Hotel, of course). **The Meredith Motel,** 4300 Westcliff Dr., 541/386-1515, has Eisenhower-era furnishings as well as panoramas from most rooms. The only drawback is that its proximity to the freeway might impact light sleepers. **The Vagabond Lodge,** 4070 Westcliff Dr., 541/386-2992, has lovely landscaped grounds with a playground for kids, and is a bit more set back from the highway. It is close to the Charburger Restaurant, a basic family-fare type of place, with cheap but filling breakfasts. Both motels are in the $50–80 range and are two miles from downtown. In the same area but in a different price range is **Lakecliff Estate B&B,** 3820 Westcliff Dr., 541/386-7000. Designed by A.E. Doyle, famous for such landmarks as Multnomah Falls Lodge and the Portland Public Library Central Branch, this 1908 bluffside summer home sits secluded in acres of forest. Three rooms have their own fireplace and one has a window that lets you gaze down at the Columbia from bed. There are two units that share a bathroom for $90 and two with private bathrooms for $110. Closed Oct.–April.

Three relatively new hotels can be found along the main drag (West Cascade Street), about a mile from downtown on the west side. **Comfort Suites,** 2625 W. Cascade, 541/308-1000, is the newest and fanciest of the three. To balance out its rather uncharming location, it offers immaculate rooms and amenities such as a pool and spa and some suites with kitchens. Rooms range $80–140. **The Sunset Motel,** 2300 W. Cascade, 541/386-6098, offers a good budget option, with rooms ranging $55–65. It also operates a small RV park on the premises (see Camping, below). Both of these places are walking distance to Cascade Commons, Hood River's new shopping center.

Love's Riverview Lodge, 1505 Oak St. (the main street becomes Oak Street from here east, through downtown), 541/386-8719, offers some suites with kitchens, plus a pool. Rooms run $70–125.

Closer to downtown, there are plenty of options, both bed and breakfasts and hotels. Three quaint B&Bs are located in the leafy old neighborhood near the historic center. **The Inn at the Gorge,** 1113 Eugene St., 541/386-4429, is a 1908 Victorian that can be summed up thusly: a windsurfer hangout in a classy bed-and-breakfast. Offerings include windsurfing instruction, equipment rentals and storage, group and off-season rates, and a complete kitchen in three of the four rooms. Even if you're not a "boardhead," the large and tasty breakfast served here would be reason enough to give this place a look. Rates run $80–105. Along similar lines, the **Gorgeview Bed and Breakfast,** 1009 Columbia, 541/386-5770, is a

windsurfer-oriented spot in a historic house with a great porch view and a hot tub. Rooms are quite affordable at $65–75. New on the scene, **The Cat's Meow,** 821 Oak St., 541/386-1204, is in a Queen Anne–style house a block from the east end of downtown that also offers nice views from its rooms. Doubles start at $75.

The Oak Street Hotel, 610 Oak St., 541/386-2845, is centrally located on the main street and next to a great restaurant—Brian's Pourhouse. It also has attractive rooms for a reasonable $55–67. In the heart of downtown is the **Hood River Hotel,** 102 Oak St., 541/386-1900 or 800/386-1859, an impeccably restored turn-of-the-century hotel with a first-rate restaurant (Pasquale's Ristorante). Most of the rooms go for $90–120, with a few that are more reasonable, and a few higher-priced suites with kitchens; all come with continental breakfast. Special vacation packages are also featured. The oak-paneled, high-ceilinged lobby, with cozy fireplace and adjoining lounge/restaurant, is particularly inviting. Some rooms facing the river are exposed to periodic train noise that's not likely to bother anyone except perhaps very light sleepers. All in all, "the Hotel" (as locals call it) is a nexus of activity, and the most charming in-town digs to be found.

If being on the river is essential to you, **Best Western's Hood River Inn,** 1108 E. Marina Way, 800/828-7873, is the only place in town to boast direct river frontage and even a small private beach. Its location (next to fast food places off Exit 64 of the freeway, and isolated from downtown), however, is less than ideal. Nonetheless, the rooms ($80–120) provide great opportunities to watch windsurfers, and there's a decent restaurant on the premises (Riverside Grill). Best of all is its heated outdoor pool and spa.

Another option for accommodations is to stay outside of town in the Hood River Valley. Here you'll find several nice bed-and-breakfasts in bucolic settings a short drive from the Gorge and downtown. The closest of these to the town, **Panorama Lodge,** 2290 Old Dalles Dr., 541/387-2687 or 888/403-2687, is nestled in the wooded hills on the valley's east side. Its five rooms, most with Mt. Hood views, go for $70–90, tasty breakfast included.

Spectacular views from every window are found at **Beryl House Bed and Breakfast,** 4079 Barrett Dr., 541/386-5567. This 1910 farmhouse is only four miles from town in the midst of fruit orchards below Mt. Hood, and it's not surprising to find a hearty farm breakfast awaiting you each morning. What is surprising is the budget-friendly rate of $60–70. Located halfway between Flerchinger and Hood River vineyards, this B&B is especially recommended for oenophiles. In addition, guests benefit from the innkeeper's expertise on local restaurants and windsurfing.

Another farmhouse turned bed-and-breakfast in the orchards, the **Bella Vista Bed and Breakfast,** 3000 Reed Rd., 541/386-1545, offers two rooms at $65. Farther from town in the gorgeous upper valley are two more B&Bs. **The Old Parkdale Inn,** 4932 Baseline Rd., Parkdale (terminus of the Mt. Hood Railroad), 541/352-5551, offers three rooms, two of which are spacious suites. The tab runs $115 ($135 for the suites), but the breakfast is gourmet-quality and the peaceful village will satisfy those looking for an escape from the rat race. The gardens, full kitchens, mountain views, and private baths are also appreciated. The **Mt. Hood Hamlet Bed & Breakfast,** 6471 Hwy. 35, 541/352-3574 or 800/407-0570, has good Mt. Hood views, full breakfasts, and a nice mix of modern conveniences and a historic feel for $95–115.

A distinctive 1904 Queen Anne home built near the bluffside cherry orchards by the son of J.H. Mosier, the town's founder, is today a bed-and-breakfast known as **Mosier House,** 704 3rd Ave., 541/478-3640. Mosier's church and library date back to this era as well. There are four rooms with shared bath ($85) as well as a master guest room with private facilities (featuring a vintage claw foot tub).and its own entrance and porch ($125). Weekend guests are asked to book two nights. A full breakfast (artichoke fans will like their eggs Sardu) and tea with baked goods each afternoon are included. If you don't care to stray too far from the bucolic surroundings for dinner, by publication time Mosier should have its first restaurant. You might also ask the innkeepers for directions to the interesting Pioneer Cemetery perched on a hill overlooking Mosier Creek. The

dozen graves date back to the late 19th century when Mosier was settled as a timber town. A cycle of floods wiped out the lumber mill here, adding impetus to the growth of orchards.

Camping

Hood River County runs three parks with campgrounds in the Hood River Valley. **Tucker Park,** 2440 Dee Highway (Hwy. 281), 541/386-4477, is only four miles from town, in a lovely spot along the banks of the gurgling, boulder-strewn Hood River. It's the most developed of the three county parks, with a store, restaurant, laundry, and ice machine close by. It features 14 sites with water and electricity ($14), and 67 tent sites ($13). **Toll Bridge Park,** Hwy. 35, 541/352-5522, is also set along the Hood River but in the upper valley. It's 17 miles south of Hood River. It offers showers and two grocery stores a short distance away. Full hookup sites are $15, $14 for water/electric, and $13 for tent sites. **Routson Park** is off Hwy. 35, along a roaring stretch of the Hood River's East Fork, at the gateway to the Mt. Hood National Forest. It provides a more rustic setting higher in the mountains, only 25 minutes from town. Amenities are more spare (flush toilets and drinking water available), and trailers are not recommended.

Oregon State Parks offers two full-service campgrounds right on the Columbia Gorge. **Viento State Park,** eight miles west of Hood River on the river side of I-84, Exit 56, offers direct recreational access to the mighty Columbia, making it a windsurfer favorite. From mid-March to late October, you'll pay $14–19 for one of the 58 sites with water and electric, or $13 to pitch your tent at the other 17 sites. These sites are first come, first serve but call 800/551-6949 for information. To avoid train noise, try to get a site across I-84 from the main campground. This more forested, less populated loop is far enough from the train tracks to minimize noise.

Memaloose State Park, 11 miles east of Hood River on I-84, is accessible only from westbound lanes (Exit 74) of I-84. On the Columbia with limited river access, the park offers 43 full hookup sites and 67 tent spaces, showers, and an RV dump station. Sites cost $13–19. It's only fair to mention that this campground is not far from a main freight train line, so expect to hear the trains go by, even at night. Call 800/452-5687 for reservations, mid-March to mid-October. Placards in the nearby rest area detail Oregon Trail information as well as how Natives were buried on the island to the north.

Two private RV parks are also located in the Hood River area. **The Sunset RV Park and Campground,** located right in town at 2300 W. Cascade, 541/386-6098, has a laundry, restroom, and showers on the premises, as well as 16 tent spaces and hookups for seven RVs. **The Columbia River Gorge Resort,** 2350 Carroll Rd., Mosier, 541/478-3070, is four miles south of Mosier and 10 miles from Hood River. It features a broad range of amenities, including a nine-hole golf course, store, and clubhouse. RV sites are $20; tent sites will run you $15 at both campgrounds.

There are several nice but semi-primitive Forest Service campgrounds in the Mt. Hood National Forest, which surrounds the valley on three sides. All are in pleasant settings. You can call the Hood River Ranger Station for information, 6780 Hwy. 35, 541/352-6002, or the Portland office at 503/666-0701. Some of the Forest Service campgrounds within 45 minutes of town are Sherwood, Robin Hood—both on Hwy. 35—Lost Lake, Wahtum Lake, and Laurance Lake. The latter three campgrounds are in the mountains west of the valley.

Food

Hood River's status as the premier windsurfing town in North America and a tourist mecca has brought sophisticated tastes and higher prices. No other small town in the Gorge (or the Pacific Northwest, for that matter) can boast such a roster of fine restaurants, not to mention gourmet coffee and options for vegetarians. For that matter, there aren't too many towns of a few thousand souls anywhere in the world with their own coffee roasters (Hood River Coffee Co.), several wineries (Flerchinger, Hood River), three microbreweries (Full Sail/White Cap, Big Horse, and Eliot Glacier), and some of the finest fruit in the world. The only thing to keep in mind is

that most restaurants here close early (by big city standards), so plan accordingly.

The brightest spot in Hood River's dining scene is **Brian's Pourhouse,** 606 Oak St., 541/387-4344. No Gorge establishment that we visited can match Brian's for sheer culinary creativity—a fact immediately evident upon tasting such appetizers as the chili-flaked calamari with lemon aioli and soy ginger dipping sauce and skillet roasted mussels in a red curry coconut broth. Dinner standouts include fettuccine con vongole (clams) and sesame-crusted ahi, served up with shiitake mushroom roll and grilled Asian beans. And leave room for the Dutch apple pie. Most entrées are $12–18. A Sunday brunch is served till 3 P.M.

Downtown is blessed with four other restaurants that will please discerning palates, particularly those partial to Italian food. **Pasquale's Ristorante,** 102 Oak St. (in the Hood River Hotel), 541/386-1900 or 800/386-1859, offers Italian and continental dinners, good breakfasts, and some outdoor seating (the closest thing to a sidewalk café in Hood River). Most dinner entrées fall between $14 and $19. Standout items include the rack of lamb in rosemary garlic sauce with mint jelly, and duck boscaiola with shiitake mushrooms and cranberries, draped in a balsamic vinegar glaze. The quiet elegance of the surroundings is a delight at breakfast as well with such specialties as eggs Florentine ($6.25) and homemade Italian chicken sausage ($3.50). In a similar dinner price range and culinary genre are two new Italian restaurants. **North Oak Brasserie,** 113 Third St., 541/387-2310, offers a solid repertoire of regional Italian dishes served in the warm-colored, cozy confines of a cellar below a historic building. The Brasserie has already developed a reputation for delectable appetizers and such as grilled goat cheese and roasted garlic, shiitake mushroom ravioli, and other creative fare. Vegetarians will also appreciate the gorgonzola gnocchi, lasagna, and butternut squash ravioli. The roasted garlic and brie soup is the house specialty, and serious oenophiles will be drawn here to sample the finest wine collection in town. **Abruzzo Italian Grill,** 1810 W. Cascade, 541/386-7779, features a rustic Mediterranean setting, old country culinary traditions, and a highly regarded chef, Mark DiResta. Main courses range $8–18, with most pasta dishes below $15. Indoor and outdoor seating is available. Open for dinner Tues.–Saturday.

The Sixth Street Bistro, 6th and Cascade, 541/386-5737, has a good selection of microbrews on tap and an eclectic menu featuring fresh Northwest and pan-Pacific elements. A nice herb bread comes with your meal. Dinner prices are typically in the $10–15 neighborhood.

Lighter, moderately priced dishes ($5–7) are served up in two new downtown restaurants. **Blossoms Eatery,** 106 Oak St., 541/386-1903, is a pan-Asian restaurant featuring a menu that spans the Far East. A "must" dish is the Thai green papaya salad ($5). **Anz Cafe,** 315 Oak St., 541/387-2654, has soups, sandwiches, and other luncheon fare inside Hood River's premier cookware shop, Anz Panz. This is a great place to come for coffee and desserts. Speaking of dessert, don't miss the award-winning truffles and other goodies at **The Carousel Candy Company,** 3rd and Cascade, 541/387-2737.

On "The Heights" (the plateau forming the start of the lower Hood River Valley, a few hundred feet above downtown), you'll find three noteworthy eateries that define the Hood River "hot zone." **Fiesta Restaurant,** 1310 13th St., 541/386-7121, offers the most authentic Mexican food in town, in humble but pleasant surroundings. It's the only one of the five Mexican restaurants in town that members of the local Mexican-American community regularly frequent. The carnitas (fried pork) and camarones con mojo de ajo (shrimp in garlic sauce) are especially good. All this can be had for around $10 per person, not to mention continuous Mexican pop music to accompany your meal. Right next door **Big Easy,** 1303 13th St., 541/386-1720, spices up the local restaurant scene with cajun, creole, and barbecue, from sweet and mild to hot and wild. Expect dinner bills to run $15–22.

For the truly carnivorous, there's **The Mesquitery,** 1219 12th St., 541/386-2002, where wood-smoke and barbecue flavors issue a wake-up call to your taste buds for lunch or dinner. You'll find the best ribs in town here, not to mention

steaks, fish, and many other dishes. Particularly recommended is the pollo vaquero (cowboy-style chicken), mesquite-grilled chicken doused in pico de gallo sauce and rolled up in a taquito. Prices run $10–18 for dinner, depending on how many side dishes you tack on to the main course.

Two other highly recommended restaurants are ensconced at opposite ends of town. To make a special occasion of your evening, try **Stonehenge Garden,** 3405 W. Cascade, 541/386 3940, located in a historic house in a romantic wooded setting on the west end of town. Stonehenge specializes in classic renditions of aged beef, fresh seafood, and fine wines. A must-try dessert is the bread pudding, finished with crème brûlée and bourbon caramel sauce. The setting and quality justify the prices of $15–25 per dinner. If you're coming off Exit 62 of I-84, look for it just past the gas station across the road. Follow the signs on the right up the dirt road about a mile.

East of downtown, in the Best Western Hood River Inn, is the **Riverside Grill,** 1108 E. Marina Way, 541/386-2200. Featuring a riverside perch along the Columbia, the locale allows diners to enjoy a fine view while dining on superb Northwest cuisine. The prices average $15–20 for dinners, about half that for breakfast and lunch. The inn is located on the north (river) side of I-84, just off Exit 64.

A cluster of informal but good deli/lunch/coffee places is located along Oak Street in the downtown area. **Andrew's Pizza and Bakery,** 1070 Oak St., 541/386-3940, easily wins our vote for best pizza in the Gorge. East Coast transplants will especially appreciate the thin-crusted triangles, so reminiscent of the Big Apple. Lots of extravagant toppings are available, as well as microbrews and great coffee. In the back of Andrew's is the Skylight Theater and Pub (see Entertainment and Nightlife, below). Down the street one block find **Holstein's Coffee Company,** 12 Oak St., 541/386-4115, probably the best straight-up java joint around. Walk across the street for a darn good bagel with one of seven types of cream cheese or other accompaniments at **Hood River Bagel Company,** 13 Oak St., 541/386-2123. **Mike's Ice Cream,** a few blocks uphill (walk off those calories) at 504 Oak St., serves up great ice cream and shakes from April until October. Especially noteworthy, when available, is the incomparably delicious huckleberry shake. Just around the corner from Mike's, on 5th Street between Oak and Cascade, is **Wyeast Naturals,** 541/386-6181, part natural foods store and part veggie deli. Fresh and healthy offerings include daily soups, sandwiches, and killer scones.

The Trillium Cafe, 207 Oak St., 541/386-1996, is a good option for a wholesome downtown lunch at reasonable prices. They feature delicious quiche of the day specials, soups, and more. Not far from downtown, the **New York Sub Shop,** 1020 Wasco Ave., 541/386-5144, makes giant sub sandwiches which, true to East Coast tradition, are amply stuffed with piquant ingredients and very reasonably priced. You are guaranteed to leave satisfied.

For sojourners wandering through the valley to admire the pastoral beauty of the orchards or Mt. Hood views, **Santacroce's,** 4780 Hwy. 35, 541/354-2511, will satisfy your hunger with good, basic Italian food and pizza. Homemade sausage is a specialty. Open for dinners only, prices here are moderate ($5–13) and the atmosphere decidedly informal and family-friendly. In the lower valley there's **McNew's Clubhouse Restaurant** at the Hood River Golf Course, 1850 Country Club Rd., 541/386-5022. This is the only pace in town with German cuisine.

Finally, fans of Mexican street food should keep an eye out for a food trailer in a parking lot just east of Cascade Commons, in the lot next to Zeman's Music, 1819 W. Cascade, on the south side of the road. **El Rinconcito** serves up tacos, burritos, and other down-home south-of-the-border goodies at rock-bottom prices. Along with traditional carnitas (pork), chicken, asada (beef), etc., there's a vegetarian option too. The huge, delicious burritos, which cost $3.50, are still considered the best deal around for those wanting to kill a big hunger on the run.

Entertainment and Nightlife

While not a mecca for after-hours entertainment, Hood River does have a few good offerings in this department. **The Skylight Theater and Pub,** 107 Oak St., 541/386-4888, located in the back of Andrew's Pizza, brings first-run Hollywood movies and the occasional art film to downtown. It includes bar service and is really a part of Andrew's, which means you can devour a steaming slice and a frosty mug of ale while viewing a flick. Film buffs can also check out **Hood River Cinemas,** corner of 5th and Columbia Sts., 541/386-7503, featuring current, popular films at a five-screen theater.

The **River City Saloon,** corner of Cascade and 2nd St., 541/387-2583, brings big name live music acts on weekends, and features a beautiful dark wooden bar and wood dance floor. This is the "in" nightlife spot out in Hood River.

Hood River and environs has spawned its own mini-microbrew scene, with three separate establishments making and selling brews on the premises. The most famous is the **Full Sail Tasting Room,** 506 Columbia, 541/386-2247, offering beautiful river views with its renowned suds. This brewpub also attempts to showcase pub grub with gourmet ingredients culled from the region. Its hours are noon–8 P.M. daily in the summer, with winter hours limited to Wed.–Sunday. **The Big Horse Brew Pub,** 115 State St., 541/386-4411, in addition to selling several varieties of its homemade beer (the India Pale Ale is recommended), also serves up a full menu of lunch and dinner items. Most nights include live acoustic music, with many local talents featured. For other live music, keep your eye on downtown posterboards for the occasional excellent live shows (mostly regional or national blues acts) periodically playing in the ballroom of the Hood River Hotel.

Tucked away in the upper valley, in the heart of tiny Parkdale, is the charming **Elliot Glacier Public House,** 4945 Baseline Rd., 541/352-1022. They make great beers, such as an excellent Scottish ale and ample-bodied porter, and serve some dinner items, with nightly specials. It's the perfect place to stare at the awesome view of nearby Mt. Hood, while you wet your whistle.

Information and Services

The **Hood River County Chamber of Commerce,** at the Hood River Expo Center, Portway Ave., 541/386-2000 or 800/366-3530, has an extensive array of maps, pamphlets, and other

THE OREGON GORGE

information about the area. They also have a huge, 3-D model of the Gorge terrain that is an excellent way to orient you to local geography. Take Exit 63 off I-84 and head north (toward the river), following the signs to the Expo Center. Another source of local visitor information, although limited to outdoor recreation, is the **U.S. Forest Service Scenic Area Office,** 902 Wasco Ave., 541/386-2333. To get there, head down 7th Street until it winds around to the left, becoming Wasco Avenue, then follow the signs.

Downtown, you'll find the **U.S. Post Office** (97031), 408 Cascade, between 4th and 5th Streets. Just two blocks up the street, at 3rd and Cascade is the **Hood River Police Department,** 541/386-2121. There are public restrooms a block away at the old City Hall, 211 2nd Street. **Hood River Memorial Hospital,** 13th and May, 541/386-7889, is open 24 hours a day with a physician-staffed emergency room. **Care Corner,** at 12th and May, offers immediate care for illnesses and injuries. More serious cases are referred to the hospital across the street.

Greyhound Bus Lines serves Hood River, stopping at the Port of Hood River office at 600 E. Marina Way, 541/386-1212. Also at the same location is **Columbia Area Transit,** 541/386-4202, providing van and special bus service, but not offering regularly scheduled routes in town. **Hood River Taxi and Transportation,** 1107 Wilson St., 541/386-2255, offers taxi service in and around the city around the clock except midnight–7 A.M., OR 3 a.m.–7 A.M. on Saturday. **Blue Star Columbia Gorge Airporter,** 800/247-2272, offers airport shuttle service between Hood River and Portland International Airport. **Club Wet, Inc.,** 541/386-6084, has regular flights between Seattle and the Hood River airport. Call ahead for reservations and ticketing. The flight takes about one hour. A travel agency that can line you up with home rentals, airline reservations, windsurfing rentals/lessons, and bed-and-breakfasts is **Gorge Central Reservation Service,** 220 Eugene St., 541/386-6109.

Two laundromats are available in town. **West Side Laundromat,** 1911 W. Cascade St., 541/386-5650, has extra large capacity machines and is across the street from Safeway. You'll find **The Heights Laundromat,** 1771 12th St., 541/386-3050, in the Hood River Shopping Center a mile south of downtown.

Radio station KMCQ, 104.5 FM, broadcasts wind readings 7:20 A.M.–9:50 A.M. at half hour intervals. Local ski and road reports are also available on this station and on KIHR, 105.5 FM, the Hood River station.

The Dalles

It hits you shortly after leaving Hood River. Fir and pine give way to an oak savanna, and, eventually, the sage and grasslands east of The Cascades. You've come to The Dalles, a place Lewis and Clark in 1805 called the "Great Mart of all this Country." Instead of encountering an Indian potlatch on the Columbia however, the modern visitor will see a city of 12,000 souls living in the industrial hub of the Gorge. The cherry orchards looming above the town to the south and the aluminum plants at the western entry might be what The Dalles is more about today than tourism, but travelers interested in retracing the footsteps of Lewis and Clark and the Oregon Trail pioneers are coming here in increasing numbers. Besides pioneer wagon ruts and Lewis and Clark campsites, visitors are also discovering a first-rate museum and well-preserved downtown architectural landmarks in a National Historic District. A springtime salmon ceremony celebrated here for thousands of years can also enhance the historical reverie.

The Dalles is named for a feature of its topography that no longer exists. The name of the city goes back to early 19th-century French Canadian voyageurs. These Hudson Bay Company trappers thought that the boulders proliferating the river east of present-day downtown resembled the large flat basaltic flagstones (Dalles literally translates as "flagstones") used as gutters in the streets of Montreal. The giant trough (known as Five- Mile Rapids or The Long Narrows) created

© BRIAN LITT

The Dalles, with Mt. Adams in the background

by these rocks slowed the huge spawning runs enough to create an important salmon fishery that coalesced around a series of cascades upstream, Celilo Falls. The latter drew tribal gatherings to the river's shoreline for thousands of years. Their dipnets and spears were joined by the white man's fishwheels and canneries here in the second half of the 19th century. This same set of Dalles motivated the construction of a hydroelectric dam here in 1957 (strong currents to spin turbines) whose slackwater replaced the roiling cascades. This decimated the already beleaguered salmon runs and Gorge Native culture. Nonetheless, the Dalles Dam made inland shipping and irrigated fields possible while supplying low-cost electricity for everything from local aluminum plants to tens of thousands of households throughout the West. In short, La Grand Dalle de la Columbia may be no more, but its ripple effects endure.

DIVERSE CULTURES

The Dalles has seen many ethnic groups come and go. The Euro-American culture established by the pioneers and explorers overwhelmed these ethnic groups just as they had the indigenous peoples, giving them a more muted presence today.

The Chinese, for example, lived here during the heyday of the salmon canneries in the late 19th and early 20th centuries. At that time, waves of butchers from the Pearl River Delta put in 11-hour days at the Seufert canneries, one of which was located near the present-day Lake Celilo. The Chinese also came here to work on the railroads while Japanese toiled in the orchards. Most of the Chinese returned home after saving money to buy land while Japanese were removed to internment camps during WW II.

Today, Latino farmworkers comprise the largest minority population. Thankfully, they appear to be have greater chances for assimilation into the culture than their predecessors.

ORIENTATION

The downtown business district is located along 2nd and 3rd Streets (both one-way) near many of the landmarks mentioned in the walking tour outlined in the paragraphs to follow. Most people live in a residential section above this hub area, with access via 10th Street. Bend, a central Oregon recreation mecca, is 131 miles south via ORE 197. A bridge links up with Washington's Hwy. 14. Portland is 85 miles away via I-84.

While the heat here can be stifling by May,

wildflower displays at nearby Rowena Crest and Deschutes River Recreation Area pull petal peepers into the region. Closer to downtown, lupines bring a blue tinge to brown hillsides in late spring.

SIGHTS

The Dalles is the site of more historically significant events than any other Pacific Northwest city. Long before the advent of written history, the largest gathering of the tribes on the continent came here annually to fish for salmon, gamble, and trade. In the 19th century, the area hosted the region's seminal routes of exploration and settlement, and today has the status of being the only town where the Lewis and Clark and Oregon Trails come together. Other historical Dalles' distinctions include being the first fort west of the Rockies and the county seat of a bailiwick whose governmental reach extended into Montana. It can also claim status as the terminus of the Oregon Trail as well as of the region's first paved highway. In between these eras, prosperity came to the city when steamboats and railroads exported products from area salmon canneries, orchards, and wheat fields. These modes of transport (along with stagecoaches) also took travelers to and from this center of traders, ranchers, and miners. It also was the point of embarkation for so many gold rushes that a U.S. mint was established here.

The Columbia Gorge Discovery Center and Wasco County Historical Museum artfully exhibits all of the foregoing and more, making it the perfect place to begin a Dalles sightseeing itinerary. Situated on a bluff above the Columbia on ORE 30, the museums are accessed via Exit 82 off I-84. After turning right onto ORE 30 to head west again, follow a winding road to the parking lot.

Columbia Gorge Discovery Center and Wasco County Historical Museum

The Columbia Gorge Discovery Center and Wasco County Historical Museum, 5000 Discovery Dr., three miles west of The Dalles on ORE 30, 541/296-8600, coalesces the rich historical, geological, biological, and cultural legacies

of this region. Even its very site is on hallowed ground, having been occupied by local Indians with a burial site near the river, an overnight camp for Lewis and Clark as well as an embarkation point for Oregon Trail travelers on their way west. The Discovery Center addresses the region as a whole, articulating a 40-million-year time line with scale models and videos as well as simulated "hands-on" experiences. The exhibits follow a timeline beginning with the cataclysms that created the Gorge through its native occupation to the coming of the pioneers and subsequent domination by the White Man. Along the way, native plants and animals are given attention along with such diverse activities as road building, orchards, and windsurfing.

Of the many noteworthy exhibits, the tape recordings of tribal elders along with artifacts (check out the authentic Indian dugout canoe) and films and photos of Native American culture (don't miss the Army Corps film of Indians fishing at Celilo Falls) are especially compelling. Also worth a look is the Ford Motor company promotional film on the Columbia River Highway from the 1930s. Artistic flourishes abound in the lobby with a built-to-scale inlaid polished granite map of the Columbia and a 16-foot wooden sturgeon carved from a single walnut log nearby. Living history programs with costumed interpreters happen outside the museum on summer weekends; the programs demonstrate early lifestyles, tell stories, and answer questions. A decent cafeteria is located on-site.

A short walk away, the Wasco County Historical Museum reviews 10,000 years of Native American life, early explorers, and industry. Especially interesting are exhibits showcasing such arcane chapters of county history as the race between two competing railroads to build a million-dollar-a-mile route up the Deschutes River Canyon and the reign of Indian guru Bhagwan Sri Rajneesh. As with the Discovery Center, technology is effectively employed to tell the story of a county that saw some of the most critical early chapters of Oregon history.

Both exhibit halls are open daily 10 A.M.–6 P.M. A single admission fee pays for both venues: $6.50 adults, $5.50 seniors, $3 ages 6–16.

Wasco County Courthouse

If you retrace U.S. 30 (3rd Street) back to the western edge of town, you'll come to the restored Wasco County Courthouse next door to the chamber of commerce. The courthouse was moved from its original location where it presided over much of the country west of the Rockies in the mid-1800s. Artifacts from the jail on the first floor together with the courtroom on the second floor appear surprisingly intact for a facility that fell into disuse in 1882.

Prior to heading downtown, stop in at the **chamber of commerce,** corner of 2nd and Portland Streets, 404 W. 2nd St., The Dalles 97058, 800/255-3385, to pick up two free pamphlets, *The Dalles: Historic Gateway to the Columbia Gorge* and *Walking Tours to Historic Homes and Buildings.* While you're here, you might check on when free guided excursions are given of downtown's historical districts. You can also pick up a publication on the town's historical murals.

Downtown Walking Tour

Pamphlets from the chamber of commerce (see above) can guide you on two one-hour tours. Begin with an itinerary centered on the west end in the Trevitt Historical Area where the town's wealthy business community lived in some of the city's finest old homes. Highlights include interesting murals and a painting on the **Egbert House,** stained and etched glass windows and old-fashioned roses at the **Weiss House** and a stone root-cellar near the **Pentland House.** Ornate porch posts, gabled roofs, decorative brackets, leaded windows, and the like usher you along on this time machine voyage. Some of these homes are bed-and-breakfasts today. The chamber of commerce recommends doing this tour in the afternoon, then spending a night here in a B&B so that you can take in the Commercial District Loop after breakfast the next day when most of the buildings are open.

The **Commercial District** features structures dating from 1850 to the late 1920s. During part of this era, The Dalles was considered one of the wildest towns west of Chicago and with no shortage of saloons and houses of negotiable affection. Your pamphlet documents where much of this ac-

tivity took place and more. The itinerary will also relates the extent to which floods and fires were recurring facts of life in many frontier towns. The non-renovated, 1867 **Waldron Drug Store** (north side of 1st and Washington Streets), for example, has an entrance below street level after 1880 floods resulted in the raising of 1st Street. This building was a gold-miner provisioning store as well a ticket office and post office for steamboats. The second oldest bookstore in the state, Klindts Booksellers still shows high-water marks from 1894 floodwaters that crested at 59 feet downtown.

Local color is also imparted by downtown **murals** of historical scenes and painted ads on building facades. Historical murals are appearing in many towns with Oregon Trail heritage, and The Dalles is no exception. *Decision at Dalles,* by Don Crook, shows pioneers setting out on the Columbia River route to the Willamette Valley. Look for this 70-foot-high mural at the corner of 2nd and Federal Streets. *Ancient Indian Fishing Grounds,* by Robert Thomas, is located across the street and depicts scenes of Native fishing sites (The Long Narrows and Celilo Falls) currently submerged under slackwater behind the dam. *Lewis and Clark at Rock Fort,* by Robert Thomas, can be found at 401 E. 2nd St. on the side of Tony's Town and Country Clothing. *The Dalles: Trade Center for 10,000,* by Roger Cooke, is a third mural nearby depicting the gathering of the tribes along the Columbia described by Lewis and Clark. More murals are projected for this town so rich in history and memory. Other murals depict Gorge Natives and the U.S. government signing the 1855 Treaty, the importance of wheat farming to the region, and other such themes. The **Mural Society** provides brochures at 402 E. 2nd Street.

A handful of more prominent sites, some of which are included in the chamber of commerce walking tour pamphlet, are treated separately below. Driving directions have been included for the Native American and Lewis and Clark sites.

Klindt's Booksellers

Klindt's, 315 E. 2nd St., 541/296-3355, represents another bit of history in The Dalles. Established in

1870, it is the oldest bookstore in Oregon, complete with original wood floors, a high ceiling, and oak-and-plate-glass display cases. This is a good place to find out the "rest of the story" about the area. You might hear about visits by John Muir, John C. Fremont, Kit Carson, and Rudyard Kipling or how The Dalles had 25 saloons in town a century ago.

St. Peter's Landmark

This building, corner of 3rd and Lincoln, 541/296-5686, is featured on both walking tours mentioned above. This 1898 structure's 176-foot high steeple with the 6-foot-tall iron rooster on top welcomes visitors to the west end of downtown. Originally a Catholic church, its gothic brick facade, a statue of the Virgin Mary carved from the keel of a sailing ship, and 100-year-old stained glass have a calming effect on nerves set on edge by dodging I-84 truck convoys on the way into town. It's open every day except Monday and major holidays. Hours are Tues.–Fri. 11 A.M.–3 P.M., Sat.–Sun. 1 P.M.–3 P.M. Close by is the oldest home in The Dalles, The Rorick House, built in 1850.

The Dalles City Park

Pioneer Ezra Meeker placed a marker on this site (now at 6th and Union Streets) in 1906 to commemorate the end of the original Oregon Trail. In 1845, Samuel Barlow opened the first overland route to the Willamette Valley here, extending the initial route. Barlow Road aficionados should pick up the U.S. Forest Service brochure to guide them over much of this pioneer thoroughfare. The **Dalles Visitor and Convention Bureau,** 800/225-3385, puts out a driving-tour pamphlet that also outlines how to traverse the northernmost portions of the route.

In this park you'll also note the **Victor Trevitt House.** An interesting postscript on this pioneer printer and politico is supplied at the Memaloose rest stop halfway between The Dalles and Hood River on the west side of I-84 and at a scenic turnout on the Historic Highway east of Mosier on the way to Rowena Crest. At the turnout on the westbound interstate, is a restroom overlooking Memaloose Island on the Columbia.

Close by, a historical placard mentions that Trevitt's grave was put on the island among native burial sites at his own request, so high was his esteem for his Native friends. "Memaloose" means "to die" in Chinook, and this island experienced a death of sorts a half-century ago. At the time, water backed up by the Bonneville Dam submerged this sacred site, reducing it to its current half-acre size. Given the decimation of the Indian population and the salmon runs, this event only added insult to injury.

Fort Dalles and Surgeon's Quarters

Fort Dalles, atop the bluff at 15th and Garrison Streets, 541/296-4547, was established as Fort Drum in 1850 in response to the massacre of missionaries Dr. Marcus and Narcissa Whitman. The Whitmans had attempted to impose the white man's ways on the Native Americans with unfortunate results. For instance, the natives could not understand the concept of private property and felt that Whitman's whipping of those who inadvertently took what they considered to be communal property was unduly harsh. The last straw occurred when a measles vaccine administered by Whitman to Indian and white children killed the native children while the white children were cured. The Indians were further confused and understandably angry when they were told that their offspring's adverse reactions were due to a lack of immunities. Their violent retaliation incited Congress to establish the only military post between Fort Vancouver and the Rockies. It was the most important military installation in the West from the signing of the 1855 Treaty with Gorge Natives until 1867 when it was de-commissioned.

Several years later, in 1854, the establishment of Wasco County made The Dalles the seat of a 130,000-square-mile bailiwick stretching from the Cascades to the Rocky Mountains. This was the largest county ever formed in the United States. Stretching from latitude 47 to latitude 46, 17 other counties were established in central and eastern Oregon. After being platted in 1854, The Dalles' charter was granted in 1857.

The Surgeon's Quarters, dating back to 1856, serves as a museum for armaments, period furniture crafted by Oregon Trail migrants (as well as treasures shipped around Cape Horn), and other pioneer-era artifacts. The historic photos here of Celilo Falls and The Long Narrows fishing areas in their glory are especially interesting. This building is the only remaining part of the original fort complex, and the museum is Oregon's oldest—dating back to 1905.

Hours at Fort Dalles are daily 10 A.M.–5 P.M. March–Oct.; Monday, Thursday, Friday noon–4 P.M. and Saturday 10 A.M.–4 P.M. Nov.–February. Admission is $3 adults with discounts for children and seniors. To receive information by mail, write: City of The Dalles Museum Commission, P.O. Box 806, The Dalles 97058.

Rock Fort

Lewis and Clark aficionados will undoubtedly notice pamphlets, signs, and murals referring to a site called Rock Fort. This was one of the few places that the explorers stayed on two occasions. Coming from downtown, take Exit 83 (W. 6th Street), turn left and then make your first right onto Webber Street to the port area. Go a mile on Webber toward the river and make a right on W. 1st Street. As you drive east past the ware-

LEWIS AND CLARK'S BOTANICAL LEGACY

President Thomas Jefferson, who conceived of the Lewis and Clark Expedition, intended it to break new ground scientifically, keynoting this desire with the statement, "The greatest service that can be rendered any country is to add a useful plant to its culture." With one of the most diversely ranging set of botanical species found anywhere, the Columbia River Gorge gave the explorers ample opportunity to give form to Jefferson's vision. The mere fact that they described, drew, and sometimes named species never seen before made their discoveries valuable. Those species that were able to make it back to Philadelphia for further study were the moonrocks of their day. Whether it was collecting Oregon grape (which eventually became the state flower) at Celilo Falls, noting vine maple at the Bridge of The Gods, or bigleaf maple at Bradford Island (site of the present-day Bonneville Dam) the botanical training the explorers received from Benjamin Barton in Philadelphia prior to their trek proved invaluable.

Two Lewis and Clark discoveries modern travelers especially covet are balsamroot and thimbleberry. The springtime spectacle of balsamroot's ubiquitous yellow blossoms atop Rowena Crest and Dog Mountain is one of the Gorge's great visual feasts. It was first mentioned in an April 14, 1806 entry in Skamania, or Klickitat County. And one of the prime hiker snacking treats from the wild, thimbleberry, was discovered near The Dalles on April 15, 1806.

The region around The Dalles was the site of the majority of Lewis and Clark's flower-hunting forays in the Gorge. On their return trip east, the salmon weren't spawning, the weather was mild, and there was enough leisure time for this activity. The 17 species they noted during the spring of 1806 included sagebrush, which was called "southern wood" and "the aromatic shrub." This symbol of the West was noted below Celilo Falls, April 20, 1806. Important in Native American ceremonies as well as a vital food source for deer, elk, and grouse here, it is fast disappearing due to invasive plants, the natural cycle of fire being disrupted, and other outgrowths of modern civilization.

Many of the plants indigenous to the eastern Gorge noted by the explorers are currently being replanted around Rock Fort and are expected to be in bloom by the time of the Lewis and Clark Bicentennial (2003–2006). Currently, gardens filled with Lewis and Clark's plants can be enjoyed at The Columbia Gorge Discovery Center and Wasco County Museum. The latter facility also has a copy of Clark's journal, as well as other expedition artifacts. Gorge-bound visitors interested in following the botanical trail of Lewis and Clark should consult *Journals of The Lewis and Clark Expedition*, Vol. 12, by Gary Moulton, U. of Nebraska Press, 1999. The work includes plant photos from the Lewis and Clark Herbarium in Philadelphia (the facility to which the explorers brought many of the 176 species they had cataloged by journey's end), as well as a summary of the explorers' botanical explorations.

houses, several signs reassure you that you'll be at the dynamic duo's overnight bivouac shortly. The undeveloped gravel lot surrounded by big stones overlooking the river contrasts with the industrial district nearby.

Unlike the more impressive Rooster Rock, Beacon Rock, and other Lewis and Clark landmarks, this site calls upon your imagination to ward off the sights, smells, and sounds of the surrounding area. A visit to the mural *Lewis and Clark at Rock Fort,* 401 E. 2nd St., should help fill in any gaps in your visualization of the two explorers on the banks of the Columbia here. The Corps of Discovery first set up camp on this spot after portaging around Celilo Falls where they became infested with fleas. They camped here on October 25 and 27, 1805, and on their return trip, April 15–18, 1806. On the latter trip, they collected 17 area plant specimens that made it back to Philadelphia (see the special topic Lewis and Clark's Botanical Legacy). In addition to noting the abundance of plants, the expedition reveled in the area's wide open spaces and mild weather after a water-logged winter in the coastal rainforest. Expedition journals describe the eastern Gorge thusly:

> *As the ripples gently lap against the Lake Celilo shoreline, try to imagine yourself standing here amid throngs of Indians and racks of drying salmon with the roar of waters abruptly dropping 20 feet at Celilo Falls.*

> *. . . a beautiful seen. . . particularly pleasing after having so long been imprisoned in mountains and these almost impenetrably thick forests of the seacoast.*

The Dalles Dam and Celilo Falls

While a hydroelectric dam built in 1957 might seem out of synch with a venue whose early history is its greatest appeal, a visit here offers a look at petroglyphs and displays on Lewis and Clark as well as the fate of Celilo Falls. The latter was a staircase of rapids over which Indians fished from wooden scaffolds until they were submerged by Lake Celilo, which was created by dam construction. The dam tour details the workings of the world's fourth largest hydroelectric project (largest dam on the lower Columbia). To get

there, take I-84 to Exit 87 and the Frontage Road to the visitor center, a staging area for the free train that tours The Dalles Dam. For information on tour hours, call 541/296-9533.

You might notice that the dam's longest arm runs parallel to, rather than across, the river. This is because the trough through which the Columbia runs here is so narrow that there wouldn't be room for navigation locks, generators, fish ladders, and spillways with a conventional design. From 1863 to 1915, travelers and commerce went around the rapids on a portage railroad. Thereafter, a canal enabled vessels to bypass the tumultuous waters. This canal was buried beneath waters backed up by the dam in 1957. Since that time, water traffic has gone through the locks on the Washington side.

The visitor center is open from early June to Labor Day, but you can visit the powerhouse (Exit 88) 9 A.M.–4 P.M. the rest of the year to see the petroglyphs and pictographs removed from the area that is now under water.

The first weekend of April, the age-old Native American ritual of welcoming the first salmon upstream takes place at Celilo Village, 12 miles east of The Dalles (take the Celilo Exit off I-84) on a shelf at the foot of a bluff overlooking the interstate. The public is welcome to join the celebrants free of charge for fry bread, huckleberries, and salmon cooked over an open fire and served with boiled roots and venison. Look for the ceremonial lodge a short distance southwest of the exit. Contact the chamber for more details.

Today, Celilo Village is cut off from the river by railroad tracks and the freeway. For a perspective on the 24-mile-long Lake Celilo created by the backup of dam waters, take Exit 96 and stand on the small gravel beach. As the ripples gently lap against the shoreline, try to imagine yourself standing here amid throngs of Indians and racks of drying salmon with the roar of waters abruptly dropping 20 feet at Celilo Falls.

© ALBERT BARNES/MARYHILL MUSEUM

Celilo Falls as pictured in 1938

THE OREGON GORGE

RECREATION AND ACTIVITIES

The Dalles Art Center and Gallery

Enjoy rotating exhibits of local artists in various media in the beautiful 1910 Carnegie library that's listed in the walking tour pamphlet on the corner of E. 4th and Washington Streets. Hours run Tues.–Sat. 11 A.M.–5 P.M. Call 541/296-4759 for information.

Windsurfing

Besides its historical significance, The Dalles is gaining a reputation as the best place in the Gorge to learn windsurfing. The bowl-like contours of **Riverfront Park**—easily accessible by Exit 85—mute the power of the winds while isolating the area from the Columbia's stiff current and keeping the waves down. With wind currents that always seem to blow you back toward shore, beginning windsurfers can venture out with a greater feeling of security here than elsewhere in the Gorge. Park amenities include a restroom and picnic area.

Mayer Park West, located below the Rowena bluffs about seven miles west of town features strong west winds and easy access to open water with good chop. Portable toilets and a picnic area are onsite. To get there, take Exit 76 off I-84

and go north across the railroad tracks. Turn right (east) and follow the road to its end.

Another site appreciated by advanced sailors is **Celilo Park,** nine miles east of The Dalles. Both the wind and the currents can get strong here. It has an attractive park atmosphere, with lots of shade, a grassy rigging area, and restroom facilities.

White-water Rafting

You'll find a popular run just a 45-minute drive south of The Dalles. The put-in is at Maupin, a dusty but cute town straddling U.S. 197. Class III white water makes this a popular experience for beginners who like thrills without spills. **CJ Lodge Whitewater Rafting,** 800/395-3903, offers expert guides for day trips. Their offerings include packages with meals and overnight lodgings.

Fishing

Steelhead and trout fishing are renowned at the mouth of the Deschutes River. It's possible to hike into remote fishing holes here (see Hiking/Biking at Deschutes River Recreation Area, below). At Lake Celilo close by, anglers will find sturgeon, walleye and steelhead.

Oregon Guides and Packers, P.O. 673, Springfield 97477, 541/937-3192, produces a free catalog of outfitters, including fishing guides and white-water rafting companies on the Deschutes and other area waterways. Otherwise, call **Young's Fishing Service,** 800/270-7962, for overnight packages on the Columbia and Deschutes Rivers.

Orchards of The Dalles Driving Loop

A scenic drive beginning on 2nd Street goes south along Mill Creek or Dry Hollow Roads through orchards on Olney, Skyline, and Threemile Roads. This drive is best savored during April's cherry blossom season.

Hiking/Biking at Deschutes River Recreation Area

About a dozen miles east of town, the riverbank of the Deschutes near its Columbia confluence is a mecca for several different kinds of explorers. Fishing, wildflower, and bird-watching enthusiasts as well as history buffs (thanks to area Lewis and Clark and Oregon Trail heritage markers) all set out on adventures here, but hikers and mountain bikers predominate.

Gentle and scenic hiking and biking trails parallel each other along the **Lower Deschutes River.** To get there, take I-84 east from The Dalles to the Celilo exit (#97). Turn right and then immediately left, following the frontage road several miles. Immediately after the Deschutes River Crossing, the trailhead is on the right. These trails meander for 25 miles past old homesteads, springs, and groves of willow and locust trees. The bike trail is on higher ground, while the walking trail hugs the riverbank. Around 1860 part of the trail was the location of a historic wagon road to the gold mines near Canyon City. Later, this thoroughfare became the focus of a great rivalry between two competing railroads. A Wasco County Museum exhibit details the attempt to build a railroad line through this canyon to Bend. While this effort failed, the railbed has enjoyed a new incarnation as the Deschutes River Trail. The prime time to visit this area is fall when cooler temperatures (avoid the inferno in July and August) and red-tinged sumac are an epiphany amid the 10-foot tall sagebrush and other desert scenery.

Other Activities

A visit to the restored Moorish-style **Granada Theater,** 223 E. 2nd St., 541/298-4710, lets you enjoy music and movies in a theater that dates back to the days of vaudeville. Later, it was the first theater west of the Rockies equipped for talkies. Recently, the long, thick red curtains have been coming up on *Northwest Passages.* With productions showcasing the gamut of regional history, these musical interludes take place every Saturday at 8 P.M. between Memorial Day and Labor Day except during Neon Nights (see Events, following).

Columbia Cinemas, 2727 W. 7th St., 541/296-8081, is located behind Kmart and has early matinees all week supplementing evening show times. **Cascade Cinemas,** 1410 W. 6th St., 541/296-8081, also shows first-run flicks.

Sorosis Park serves as a backyard for the locals to enjoy tennis courts, picnic areas, and just plain beautiful views. To get there, take Trevitt Street south and follow the signs.

Events

Find out more about the following events online at www.thedalleschamber.com. **Fort Dalles Days Rodeo,** 541/296-2231 or 800/255-3385, is the only "serious" rodeo in the Gorge, replete with clowns, buckin' broncos, and steer ropers. Admission is $10 per night at this third weekend of July (starting Thursday) affair. The rodeo grounds are located just west of downtown on River Road. Take Exit 83 off I-84, then a quick left onto Webber, go under the freeway, and left again on River Road.

The fourth weekend of April marks the **Cherry Festival,** a local favorite. This event features parades with antique cars downtown, live music, and beautiful cherry blossoms (several months before the harvest itself).

Neon Nights, is the big musical event here, taking place outdoors at Riverfront Park the second weekend of August. Call the chamber, 800/255-3385, for more details.

Historic Dalles Day takes place the second Saturday in October. The downtown National Historic District comes alive with interpreters staffing many of the downtown historic landmarks to help evoke the pioneer past. The chamber of commerce provides information on this event.

PRACTICALITIES

Accommodations

As in the rest of the Gorge, the rumble of freight trains and barge and freeway traffic are never far away from a good night's sleep. At least The Dalles has a selection of lodgings with diverse appeal. Given the rich history here, a bed-and-breakfast is more in keeping with the surroundings and not appreciably more expensive than many motels.

The **Columbia Windrider,** 200 W. 4th St., 800/635-0051, is recommended for outdoorsy folks. Set in a rambling old home on the edge of the historic district, it features a pool, hot tub, and four units sharing a bath. When you're through relaxing, the innkeeper can offer windsurfing tips and point the way to other outdoor attractions. Singles can get a room here for $45 and doubles $56. A foursome can get away with $65 for a large room. A kitchen and laundry are available.

More elaborate quarters can be found at **Columbia House B&B,** 525 E. 7th St., 800/807-2668. This 13-room movie-themed manse with 1930s art deco styling sits above the city and the river. The four guest rooms have private baths and are well-situated for a good night's sleep. This 1939 home sits on acreage set back from the street (with no alley or street behind) to insure quiet. Guests also appreciate the seven-mile river view from the shaded patio deck and from the house. Rates range $65–85.

The **Liberty House,** 514 Liberty St., 541/298-5252, is located in the 1892 Weiss House. Despite a location in an industrial neighborhood, the Victorian theme pervades right down to the antique dolls and bedspreads. Choose between a double bed for $65 or a queen and day bed for $75.

Close by the Windrider bed-and-breakfast you'll find a budget motel, **Oregon Motor Motel,** 200 W. 2nd St., 541/296-9111. Rates are $40\#208>50.

Three chain motels are clustered in the suburban west side of town. **Quality Inn,** 2114 W. 6th St., 800/848-9378, features rooms ranging $64–75 and offers a pool, hot tub, guest laundry, and some kitchenettes. Next door, **Days Inn,** 800/991-0801, charges $57–69 and has an indoor pool and some kitchenettes. A family-style restaurant, Cousins, is

convenient to both of these hotels. The **Super 8,** 609 Cherry Heights, 800/800-8000, lies in a shopping mall area a half-mile closer to town. It charges $79 for a king, $47 for a single.

The Best Western Umatilla House, 2nd and Liberty, 541/296-9107, boasts an on-site restaurant and a downtown location, charging $47 for a single and $69 for a room with 2 queen beds.

The **Shilo Inn,** 3223 Bret Clodfelter Way (near The Dalles Dam), 800/222-2244, offers mini-suites for $109, or river-view kings for $129. While it's possible to get non-view rooms here for below $70 certain times of year, it would defeat the purpose of staying, given Shilo's excellent location on the river. From the Frontage Road you can step onto the low rocky bluff over the Columbia and look at Lone Pine Indian village. This handful of weather-beaten huts was left by a group of Shakers, a Native cult incorporating some aspects of Christianity that flourished here at the turn of the 20th century. This area also was the site of the Seufert Cannery, which is detailed in a Wasco County Museum exhibit. The Dalles Bridge reaches across the Columbia just past Lone Pine. The Dalles Dam Visitor Center is less than a mile away from the motel. Under the bridge look for Native fishing scaffolds. The river-view dining room and lounge offer moderately priced meals. There's also an outdoor pool, hot tubs, sauna, and fitness room as well as guest laundry facilities on-site.

Camping

Deschutes River Recreation Area, 800/452-5687, boasts 34 primitive sights for tents, trailers, or self-contained RVs. Campers enjoy picnic tables and fire grills; piped water and flush toilets are available. No reservations are accepted and the fee is $10–13. Open mid-April to late October, take Celilo Exit 97 off I-84 and turn south on Hwy. 206, then drive five miles to the park. This is a popular place when the steelhead are running. For 25 miles upstream, the river is inaccessible from the road. Immediately past this point is **Mack Canyon,** an idyllic spot where you can fish for steelhead and try to spot a bighorn sheep, reintroduced here in 1993. Just be on the lookout for rattlesnakes. Call the Bureau of Land Management at 541/416-6700 for information on the 19 sites for tents and RVs (no hookups here) as well as driving directions.

Food

Begin the day with the best coffee in town and an array of baked goods at **Holsteins,** 3rd and Taylor, 541/298-2326, at the east end of downtown. On weekend nights, enjoy dessert and occasional live acoustic music here.

Two Mexican restaurants, located at opposite ends of downtown are reliable choices for variety and reasonable prices. Our preference, **Ixtapa,** 728 E. 3rd St., 541/298-1265, serves up such *estilo Jalisco* specialties as camarones del diablo (devil's prawns). Prices run $8–12. In this price range, **Casa del Mirador,** 302 W. 2nd St., 541/298-7388, also serves south-of-the border dishes. Their signature plate is panchita del mar (belly of the sea)—a combo of prawns, crab and orange roughy cooked in a foil pouch with a secret sauce.

Two other ethnic choices occupy a moderate price range. **The Lighthouse Restaurant,** 802 Chenoweth St., 541/298-8896, has the only sushi you'll find east of the Gorge's Cascade crest. Tempura and rice bowls run $5–12 here. **Hunan One Express,** 421 Union St., 541/296-7118, can be found on the corner of 4th and Union Streets. Most dishes cost $6–10 on a menu of Szechwan and Cantonese favorites.

After visiting St. Peters, the century-old Gothic revival landmark, you can delay your reentry into the 20th century by grabbing a bite in the shadow of history at the **Baldwin Saloon,** 1st and Court Sts., 503/296-5666. This 1876 building (it was a restaurant then, too) is a repository of turn-of-the-century oil paintings adorning the restaurant's high-ceilinged brick walls. The cast-iron facade, 18-foot mahogany bar, and the pendulum clock also ensure a historical reverie. We enjoyed the fresh oysters (pan-fried, $12), homemade soups, and smoked salmon mousse here. Oysters Rockefeller and pork Roberto are touted by regulars. Peanut butter pie and hazelnut cheesecake are recommended for dessert. Main courses range $6–16.

Close by the Liberty House bed-and-breakfast, **Bailey's Place,** 515 Liberty St., 541/296-6708, is known as one of the best places in the region for prime rib. In addition, well-prepared steak and seafood are served in the confines of the 1865 Italianate Edward French House. Prices run $10–20 for main courses in this local favorite for romantic fine dining.

Getting Around

Five buses a day go between The Dalles and Portland for $13 one-way on **Greyhound,** 201 E. Federal (corner of 1st), 541/ 296 2421 and 800/ 231 2122. The transportation center is a copy of the old railroad depot.

Blue Star Columbia Gorge Airporter, 800/247-2272, has shuttle service to the Portland airport.

Information

The Dalles **chamber of commerce** is located at the corner of 2nd and Portland Streets, 404 W. 2nd St., The Dalles 97058, 800/255-3385. Their website is www.thedalleschamber.com. Additional information on this area can be had by calling 800/98-GORGE.

Two historic buildings on the walking tour also serve utilitarian functions. The **post office,** 100 W. 2nd St., 541/296-2609, housed in a 1915 classic structure, is the oldest federal building still in use in the Gorge. In like measure, the city **police,** 313 Court St., 541/296-2613, hold court in a 1908 stone building.

By contrast, the **Mid-Columbia Medical Center,** 541/296-1111, offers facilities so modern that they were praised by Bill Moyers as being in the vanguard of medical care in his public television documentary on the subject.

Wash clothes at **The Washin' Shop,** 1256 W. 6th St., 541/296-9722.

Washington Gorge

Washougal to Dog Mountain

The gateway to the Columbia River Gorge Scenic Area in Washington begins at milepost 18 of Hwy. 14 two miles east of Washougal. Before this boundary was established in 1986, what *The Oregonian* described as a "creeping social glacier," the Portland-Vancouver area had festooned hillsides and riverfront with housing and industrial development and was threatening to move farther east. Today, the border of the Scenic Area is a place where the sights, sounds, and smells of Clark County paper mills and waste treatment plants begin to abate. As traffic thins, forested hillsides, wetland wildlife preserves, and river vistas welcome you to western Washington's Columbia Gorge.

If you've only experienced the western Gorge in Oregon, be prepared for some differences. The 43 miles between Washougal and Dog Mountain is still on the wet side of the Cascades Range, but the shoreline's southern exposure gives it more sunshine than its Oregon counterpart. You'll also appreciate less traffic than the glut of cars careening down Oregon's I-84. Despite the rural, country-road feel that pervades the western Washington Gorge, you'll

Castle Rock, also known as Beacon Rock

find an award-winning museum, two health spas, and the Gorge's premier destination resort. Natural highlights include the springtime floral fest atop Dog Mountain, the region's only natural hot springs located in the forest primeval, and diverse outdoor recreation activities at Beacon Rock State Park.

The Land Ethic

The Washington side boasts one of the first and one of the most eloquent expressions of the land ethic in the Gorge. In 1915, Henry Biddle, a descendant of Nicholas Biddle, who helped finance Lewis and Clark's expedition and later edited their journals, bought an 848-foot basalt monolith 23 miles east of Washougal that industrial interests had been wanting to quarry. He recognized that Beacon Rock had geological (the nation's largest freestanding monolith), historical (Lewis and Clark named it in 1805 and used it as a navigational reference point), and scenic value. To make it a recreational resource, he built a trail to the top. Upon his death, his heirs attempted to donate it to Washington State Parks, but received a lukewarm reception. When the Army Corps of Engineers wanted a piece of the rock as material for a jetty at the mouth of the Columbia, the family offered it to Oregon State Parks who were very much interested. This compelled Washington to reconsider and establish the 4,000-acre Beacon Rock State Park in 1935.

HISTORY

The Chinook Indians populated this region and had extensive contact with Lewis and Clark, who camped near the river at present-day Cottonwood Beach in Washougal during the first week of April 1806. Expedition journals imply that the Corps of Discovery might have intended to stop there only overnight March 31, 1806. But the next day, they saw Native American canoes moving downstream and learned that the people were escaping famine in the east. The expedition remained at the beach until April 6 and hunted and dried elk.

French Canadian voyageurs in search of pelts for Britain's Hudson Bay Company came in the wake of Lewis and Clark, leading to the establishment of that firm's western headquarters in 1824 at Fort Vancouver. With lots of single men and a shortage of women, it was hard for the British to sustain a permanent claim to the region. Even though a Hudson Bay Company trapper married a Chinook maiden and established a small settlement at Washougal (Land of Rushing Water) by 1847, it was already clear that the sun had set on the British empire along the Columbia River.

As Oregon Trail emigrants streamed into the Gorge, the truth of U.S. Secretary of State John C. Calhoun's words became clear. He had said, "the battle for the West would be won in the bedroom," predicting that pioneer couples would simply outbreed the mostly single trappers and merchants in the Hudson Bay Company's employ. By 1848, England decided to let go of her claim on the region, established in 1792 by Vancouver.

Shortly thereafter, the settlers encountered another foe. When more pioneers arrived to take advantage of 1850 government land giveaways that usurped tribal claims, tensions grew. After an 1855 treaty with Gorge Natives further encroached on Indian lands, a series of skirmishes at several forts ensued in 1856. These uprisings were put down (see Fort Cascades under Sights, following) and increased military presence gave further impetus to the already fast-growing population, transportation, and trade in the Gorge's first official town on the Washington shoreline, Cascades. Several years later, many of the troops were called back to the East Coast for the Civil War. The town continued to flourish, however, because of its legacy as a portage around the Great Cascades of the Columbia.

As military portage roads, tramways, shipping locks, and railroads made the movement of people and commerce around these rapids easier, other towns sprang up including Washougal, Cape Horn, Skamania, and Stevenson. Cordwood to fuel steamboats became a major cottage industry in the region during the second half of the 1800s. Area forests also supplied lumber destined for a mid-19th century housing boom in Gold Rush–era San Francisco and firewood for such upriver locations as The Dalles.

Outside of hot springs resorts that developed around the turn of the 20th century in Skamania and Carson, the region maintained a largely resource-based economy that went up and down with the allowable cut for the better part of the last century. This began to change with the 1993 opening of Skamania Lodge in Stevenson, a luxury destination resort highlighting the natural beauty of the Gorge. The nearby Columbia Gorge Interpretive Center has also attracted cruise ship shore excursions and bus tours to town. Plans to develop more recreational resources also promise to diversify the economy of the Washington side of the Columbia River Gorge.

SIGHTS AND ACTIVITIES

Lewis and Clark Campsite
Reportedly, the Port of Camas/Washougal has decided to establish a park with heritage markers at Cottonwood Beach for the 2006 bicentennial of the explorers' stay here. In the meantime, those following the Lewis and Clark Trail (note markers all along Hwy. 14) can find this site with the following directions: from near milepost 17 on Hwy. 14 at the east end of Washougal, turn on 32nd Street at the sign for Port Industrial Park. Go four-tenths of a mile to Index Street and park at the base of the dike.

Two Rivers Heritage Museum
Marked by a sign on Hwy. 14, Two Rivers Heritage Museum, Front and 16th Sts., Washougal, 360/835-8742, shares a parking lot with a Pendleton Outlet Store. A block north is the Washougal Post Office. This small museum's highlights are the Native American baskets to your left upon entering, a fascinating collection of out-of-print photo books on the early days in the region, and a gallery of old Gorge photos and paintings that trace the history of the region from ancient times to the present. Of arcane interest in this assemblage is an August 1970 article on the wall about the Sky River Rock Festival

set up by politicians in this conservative mill town to divert protestors from picketing an appearance by President Richard Nixon in downtown Portland. The admission is $2 and the hours Tues.–Fri. 11 A.M.–3 P.M. all year.

Pendleton
Washougal's claim to fame is the **Pendleton Woolen Mill**, 17th and A Sts., 800/568-2480, in operation since 1912. Hour-long guided tours (no cameras allowed) are given weekdays 9, 10, and 11 A.M. and 1:30 P.M. Detailed information on this company is offered in *Moon Handbooks: Oregon* by Stuart Warren and Ted Long Ishikawa. An outlet sells seconds and overstocked items.

Steigerwald National Wildlife Refuge
Two miles east of Washougal, if you look south from milepost 18 near the beginning of the western border of the Scenic Area, you'll see the marshes and meadows of the Steigerwald Refuge. This area will eventually become a gateway visitor center to the Columbia River Gorge Scenic Area. By 2005, the facility will feature trails through natural habitat, an elevated viewing structure overlooking wetlands, an information booth, classrooms, a gift shop, and parking. Call 541/386-2333 for more information. In the meantime, more than 100 species of birds have been seen here, among them tundra swans, bald eagles, and wood ducks.

Cape Horn
Driving east from Washougal, Hwy. 14 begins to ascend from the Columbia River and the railroad tracks. After about five miles, the highway reaches its highest point and is clinging to rock cliffs. A couple of road turnouts with a commanding view of the Columbia looking east toward Beacon Rock and beyond has been labeled as Cape Horn. While limited space to park at the viewpoints might compel you to drive on and the chicken wire inhibiting rock-slides off the sheer cliffs across the highway doesn't inspire confidence, Cape Horn is a "must" photo opportunity. The sweep of river and cliffs here make up the preeminent vistas on the Evergreen Highway.

THE MYTHIC LEGACY OF THE COLUMBIA GORGE

Modern-day history books include Lewis and Clark and the Oregon Trail pioneers in their writings about the Columbia River Gorge. Future tomes on the region will add Woody Guthrie, D.B. Cooper, and perhaps Bigfoot to the Who's Who of area notables. While their relationship with the only sea-level cleft in the Cascades was transitory, each of these Gorge travelers has carved out a permanent niche in the psychic landscape of the Pacific Northwest.

Perhaps the most tangible remnants of this legacy are the 26 tunes penned by Woody Guthrie here during one month in the spring of 1941. He had been hired by the federal government (for $266.60) to write songs to help sell the public on the Bonneville Dam's goal of harnessing the river for irrigation, flood control, and cheap electricity. Out of this effort came such standards as "Roll on Columbia" ("your power is turning our darkness to dawn"). Considering his forebears in the Columbia Gorge, it's altogether fitting that the folksinger laureate of our country reached his creative peak in this storied landscape.

Despite Guthrie's predominant themes of social justice and environmental grandeur, a song about the heist of the century might have been forthcoming had this troubadour been writing after November 24, 1971. On that day, D.B. Cooper bailed out of a Boeing 727 over southwestern Washington with $200,000 in cash—after executing the world's first successful airplane hijacking/extortion. It all began when someone calling himself Dan Cooper (later misidentified to a UPI reporter as "D.B." by the FBI) commandeered a Portland-to-Seattle flight by handing the stewardess a note about a bomb he said would explode unless he received a large sum of money and some parachutes. To underscore his threat, he opened his briefcase to reveal a foreboding network of wires and sticks. After his request was granted at the Seattle airport, the flight headed back toward the Oregon border, where he jumped out of the plane and into history. He also might have jumped into the Columbia River if a small portion of the money recovered along its banks in 1980 is any indication. Some years later, a diver found what he claimed was Cooper's parachute not far from this site. In any case, the derring-do of this modern-day Jesse James was the high-tech equivalent of a stage robbery committed at a full gallop. With only unconfirmed sightings of the mysterious Mr. Cooper over the last two decades, all that remains of this crime is the poetic justice of its Old West backdrop to stir imagination and wonder.

For years, Cape Horn's cliffs had been an obstacle to road construction until 1929 when the Shed Bridge supplanted the old roadbed which went through the Washougal Valley. This broad promontory, which sits 400 feet above the river, was named in the first decades of the 19th century by French Canadian voyageurs who thought it evoked Cape Horn in South America. Reportedly, faint pictographs and petroglyphs can be seen near the base of the cape. During the late 19th-century heyday of steamboats, a small settlement thrived here.

For a short and scenic side trip, head east downhill from the viewpoint and take Cape Horn Drive down to the river, through overhanging maples and Douglas fir trees. This steep, narrow, serpentine road is not recommended for large vehicles. In August, look for bluebells along Hwy. 14 in the Cape Horn area. A proposed Cape Horn Park featuring cliff-top viewpoints, large trees, and grassy meadows is currently under consideration.

Franz Lake

About seven miles downhill from the Cape Horn viewpoint, look for a small turnout on the south side of the highway. A walkway leads a short distance to viewing platforms and interpretive placards. Franz Lake, a wetland wildlife refuge, features an abundance of waterfowl, birds of prey, tundra swans, bald eagles, and snow geese. The tundra swans are best seen in February and sightings of the other species also tend to be best during winter. Wapato, a sweet bulbous root that was an important form of sustenance for Gorge tribes until its decline, re-established itself here in the second half of the 20th century.

Another secret the Columbia Gorge might share if it could talk would be the whereabouts of the abominable snowman, aka Bigfoot or Sasquatch. Native American tribes of the region regarded this creature as a fact of life and celebrated its presence in art and ritual. Whether it exists outside the mind or not, the King Kong of the Northwest forests has attracted to the region everyone from hunters and academics to curiosity seekers and *National Enquirer* reporters. Although the notion of a half-man, half-ape eluding human capture seems implausible at first, a brief look at some of the evidence might convince you otherwise. As recently as the winter of 1991, reports from a remote area of the Blue Mountains (whose chief drainage is the Columbia River) spoke of more than 60 miles of tracks left in the snow by a large five-toed creature. Scientists on the scene were of the opinion that the pattern of the prints and the gait could not have been fake. A similar conclusion was reached in 1982 about a plaster cast of footprints taken from the same mountain range. A Washington State University professor detected humanlike whorls on the toe portions of the prints, which he said showed that the tracks had to have been made by a large hominid. Reports

and evidence of actual encounters abound in the annals of the Northwest, compelling the U.S. Army Corps of Engineers to list it as an indigenous species, accompanied by a detailed anatomical description. Skamania County, whose southern border is the Columbia River shoreline, declared the harming of these creatures a gross misdemeanor punishable by a year in jail and a $1,000 fine.

The unwavering belief of Bigfoot adherents among the scientific community, and the Native insistence that it's a living entity, has naturally met with skepticism. But considering that stories about two-toned black and white bears roaming the alpine hinterlands of China persisted for centuries until the 1936 discovery of pandas, there could be something new under the sun in the 21st century.

In any case, Bigfoot, Woody Guthrie, and D.B. Cooper all possess a mythic aura that will last as long as people gather round the campfire to sing songs and tell stories. And in the flickering firelight, there might be a shadow or an echo of someone or something that'll give you pause. It's all happened many times before here in the Columbia River Gorge.

Beacon Rock State Park

One mile after passing through the town of Skamania (gas and food available at the General Store), this 848-foot rock appears on the south side of the highway. It is the heart of an ancient volcano whose outer layer was worn away by the Missoula floods. Besides its Guinness-like dimensions, the rock provides a recreation mecca. Camping (open year-round, no reservations, lots of amenities for $10 a site), 14 miles of trails (see Hikes, following), and a swimming beach are within the park's confines. Climbing routes, a nearby boat launch, horseback riding, and mountain biking round out the activities here. In addition to the land surrounding the rock on the south side of the highway, the park's campground and the Hamilton Mountain Trailhead lie across the highway up a service road.

Fort Cascades

A mile beyond Beacon Rock is the town of North Bonneville, relocated from its old location a short distance upstream in the late 1970s to make way for the Bonneville Dam's second powerhouse. Today, this small residential community is home to Army Corps of Engineers and other dam workers. The convenience store and gas station might be the only reason to make a right at the main town site. Farther east on Hwy. 14 however, turning right on Dam Access Road (milepost 38.5) takes you into Fort Cascades—the location of Washington's first official town and an Indian conflict known as The Blockhouse Wars.

The latter term refers to the 1856 attacks by Gorge tribes on area forts, the designs of which had block-like contours. A series of information kiosks near the parking lot recount the conflicts as well as subsequent developments, featuring photos taken of the area in 1867. Throughout the second half of the 19th century, this settlement served as headquarters for efforts to portage the Great Cascades of the Columbia. Today, markers along a 1.5-mile self-guided hiking loop just beyond the information kiosks denote the sites of the old town and fort as well as other landmarks. An 1860 gravestone, remnants of a portage railroad track, and other artifacts enhance this time machine voyage to what may be termed the cradle of pioneer settlement in the western Gorge. A drop-box with pamphlets (none were there when we visited) at the trailhead should help you get more of a sense of this history and perhaps avoid getting sidetracked off the interpretive loop which has several confusing spur trails.

A Damsite Better

Located a short distance east of Fort Cascades is Washington's branch of the **Bonneville Dam,** milepost 39 on Hwy. 14, 509/427-4281. Opened in 1982, turbines here, together with Oregon's facility, produce over a million kilowatts of power that feed into Northern California's grid. The latter fact took center stage during the California energy crisis of 2001 when a Northwest drought added to the Golden State's energy woes.

A tour of the powerhouse lets you peek inside a spinning turbine and gain insight into how hydroelectric power is produced. Fish-viewing windows display lamprey eels, salmon, steelhead, and other species as they head upstream each summer and fall. As in Oregon, fish counters tally the species to help make fish management decisions on such issues as catch limits and whether to run water over dam spillways to help baby salmon on their seaward migration. The visitor center is open daily 8 A.M.–6 P.M. during the summer, 9 A.M.–5 P.M. the rest of the year.

Columbia River Gorge Interpretive Center

The Columbia River Gorge Interpretive Center, 990 SW Rock Creek Dr., Stevenson, 509/427-8211, provides an excellent introduction to the history and geology here with special emphasis on the bailiwick covered in this chapter. Located a mile west of town between Hwy. 14 and Skamania Lodge, it is also easily reached from Oregon via the Bridge of the Gods, several miles east.

The exhibits proceed chronologically, begin-

the view east from Cape Horn

© BRIAN LITT

ning with a simulated basalt cliff filled with artifacts. Early photos (including some famous ones of Gorge natives by Edward Curtis), rubbings of petroglyphs, and pioneer quotations also help establish a narrative flow to the stories told here. As you move along in the museum, large displays such as a 37-foot high replica of a 19th-century fishwheel and a restored Corliss steam engine that once powered a sawmill are particularly eye-catching. There are also theaters showing features about the cataclysms that formed the Gorge and other topics pertinent to the region.

Upstairs, the focus narrows, with a room totally devoted to Skamania County (which once extended to the Rockies) history and such arcane collections as 4,000 rosaries and the personal effects of a Russian nobleman who claimed the Gorge was a spiritual vortex. In short, you'll leave here with heightened understanding of Gorge inhabitants, past and present, as well as thought-provoking perspectives on logging, salmon, power generation and other topics making up the region's complex history. The latter can be supplemented by perusing one of the excellent books in the museum shop's collection, close to the entrance. On clear days you can look across Rock Creek Cove just outside the museum at a beautiful view of the Columbia. Admission is $6 adults, $5 seniors and students, $4 children 6–12, free for children 5 and under. Open daily 10 A.M.–5 P.M. except major holidays.

Wind River Hot Spring

The only natural hydrothermal soaking pool (i.e., not piped into a tub in a building) in the Columbia Gorge is Wind River Hot Spring. As with most natural hot pools in the Northwest, bathing attire is optional and the atmosphere is decidedly casual. Located about two miles upstream from the Wind River's mouth and on its east bank, the waters here vary in temperature throughout the year. In the winter,

Henry Biddle built the path to Beacon Rock—a 4,500-foot long trail with 53 switchbacks, a 15 percent grade, and steps and catwalks—in the era prior to vehicular traffic and power tools. He had one helper; they finished the job in two years.

chilly water from the high river level dilutes the heat. Thus, the pools are hottest in late summer. The setting is gorgeous, the experience therapeutic.

To get there, head north on Berge Road from Hwy. 14 (first turn east of the Hwy. 14 Wind River Bridge) in Home Valley. Go about a mile up Berge Road, then turn left on Indian Cabin Road. Continue on this unpaved road about three quarters of a mile downhill, going under the power lines until the road reaches the canyon bottom. A small, undeveloped parking area is maintained by the private landowner, for a small fee. A rough trail along the east bank of the Wind River takes eager soakers to the hot pools, about three quarters of a mile from the parking area. Allow at least 30–40 minutes for this walk, which is really a scramble over large boulders and huge tree roots. Be careful of poison oak.

HIKES

Beacon Rock

Located seven miles west of the Bridge of the Gods, the path to the top of Beacon Rock is amazing for two reasons. First, the notion of Henry Biddle building this 4,500-foot long trail with 53 switchbacks, a 15 percent grade, and steps and catwalks in the era prior to vehicular traffic and power tools with only one helper in two years defies credulity. Then, of course, there are the views on the way up and at the top. Because the trail wraps around this volcanic plug, you get ever-changing perspectives on the river, the forest, and the cliffs. As for the huge swath of Gorge visible from the top, we suggest a late June sunset hike. Because it's light so late in the Northwest during the summer and you're only a short drive from some good restaurants in Stevenson seven miles east, if you finish your meal by 8 P.M., on certain nights you could arrive at the summit in time to see the

Beacon Rock rises steeply above Gorge foothills.

Gorge bathed in alpenglow. This is a good hike for kids if you can trust them to use the trailside railings. They'll love looking down at the Burlington Northern as it chugs by, because from atop Beacon Rock the railroad looks like a Lionel Train set.

Hamilton Mountain

This trail provides an intriguing set of options for different energy levels and interests. After the first mile, you'll come to a unique and beautiful waterfall. Intrepid hikers can continue several miles to the summit for a dizzying view of the Gorge along with early June wildflowers. The trailhead is across Hwy. 14 from Beacon Rock and up a service road past the Beacon Rock Campground. In a little over a mile you'll arrive at an unmarked fork. Look for a small spur trail as it veers north (left) and up from where the main trail starts to descend to Hardy Falls. This spur trail will take you to a railed-in cliff and a rock-walled chamber wherein you see a beautiful, 50-foot cascade known as **Pool of The Winds** at Rodney Falls.

There's good news for those continuing on to the summit in April or October. Because you're on the south-facing slopes of the Washington Gorge, the snow encountered on many of Oregon's sub-alpine trails across the river in spring and fall is notably absent in upper elevations here.

Dog Mountain

During the month of May, if you drive Hwy. 14 to mileposts 53 and 54 nine miles past Stevenson you'll see a large gravel lot on the north side of the highway that's full of cars. You've arrived at the Dog Mountain trailhead. Wildflower enthusiasts come at this time of year to climb the steep three-mile trail to the 2,948-foot summit and catch the blooms at their peak. While you're likely to enjoy the vegetation and views spring through fall here, between mid-May and June is usually prime time.

Travel writer Richard Lovett described the trail's 2,900-foot elevation gain (a 22 percent grade) as the "distilled essence of StairMaster," so get here early and avoid the heat of the day. While the relentlessly steep switchbacks going up will probably punish your quadriceps, your ankles and toes will catch it on the way down. The rewards for this potential discomfort are slopes draped in springtime balsamroot as well as dozens of other multi-colored species proliferating the inclined meadows near the summit. Other enticements include all-encompassing panoramas of the Gorge from upper elevations and a summit-level loop showcasing fair weather views of Mt. St. Helens, Mt. Hood, and Mt. Adams.

Rattlesnakes and poison oak are always a possibility, so use caution. It's especially important to bring plenty of water and wear shoes with good ankle support. You can also stop at the Forest Service information desk in the Skamania Lodge lobby and ask about the newer, less steep trail to the top. It's a little longer, but you'll be able to walk around the next day without pain.

PRACTICALITIES
Accommodations

With Washougal (just west of the Scenic Area) close enough to the city to defeat the purpose of Gorge-bound travelers spending the night (not to mention a decidedly un-Gorge ambience) and a dearth of lodging options almost all the way to The Bridge of the Gods (just past milepost 41), our listings begin halfway through western Washington's Gorge. At press time, **The North Bonneville Spa and Resort,** P.O. Box 356, 509/427-7767, was anticipating opening in the fall of 2001. Drawing on healing waters from nearby Moffat Creek (a traditional place to soak for Gorge Natives), this hostelry offers a complete spa experience in the European tradition amid Northwest Cascades decor. Upon entering the lobby, a 35-foot-tall river-rock fireplace and nine windows—each 30 feet tall and nine feet wide—immediately evoke *The Hall of the Mountain King*. The Paul Bunyanesque motif is seen again in the huge high-ceilinged building housing a nearly Olympic-sized pool filled with 98° mineral water. Other spa facilities include two dozen soaking tubs and 11 massage rooms. Ornate Oregon white oak woodwork, wrought-iron light fixtures and other aesthetic refinements seem to greet the eye at every turn in this 74-room lodge. An on-site restaurant, a big garden, and a landscaped outdoor spa should also soothe mind, body, and spirit. To find this remote retreat, turn right at Hwy. 14's milepost 38.5 (Dam Access Road), then head east until you come to a tunnel under the highway. On the other side of the tunnel, follow Cascade Drive east and north to the resort. Rooms will begin at $136.

About seven miles east from North Bonneville, another bastion of Gorge hospitality awaits. The immense picture windows of **Skamania Lodge,** 1131 SW Skamania Lodge Way, 509/427-7700 or 800/221-7117, look eastward towards a river view that feeds the soul. Even if you don't spend the night here, come to take it all in from the high-ceilinged sitting room just past the front desk. Besides the view, the high ceilings and immense rock fireplace evoke the warmth and grandeur of a classic national park lodge. From the petroglyph rubbings, pictographs, and other Native American motifs decorating the public rooms to the Pendleton blankets in the guest accommodations, Skamania's decor instills a sense of place. The food in the dining room follows suit, drawing on a regional bounty of Northwest fish, lamb, and produce in a menu featuring dishes such as chinook salmon roasted Indian-style on an alder plank. The active traveler will enjoy the resort's golf course, exercise room, pool, tennis courts, and horseback riding and hiking trails. In this vein, don't forget to bring a swimsuit to experience unparalleled views from an outdoor hot tub seemingly carved from stone.

A Forest Service information desk sits across the hall from registration to the left of the front entrance with free Gorge information pamphlets as well as a ranger on duty to answer questions and sell Northwest Forest Passes. A bookstore here sells titles relating to Gorge human and natural history. Rates vary with the season and the type of room (forest or river view), but expect to pay anywhere from $130 to $279 for a modified American plan bed-and-breakfast package. Check out Skamania's website, www.skamania.com, for more information.

One lodging in Stevenson also offers an experience in keeping with the magnificent natural surroundings. **The Columbia Gorge Riverside Lodge,** 200 SW Cascade Ave., 509/427-5650, features shore-side contemporary log cabins, some with deckfront hot tubs overlooking the river. Most of the eight units also have hot tubs in the bathroom. Fully equipped with kitchens and gas fireplaces, each room sports its own unique decor conforming to different parts of the globe as well as Northwest history and Native American culture. The romantic and intimate ambience here is sustained by the lack of TVs and phones, although there is a public room to watch videos and read complimentary newspapers. Its location on Bob's Beach, a well-maintained park-like windsurfer hangout, makes this especially appealing to boardheads. However, even sedentary types will enjoy watching the sternwheeler tour boats, cruise ships (both of which dock just east), and barges pass by. Proximity to the best brewpub and restaurants in this part of the Gorge (see Food, following) is another plus. Best of all, however, are the rates. During school vacations, weekends, and holidays, the upper units go for $84 single and double. The lower units cost $69 single and double. The front cabin commands $149 for 1–4 people. From Sunday to Thursday in off-peak months, these rates also apply but with a three-night stay, so one night is free. The only drawback to staying here is the problem endemic to almost all Gorge lodgings—noise. The difference here is that the innkeepers offer complimentary earplugs in the rooms to ward off the occasional rumble of trains or foghorns on the river. For more information, visit www.cg.riversidelodge.com.

Finally, we'd like to recommend an overnight stay or at least a visit to a Gorge landmark, **Carson Mineral Hot Springs Resort,** P.O. Box 1169, St. Martin Rd., Carson, 800/607-3678 or 509/427-8292. After a long hike or drive there is nothing quite like soaking in huge bathtubs filled with 126° mineral water. To sustain the soothing effects on nerves and muscles, you're wrapped in towels then massaged. While the huge tubs and dank locker rooms might evoke all the charm of a 19th-century tuberculosis sanitarium (this place began in 1897), the feeling of well-being resulting from the therapeutic regime is hard to beat for $12. Thereafter, you can stay in very basic cabins ($60) or hotel rooms ($35–45) and/or dine on good old-fashioned home-cooking (from veggie stir-fry to prime rib). Call ahead to the hotel for directions. You might also call the

Wind River Ranger Station, 509/427-3200, for information on area camping, trails up Wind Mountain, and such north-of-the-Gorge adventures as the Trapper Creek Wilderness, cross-country skiing at Old Man Pass, the cyclo-crane (for aerial perspectives on an old-growth forest), and Mt. St. Helens.

Food

While most western Washington Gorge dining choices will be found in Stevenson, **Publisher's Café,** 2131 B St., Washougal, 360/835-7637, can get travels here off to a good start. Imagine eating a delicious homemade meal—roast pork loin, homemade soup and breads, fresh-baked lemon meringue pie for under $12—in the living room of an older house while listening to soothing music. The quaint teapots, lace linens, and attentive service are the perfect preamble to an afternoon wilderness adventure. Open Tues.–Sat. 11 A.M.–3 P.M.

In Stevenson, for upscale contemporary dining at moderate prices, **Big River Grill,** 192 W. 2nd, 509/427-4888, is the ticket. Lunch, dinner, and weekend breakfasts in this early 20th century building decorated with a *Field & Stream* motif feature dishes evocative of the locale. Lunchtime standouts include a smoked sturgeon mousse appetizer ($6.95), a grilled steelhead sandwich ($7.95), and the ultimate cheeseburger topped with Oregon's award-winning Tillamook cheddar ($7.95). For dinner, go with pepper-crusted steelhead ($15). Wash it all down with the hoppy Pale Strider ale from the local **Walking Man** microbrewery (240 SE 1st Ave., #3, 509/427-5520). Lunch is served from 11:30 A.M.–5 P.M.; dinner from 5–9:30 P.M. Breakfast at Big River Grill is served on weekends only 8:30–11:30 A.M.

Across the street, **The Rio Café,** 509/427-4479, serves tacos, burritos and enchiladas filled with home-smoked meats. Chicken mole, chile verde and other traditional mainstays round out the menu. Two can dine well here for around $20.

White Salmon and Mt. Adams Area

In the heart of the Columbia Gorge on sunny, south-facing slopes, the White Salmon area has perhaps the best climate and scenery in the region. Here, just east of the Cascade divide, prodigious storms drench the west slopes of the mountains. The rainfall (averaging 30–35 inches annually) is just enough to support forested hillsides and open, drier woods interspersed with grassy clearings. Head east for a half-hour and the trees all but disappear; go west a similar distance and you've doubled the annual rainfall.

Signs of urban life in this rural stretch of the Gorge are confined to the neighboring towns of White Salmon and Bingen. Be that as it may, many residents of the area still rely on Hood River for employment, shopping, and services. White Salmon (pop. about 2,000), with its all-encompassing view of the Gorge and Mt. Hood, sits atop a 500-foot high basalt bluff rising out of the Columbia's narrow floodplain. It's primarily a residential community, with small businesses clustered along a turn-of-the-century main street called Jewett Boulevard. Bingen (pop. about 1,000) has a decidedly more industrial character, with its lumber mill and fruit-packing plant. Due in part to its location along the main highway (Hwy. 14), Bingen has a few funky bistros opened recently to serve an influx of windsurfers.

Backdropping it all is the massive glaciated sentinel of Mt. Adams, much broader and over 1,000 feet taller than its rival volcano, Mt. Hood. Between Mt. Adams and the Gorge, the rushing White Salmon River carves out a lush agricultural valley dotted with a few small settlements.

HISTORY

The archaeological record of this region has documented a Native American presence for millennia. The Natives in this part of the Gorge consisted of two tribes, each from distinct cultural/linguistic groups. Along the immediate shore of the Columbia, bands of upper **Chinook** Indians lived a settled, village-based life focused on the river's rich bounty of fish. They shared a language and customs with other Chinook river tribes, whose villages stretched from thundering Celilo Falls on the east to the mouth of the great river near Astoria. The **Klickitats,** whose territory covered the uplands and river valleys to the north of the Gorge, were known to be a more aggressive, nomadic tribe. They spoke a dialect of the Sahaptin language, shared by other tribes of the Columbia Basin and high plateaus. This linguistic connection included their cousins, the **Yakamas,** an occasionally quarrelsome tribe of expert horsemen who shared villages with the Chinook bands. Mt Adams (Pa-toh in the Klickitat language) was especially revered by the Klickitats. The mountain's relative obscurity to the outside world was sustained by Lewis and Clark, who set eyes upon the peak and mistook it for Mt. St. Helens (as had been previously noted in 1792 by the Vancouver expedition), recording their error in those famous journals.

Early Euro-American settlements in the area focused on fertile flatlands along the river. The Joslyn family built the first homestead in present-day Bingen in 1853. It was the first permanent European settlement on the north bank between Fort Vancouver and distant Walla Walla. During those early years, settlers trickled in, mostly from the Oregon Trail. The trickle increased in volume during the 1870s, with easterners and midwesterners of Norwegian and German descent drawn to the area. A German influence can clearly be seen in both towns' Bavarian-style, half-timbered building facades and other architectural details.

In 1874, two prominent families who had settled in the area waged a long-standing Hatfields and McCoys–style conflict that sharply divided hill dwellers and flatlanders into White Salmon and Bingen. The Suksdorf family (German immigrants) settled in the lowlands near the original Joslyn homestead. The Jewetts, transplants from Wisconsin, were attracted to a panoramic perch atop the White Salmon bluff where they planned to develop a utopian, socialistic community. It wasn't long before conflicts flared over that most

apple blossoms in White Salmon

© BRIAN LITT

crucial of western resources—water. Irreconcilable differences over drinking water and irrigation allocations drawn from Jewett Creek by both families led to a bitter feud. In 1892, Theodore Suksdorf (later, a descendant, Wilhelm Suksdorf became a prominent Gorge botanist) filed a separate town plat for the lowlands, calling it Bingen after the family's ancestral hometown along the Rhine River. Although the whole area had been called White Salmon since about 1870, White Salmon now became the settlement "up on the bluff" and Bingen got the flatlands. A few years after this division, a Bingen farmer defiantly closed the gates on his property along the road leading from White Salmon, through Bingen, to Palmer's Landing (near the present-day site of the Hood River Bridge). Frustrated White Salmon citizens decided to carve a shortcut road down to Palmer's Landing—an important river access spot. Today, the shortcut, now called Dock Grade Road, allows passage from White Salmon down to the Hood River Bridge, completely bypassing Bingen. Highway 141 is a longer, main thoroughfare that still follows the original, historic route between the two communities.

The local area grew slowly during the late 19th and early 20th centuries as timber and apple harvests and riverboat traffic boomed. It was the

heyday of great sternwheelers plying the Columbia, yet these two towns remained sleepy compared to the Oregon side. The North Bank Highway (Hwy. 14) traversing White Salmon and Bingen wasn't completed until 1938.

SIGHTS

National Fish Hatcheries

Two major, federal salmon hatcheries west of White Salmon will appeal to the whole family as well as anyone intrigued by the fascinating story of the world-famous Columbia River salmon. The two sites are managed as one complex although five miles apart. The **Little White Salmon/Willard National Fish Hatchery Complex** is the oldest of three federal hatcheries on the Gorge, established in 1896 at the mouth of the Little White Salmon River. Visitor facilities are located at the Little White Salmon hatchery. The Willard hatchery, five miles upstream, is also open to the public through pre-arranged group tours.

The hatchery complex raises both spring and fall chinook salmon and coho (silver) salmon species. Visitor facilities at the Little White Salmon hatchery include underwater viewing windows and an observation deck overlooking the Little White Salmon that allows views of salmon spawning in native habitat. Best times to visit are May through August, to view large adult spring chinook; late July through August to see spring chinook; and late October through late November to witness the spawning of both fall chinook and coho salmon. The Little White Salmon Hatchery is about eight miles west of White Salmon, along Hwy. 14. The hatchery road entrance is at the west end of the Little White Salmon Bridge at Drano Lake. Go about a mile up this road to the hatchery. The Willard facility is located five miles north, along the north side of Cook-Underwood Road, which can be reached just past the Little White Salmon Bridge off Hwy. 14. Both facilities are open daily 7:30 A.M.–4 P.M. For more information, call 509/538-2755.

The **Spring Creek National Fish Hatchery,** 509/493-1730, is located four miles west of White Salmon, just south of Hwy. 14. Spring Creek (the entrance to which has become a top windsurfing launch) was opened a few years after the Little White Salmon Hatchery began its fish rearing programs at the turn of the century. Fall chinook salmon return to Spring Creek each September, which is the most interesting time to visit. The hatchery is open daily 7:30 A.M.–4 P.M. from September through May, and on weekdays only from mid-May to August. More information on both hatcheries is available on the Internet at www.r1.fws.gov/gorgefish/.

Gorge Heritage Museum

While in Bingen, visit the Gorge Heritage Museum, 202 East Humboldt St., one block north of Hwy. 14 (left at the only traffic light in town, then first right). The museum houses a small but fascinating collection of regional artifacts in a historic church building. Display items include relics from old post offices, military gear, period photos, and Native American artifacts. Hours are Thurs.–Sat. 11 A.M.–4:30 P.M. from Memorial Day to Labor Day.

Glockenspiel Tower

For lovers of small town trivia or things faux-German, drive a mile up the hill on Hwy. 141 to the center of White Salmon. Here, you can see the only glockenspiel tower west of the Mississippi. It's located at the corner of Jewett and Main, in the White Salmon city hall, and reflects the German heritage of many of the area's early settlers.

Scenic Drives

The rolling green carpet of the **White Salmon River Valley** spreads out along Hwy. 141 between White Salmon and Trout Lake, offering one of the most scenic, relatively unpeopled drives to be found anywhere. You'll pass fruit orchards, vineyards, verdant stands of old timber, and catch glimpses of rapids tumbling down hillsides. The most impressive white water is the churning cauldron of Husum Falls (Class V), visible just north of the bridge where the highway crosses the White Salmon river about six miles outside the town of White Salmon. Start the route by taking the Hwy. 141 Alternate on the east side of the Hwy. 14 bridge crossing the White Salmon River, which is about a mile east of the Hood River Bridge over the Columbia. This cutoff hugs the slopes above the calm lower reaches of the White Salmon, and bypasses the town of White Salmon on the main highway. The alternate joins up with main Hwy. 141 a few miles from the Columbia, and begins its meandering climb toward the foothills of majestic Mt. Adams. The ride from the Columbia to the little town of Trout Lake at Mt. Adams' base will take about a half-hour without stops. Drop in at The Logs Bar and Restaurant in BZ Corners along the way, for a distinctly local meal (see Food under Practicalities, below).

For those who want to drive a loop, take the **BZ-Glenwood Highway** (right at BZ Corners) about 20 bucolic miles to Glenwood, then go right on the Goldendale Highway as it follows the scenic upper Klickitat River. After about half an hour, turn right on Hwy. 142, following this lovely state highway down the steep Klickitat River canyon to the town of Lyle, where it joins Hwy. 14. A right turn on Hwy. 14, past the crags and soaring cliffs of the Gorge, will get you back to the White Salmon/Bingen area in 10 minutes. The whole loop provides a couple of hours of photo-ops, capturing pastoral, forest, and alpine landscapes.

A much shorter, but equally scenic loop is the **Cook-Underwood Road.** Take Hwy. 14 west from the Hood River Bridge about a mile, then turn right on the first road after the Hwy. 14 bridge over the White Salmon River. The road gradually climbs about 1,000 feet, skirting along the edge of steep bluffs rising above the Columbia River. Vineyards, orchards, and woods line the road. Numerous pullouts along the south side of the road, several miles up from Hwy. 14, offer spectacular vistas of the Gorge, Mt. Hood, and the Hood River Valley below. The 12-mile journey eventually ends back at Hwy. 14, about 10 miles west of White Salmon.

Mt. Adams and Vicinity

The most compelling attraction in this entire area is 12,276-foot high **Mt. Adams,** a gigantic Cascade volcano covered with numerous glaciers, and surrounded by thousands of acres of unspoiled, lightly-visited wilderness. To get a sense of its immensity, consider these facts: this hulk of a mountain covers over 230 square miles of land; its potential volume of lava eruption is almost 50 cubic miles, enough molten rock to bury all of Manhattan Island and its skyscrapers, with plenty to spare. That amounts to about four times the volume of its neighbor volcano, Mt. Hood. Despite its massive dimensions and scenic splendor, Mt. Adams remains one of the least visited of the huge volcanoes of the Cascade chain, prompting its nickname, Sleeping Giant. Resting Giant would be more apt, as it is a dormant, active volcano that erupted dramatically about 1,000 years ago. The surrounding volcanoes of Mts. Hood, St. Helens, and Ranier all have higher public profiles and high visitation levels for their own reasons. Mt. Hood, the quintessential symbol of Oregon, has been blessed (or cursed) with easy highway access for decades. Mt. Rainier, gorgeous backdrop and the pride of Puget Sound's cities, draws millions annually to the splendor of its national parks. And Mt. St. Helens offers a unique chance to visit the only recently active volcano in the lower 48 states. Bottom line: Mt. Adams can match any of these for visual beauty, and far exceeds them all in access to wild solitude minus traffic jams and gift shops.

The northern, western, and most of the southern faces of the mountain are protected in perpetuity by the U.S. Forest Service in the **Mt. Adams Wilderness.** It's an area that covers almost 50,000 acres of old growth forests, countless alpine ponds, meadows, and massive ice fields. Diverse recreational opportunities abound on and around the mountain, including hiking, mountain climbing, camping, cross-country skiing, fishing, and snowmobiling (see Recreation and Activities, below, for details). Take Hwy. 141 to the hamlet of Trout Lake, with several well-maintained roads heading out of town to the north and east up Adams' slopes. Maps and other information can be obtained at the Mt. Adams Ranger Station in Trout Lake, 509/395-2501, or the Gifford Pinchot National Forest headquarters in Vancouver, Washington, 360/696-7500.

A notable attraction close to Mt. Adams is **Guler Ice Caves,** located about five miles west of Trout Lake on Hwy. 141 (turns into Forest Service Road 24 for the last mile). A series of underground lava tubes that harbor perpetual ice formations, the caves were reputed to be an ice source for pioneers seeking cold beverages long before the age of refrigeration. A few more miles past the ice caves, along Forest Service Road 60, lies another site worth a stop—**Big Lava Bed,** a rugged jumble of 12,000 acres of lava originating from a 500-foot crater. There are no marked trails, so you might just want to skirt the edges of this vast, barren landscape. Compass readings here may be unreliable due to local magnetic influences from the surrounding expanse of rocks.

Despite its massive dimensions and scenic splendor, Mt. Adams remains one of the least visited of the huge volcanoes of the Cascade chain, prompting its nickname, Sleeping Giant. Resting Giant would be more apt, as it is a dormant, active volcano that erupted dramatically about 1,000 years ago.

RECREATION AND ACTIVITIES

Windsurfing

Hood River's well-deserved title as "windsurfing capital of the world" has been earned, in part, by some awesome windsurfing sites on the Washington side of the river. Two of the very best around are right next to each other only four miles west of the Hood River-White Salmon Bridge. **Spring Creek Hatchery,** aka "the Hatch," is a rocky shoreline area at the entrance to a federal salmon hatchery. Local sailors discovered this outstanding spot to ride big swells and "catch air" in the 1980s. Limited parking and facilities include portable toilets. On high west wind days (common in late spring and summer), expert windsurfers can be seen slicing through waves and doing occasional "loops," whereby sailor and rig are launched skyward in a circle by the synergistic combination of wind and wave. This is also one of the most exciting places for windsurfing voyeurs to watch the action. Tiny **Swell City,** offering access to wet 'n wild rides available at its big neighbor to the east, is a small parking lot on the south shoulder of Hwy. 14, just west of the Hatch.

Somewhat less glamorous than those two hot-dogger havens, **Bingen Point** lies about two miles east of the Hood River Bridge, at the end of a long gravel road. To get there, turn right off Hwy. 14 at the "Bingen Marina" sign, a block east of the only blinking light in Bingen. With gentler water, especially near shore, this is a good spot for the less-than-expert windsurfer to practice basic skills. A nice grassy area for rigging your sail and board and picnicking are offered here, along with a comfort station.

Hiking and Mountain Biking

Six miles east of Bingen, **Catherine Creek** is a beautiful oak-pine savannah with one of the most impressive wildflower displays (April–June is best) in the Gorge on several thousand acres of federal lands. A transition zone between rain forests on the west and grasslands on the east side, it has miles of gentle to moderately steep hiking trails with great Gorge views from higher elevations. It also offers a trail to the top of the only big rock arch in the Gorge. Go east from Bingen on Hwy. 14 for four miles, turning left onto County Road 1230 at milepost 71 and a sign for Rowland Lake. After a mile and a half on this old highway, you'll come to a small, unmarked parking area on your left. The main trail and its spurs take off north of the road. A lovely, mile-long paved trail that is wheelchair-accessible and especially nice for families with small children is located on the south side of the road. A pretty cascade is the highlight of this lower trail. A rock arch above the remains of an old homestead will intrigue hikers who follow the trail north from the parking lot. Springtime hikers are advised to watch out for ticks and poison oak.

Well-tuned, fit folks on mountain bikes will enjoy pumping up **Hospital Hill** (technically known as Burdoin Mountain). Named for its location directly behind Skyline Hospital (as opposed to its potential health effects), the hill's steep grades ensure a cardiovascular workout and stunning views of the Gorge and Mt. Hood from the top. To get there, take the Skyline Hospital driveway on the north side of Hwy. 141 (Jewett Blvd.), veering to the left just before the road curves to the right to the hospital parking lot. Park just to the left of the electric substation. This trail runs through private land, and bikers must stay on the trails, respecting private property rights and No Trespassing signs. For more information on this and other mountain bike trails in the area, go see the pros at **Sunset Cycles,** 509/493-3117.

Also in the White Salmon area, the **Buck Creek Trail** system features miles of trails shared by hikers, bikers, and equestrians on state lands in the thickly forested foothills of the Cascades. Ambitious hikers who climb to some of the 3,000-foot or higher summits such as Nestor

BOB RACE

WASHINGTON GORGE

Peak are amply rewarded with "double-volcano" views of Mt. Adams and Mt. Hood. The Northwestern Lake Road, six miles out of White Salmon on the west side of Hwy. 141, gets you to Buck Creek. Another option for mountain bikers is the historic **Weldon Wagon Road** running about six miles uphill or downhill, depending on where you begin. The bottom of the road intersects Highway 141 just south of Husum, 10 minutes north of White Salmon. The upper end links with Snowden Road, some 2000 feet above the Gorge. Snowden Road is accessed from White Salmon. From Route 141, go right on Main Street in downtown White Salmon, then turn right after about a half-mile onto Snowden Road. Continue about three miles to Weldon Wagon Raod (on the left).

Mt. Adams offers a lifetime of varied hiking and climbing possibilities, ranging from a leisurely stroll through its foothills to a grueling climb past crevasses and over huge ice fields to its 12,276-foot summit. The **Mt. Adams South Climb,** accessed from Cold Springs campground (see Camping under Practicalities, below, for detailed directions), can be done in a day but many climbers camp halfway up at the "Lunch Counter," making it a two-day climb. This is the second-highest peak in Washington state, and its ascent should not be taken lightly. Ill-prepared or casual hikers should not attempt it. This is a serious climb up a potentially dangerous mountain; only experienced, properly equipped climbers, going at the right time, are advised to take on this behemoth. For wilderness permits required for the climb, contact the Mt. Adams Ranger District at 509/395-3400.

The **Round the Mountain Trail** circumnavigates the base of Mt. Adams around the portion owned by the U.S. Government. The east face is within the Yakama Indian Reservation and is off-limits to the public, except for areas on the southeast flank. For more information, contact officials of the Yakima Indian Nation at 509/865-5121. Ranging in elevation from 5,800 feet to over 7,000 feet, this trail joins the **Pacific Crest Trail** (PCT) on the mountain's west side. It's a happy medium for folks who aren't quite ready to scale the Sleeping Giant but want an

alpine feeling, a good workout, and spectacular glimpses of the glacial wilds soaring above them. Access the trail via either Morrison or Cold Springs Campgrounds on the south side of the peak, from the PCT Trailhead off Forest Service Road 23 on the west side, or from the Takhlakh Lake Campground, also off Forest Service Road 23, but on the northwest side of the mountain.

Anyone in halfway decent condition can make the hike up to the 4,900-foot crest near **Sleeping Beauty.** The mountain derives its name from a Native American legend: a beautiful Indian princess—the object of Mt. Adams' and Mt. Hood's affections—was put to sleep in a spell and, you guessed it, turned into a mountain. Views of Adams, just a few miles to the east, from the top, are breathtaking. To get there, take Forest Service Road 88 by making a right one mile past the Ranger Station on Hwy. 141 just out of Trout Lake. After about five miles, go right on Forest Service Road 8810 to the trailhead a few miles up the road.

Indian Heaven Wilderness comprises some 20,000 acres of unique, mid-elevation (3,500–6,000 feet) subalpine meadows and 175 small lakes along the Cascade Crest west of Trout Lake. Many trails wind their way through this charming landscape important to local Native Americans for its abundance of wild huckleberry fields and traditional plants. Late summer hikers here will head back to their cars with the sweet taste of this delectable wild fruit. The area can be accessed from several Forest Service roads out of Trout Lake. Go past the Ranger District on Hwy. 141, then take either Forest Service Road 24 towards Little Goose Campground, or Forest Service Road 60 to 6035 in the direction of Forlorn Lakes Campground. Trailheads are just a short distance from either of these campgrounds.

Birding enthusiasts will discover a rich variety of waterfowl at the **Conboy Lake National Wildlife Refuge,** six miles southwest of Glenwood and about 45 minutes from White Salmon. The lake is actually a large, seasonal marsh at the base of Mt. Adams. A major hub on the flight paths of many migrating species, its visitors include graceful tundra swans and Canada geese. It is also the only known nesting location of sandhill cranes in the state of Washington. Early spring promises the most prolific and varied sightings. The refuge is located on Wildlife Refuge Road (right turn off BZ-Glenwood Highway for those heading northbound). For more information or special tours, call 509/364-3410.

White-water Rafting and Kayaking

Racing its way from the glaciers of Mt. Adams to the Columbia River, the **White Salmon River** is famous for its series of whitewater rapids ranging Class I–V. Guaranteed to get the adrenaline pumping, the adventure is an unforgettable, highly recommended highlight of any Columbia Gorge visit. Because the river is fed from springs, it maintains an ample base flow to sustain late summer rafting long after other rivers in the region have receded to dangerously low levels. The famous Husum Falls (Class V) is too dangerous for all but the most intrepid, expert paddlers, and is featured in a Gorge Games kayak event.

Two guide services provide exciting and safe white-water raft trips with Class II, III, and IV rapids down the beautiful canyon. **Phil's White Water Adventures,** 509/493-2641 or 800/366-2004, takes floaters on a three-hour drenching joyride between Husum and Northwestern Lake. Needed gear is included in the package costing $50 per person (reservations required, wetsuit rentals slightly extra). The season runs April–September, with three daily trips departing at 9:00 A.M., 12:30 P.M., and 3:30 P.M. **All Adventures in the Gorge,** 877/641-RAFT, offers a similar run for $55 per person and an optional lunch for a few more bucks.

Cross-Country Skiing, Snowshoeing, and Snowmobiling

The **Mt. Adams Winter Recreation Area** includes an abundance of recreational opportunities in the high country, unlike crowded Mt. Hood. Cross-country skiers, snowshoe hikers, and snowmobilers can enjoy themselves on miles of trails through this pristine snow country. Over 27 miles of signed ski trails and 80 miles of signed snowmobile trails crisscross the woods here. In addition, cross-country skiing and snowshoeing are permitted within the Mt. Adams Wilderness,

the unspoiled heart of an area encompassing over 47,000 acres of Mt. Adams' slopes and glaciers.

As in most national forests, access is through the sno-park permit system. Permits are available for daily or seasonal use at local sports shops and hardware or grocery stores. There are four different sno-parks (official parking areas for winter trail access) in the Mt. Adams area. All are close to Trout Lake, which is about a half-hour's drive north of White Salmon on Hwy. 141. Two of these, Pine Side and Smith Butte, are jump-off points for groomed cross-country ski trails ranging from easy to difficult. They are reached by heading northeast of Trout Lake on Forest Service Road 82 (follow the Mt. Adams Recreation Area sign as you enter Trout Lake). Pine Side, the closest sno-park, is only a few miles from the town. West of Trout Lake, the Atkisson sno-park is along Hwy. 141, about five miles past town and the Mt. Adams Ranger Station. Ungroomed cross-country trails and groomed snowmobile trails (marked with orange diamonds) start here. The Flat-top sno-park is located just off Forest Service Road 88, and also offers snowmobile trails. To get there, go one mile past the Ranger Station, then turn right on Forest Service Road 88.

Wineries

Wind River Cellars, 196 Spring Creek Rd., Husum, 509/493-2324, windriverwines@gorge.net, is reached about six miles north of White Salmon off Hwy. 141. Go left on Spring Creek Road, just north of the bridge over the White Salmon River. This winery features complimentary wine tastings daily 10 A.M.–6 P.M., with spectacular Mt. Hood views and a picnic area. Over eight varietals are grown on site, including pinot noir, merlot, cabernet, gewürztraminer, and chardonnay.

Golf

Husum Hills Golf Course, located ten minutes north of White Salmon on Hwy. 141, 509/493-1211, offers nine hilly, charming holes of golf with views of Mt. Adams. The course charges a regular fee of $9, but has senior discounts. Open to the public, the course also features a small clubhouse and cafe.

Fishing

All fishing areas require licenses. Check with the Washington Department of Fish and Wildlife, 360/902-2200 or 360/696-6211, or local sporting goods or outfitter stores for the necessary paperwork. Along the Columbia, salmon, steelhead (an anadromous, or part-time, ocean-dwelling trout species), sturgeon, and other river species can be caught. A bit inland, tributaries and small lakes offer good trout and bass fishing, among other freshwater species.

The mouth of the **White Salmon River** is a well-known haunt of salmon and steelhead anglers with lots of small boats and trailers parked along the shoulders of Hwys. 14 and 141. Peak fishing season for salmon is mid-April. **Drano Lake,** actually the broadened mouth of the Little White Salmon River, is a hot spot, despite its less-than-lovely name. A mecca for those stalking the famed Columbia River salmon, it is located eight miles west of the Hood River Bridge, with several launch lanes for small boats and portable toilets. Like the mouth of the White Salmon, this place gets crowded when the big boys are biting, as witnessed by the pickup trucks and campers lining the highway shoulder on certain spring and late summer weekends.

Northwestern Lake, just a few miles north of White Salmon on the west side of Hwy. 141, is a more tranquil retreat for those happy to take advantage of its good trout and bass fishing. A reservoir along the White Salmon River, the lake can be reached by turning left on Northwestern Lake Road, heading north out of White Salmon. **Rowland Lake,** situated four and a half miles east of Bingen on the north side of Hwy. 14, is an enclosed side bay of the Columbia River separated from the main stem by the railroad and highway. The Washington Department of Fish and Wildlife runs this peaceful site, which includes toilets, a small boat launch, and lots of trout, bass, and other fish. To reach it, turn left on County Road 1230, from eastbound Hwy. 14.

Horseback Riding

Northwestern Lake Stables, 509/493-4965, www.gorge.net/business/nwstables, is on Lakeview Drive off Northwestern Lake Road, five minutes out of White Salmon from Hwy. 141. One-hour or two-hour rides through the pretty Buck Creek watershed are offered for $20 or $40 per person. Reservations are recommended. Open daily 8 A.M.–6 P.M., weather permitting.

Events

The **White Salmon Spring Festival** celebrates the joys of spring. Featuring food, crafts, local entertainment, and a parade, it is held the third weekend in May at White Salmon City Park, in White Salmon. For more information, call 509/493-3630. The **Ketchum Kalf Rodeo,** 509/364-3355, is a real rodeo held at the Glenwood Rodeo Grounds each year on the third weekend of June. Saturday nights feature a country dance, and on Sunday there's a traditional breakfast and parade to close off the festivities.

The **Subaru Gorge Games** is a highly popular "mini-Olympics" held in early July, with many outdoor sports events throughout the White Salmon area (see the Hood River and Vicinity section of The Oregon Gorge chapter for more details). Every year, the first weekend after Labor Day in Bingen marks the **Huckleberry Festival,** a celebration coinciding with the bountiful harvest of wild berries found in the surrounding mountains. The festival features lots of food (including fresh, delicious huckleberries), entertainment, Pacific Northwest microbrews, local wines, and a parade. This annual fete is held in Daubenspeck Park, one block north of Hwy. 14, on the west side of Bingen. Call 509/493-3630 for details.

PRACTICALITIES

Accommodations

Major credit cards are accepted at most of these establishments, with the exception being some of the smaller bed-and-breakfasts. Check ahead on reservation policies and payment options. Prices are for doubles in the busy season, and do not include local sales tax.

The **Bingen School Inn,** Cedar and Franklin Sts. (two blocks north of Hwy. 14 in Bingen), 509/493-3363, www.bsi-cgoc.com, provides the only Euro-style hostel accommodations in the area, at budget rates. Located in a converted old school building, the inn is a great option for young folks and flexible travelers looking for affordable, clean, alternative lodging near Hood River, major windsurfing sites, and other recreational opportunities. Dorm-style accommodations (bring your own sleeping bag) will cost a whopping $14 ($17 with linen); private rooms are also available for $35, $10 more for each extra person. Both options feature shared bath. The inn has cooking facilities and coin laundry for guests, a gym, a rock climbing wall, and storage lockers. The Bingen School Inn is also the **Columbia Gorge Outdoor Center** (same phone number and website), which can hook you up with outdoor adventure tours, equipment rentals, and information.

Most other lodging in the area falls within the moderate price range, including a number of charming bed-and-breakfasts in the bucolic White Salmon River Valley and at the foot of massive Mt. Adams. **Bingen Haus**, on the north side of Hwy. 14, just west of the town of Bingen, 509/493-4888, www.bingenhaus.com, is located in the historic Joslyn House (c. 1860). The first house built by European settlers in the area, this nonsmoking establishment offers antique-filled rooms for $60–85, with shared bath and a hot tub for guests. **Husum's Riverside B&B,** 866 Hwy. 141, Husum, 509/493-8900, www.husums riversidebnb.com, is about a 10-minute drive north of the Columbia. It features two rooms within earshot of the gurgling White Salmon River that go for $72 each. Other extras include a hot tub and senior discounts. About 10 miles farther up the White Salmon Valley, you'll find the **Llama Ranch,** 1980 Hwy. 141, BZ Corners, 509/395-2786. Rooms range $79–99, including encounters with live llamas. Some rooms have a private bath.

For those seeking mountain solitude and great Mt. Adams views, try the Glenwood Valley, about a 40-minute drive northeast of White Salmon. From BZ Corners, just turn right (east) on the BZ-Glenwood Highway, following the signs about 20 miles to Glenwood. **Flying L Ranch,** 25 Flying L Ln., Glenwood, 888/MTADAMS or 509/364-3488, www.mt-adams.com, has both

lodge rooms and cabins with kitchens. On-premises hot tub and full breakfasts are thrown in to complete the nifty package. Prices run $85–110. **Ann's Place Bed and Breakfast,** 164 Mt. Adams Hwy., Glenwood, 888/220-7639 or tel./fax 509/364-3580, www.annsplacebnb.com, has rooms for $75–80 with private bath, in the former home of U.S. Chief Justice William O. Douglas. Use of the judge's swimming pool is a nice perk here. *Of Men and Mountains,* by Douglas (San Francisco: Chronicle Books, 1985), describes this region evocatively.

Closer to the base of Mt. Adams is the tranquil community of Trout Lake, a half-hour drive north of White Salmon along Hwy. 141. As you might expect from the name, **The Farm B&B,** 490 Sunnyside Rd., Trout Lake, 509/395-2488, fax 509/395-2127, www.thefarmbnb.com, offers guests a full farm breakfast in an 1890s vintage farmhouse. Rooms go for $78 (shared bath) or $88; no smoking allowed. **Kelly's Trout Creek Inn B&B,** 25 Mt. Adams Rd., Trout Lake, 509/395-2769, www.kellysbnb.com, has four cushy rooms in an old Victorian house. Both Trout Lake accommodations are conveniently located for hiking, berry picking, or cross-country skiing in the Mt. Adams country.

A bit more expensive, the **Inn of the White Salmon,** 172 W. Jewett Blvd., White Salmon, 800/972-5226 or 509/493-2335, www.In-noftheWhiteSalmon.com, features one of the most charming antique interiors in the Gorge. Knowledgeable about area attractions, hosts Roger and Janet Holen offer 16 immaculate rooms in this European-style small hotel. Rates range $106–143, including an excellent breakfast. **Ya-at-eeh Lodge,** 283 Courtney Rd., White Salmon, 509/493-4472, is located high atop a ridge 10 minutes east of White Salmon, with stunning views of the Columbia Gorge. Rooms are $100–125.

In Husum, you'll find **The Castle,** 92 Fordyce Rd., 509/493-0073, lodging.gorge.net/thecastle. A rather Gothic chateau, it is set in a sylvan grove along the shores of the White Salmon. Groups of up to eight can rent the entire castle for $270 (two separate suites, $135 each, with private bath); a cottage that sleeps four ($145 per night) is also available.

Camping

Camping options abound just north of the Columbia River Gorge Scenic Area, in the vicinity of Mt. Adams in the Gifford Pinchot National Forest. These camps range from RV campgrounds with all the amenities to primitive backcountry sites at the foot of a glacier. For those seeking a more developed campsite, try **Elk Meadows RV Park and Campground,** 78 Trout Lake Creek Rd., 877/395-2400 or 509/395-2400, www.elk meadowspark.com. With over 50 full and partial hookup RV and tent sites, a restroom, showers, laundry, a dump station, and BBQ and picnic facilities, Elk Meadows should suit Winnebago weekend warriors seeking a woodsy getaway without sacrificing the comforts of home.

In the middle of the cushy-to-roughing it spectrum, the Forest Service campground at **Takhlakh Lake** has tent and trailer sites, as well as basic amenities—toilets, water, picnicking, some hookups. This spot features an unsurpassed view of the Sleeping Giant (Mt. Adams). It's located about a 40-minute drive north of Trout Lake, on Forest Service Road 23 (gravel), at the northwest base of Mt. Adams. Several other Forest Service trailer campgrounds offer similar amenities, although none (except for **Ollalie Lake,** close to Takhlakh Lake) provide the awesome sight of Tahklakh enjoyed by tent campers. On the south side of the mountain, **Morrison Creek** has two camp areas, one for horseback riders, the other for tent campers. Located about 10 miles out of Trout Lake on the fairly good Forest Service Road 8040, it can be reached by taking the "23 Road" (Forest Service Road 23) from Trout Lake about a mile, then taking a right on Forest Service Road 80, following the signs to Morrison Creek. This campground is only a few miles by trail to the stunning Round the Mountain Trail skirting the massive volcano.

A couple of miles farther up the road is **Cold Springs Campground,** often used as a base for climbers ascending Mt. Adams' south route. The road to Cold Springs gets a bit dicey for all but high-clearance vehicles. Take the "23 Road" (right turn) from Trout Lake for a mile, then go right on Forest Service Road 80, following signs to Morrison Creek. Continue on the same road a few

miles past Morrison Creek to get to Cold Spring Campground. Note that this last stretch of road is quite rough. Also, both Morrison Creek and Cold Springs have only surface water available for drinking; so bring appropriate filters or tablets. For more information, contact the Mt. Adams Ranger Station of the Gifford-Pinchot National Forest at 509/395-3400.

Hearty backpackers can basically pitch a tent anywhere in the wilderness, as long as they follow the basic Forest Service rules of backcountry etiquette: 1) keep party size to 12 or less; 2) pack out all trash; 3) camp at least 100 feet from the trail and 200 feet from water sources; 4) if you make a fire, only used already-downed small wood. After that, it's up to you to make yourself a cozy bivouac and avoid becoming bear bait!

Food

The overwhelming concentration of excellent restaurants across the Columbia in Hood River can make the culinary pickins in the White Salmon-Bingen area seem slim. Places here typically serve basic, American road chow. There are, however, some notable exceptions worth a visit for their specialties.

Due to its location along the main tourist thoroughfare (Hwy. 14), sleepy Bingen has several delightfully alternative lunch spots. **Northshore Bar and Grill,** 216 W. Steuben St. (Hwy. 14), 509/493-4440, is basically a windsurfer/younger-crowd bar with good lunch fare and a few dinner specials. The limited but solid menu includes excellent burgers and Mexican-style or pasta dishes. The Northshore is also the only venue for nightlife on the north shore, featuring popular bands from all over the Northwest on weekend nights. **Mother's Market Place,** 415 W. Steuben St., Bingen, 509/493-1700, is a vegan oasis that's part natural foods store, part deli offering tasty and nutritious lunches. Try their popular and delicious sunburger, a concoction of brown rice, garlic powder, sunflower seeds, and several other ingredients "good and good for you!" Falafel, humus, soups, and salads round out the menu, any item of which will set you back less than five bucks.

Loafers Old World Bakery and Coffee House, 213 W. Steuben St., Bingen, 509/493-

3100, serves up an excellent variety of freshly baked breads, N.Y.-style bagels, and pastries, as well as delicious soups and sandwiches for lunch. Eats are always fresh and homemade, and the coffee good and strong. **The Creamery,** 121 E. Jewett Blvd., White Salmon, 509/493-4007, is another quick lunch stop. Owner Katina Putnam serves scrumptious fresh pastries daily, as well as all the gourmet coffee drinks, ice cream, and soups your grumbling belly will desire. Try one of her panini-style sandwiches with Mediterranean leanings.

Offering standard American cuisine at family-friendly rates, **Gorge House,** 201 W. Steuben St., Bingen, 509/493-5305, serves several seafood and steak dinners between $8 and $12. **Big River Diner,** 740 E. Steuben St., Bingen, 509/493-1414, is a spot where you're likely to rub elbows with cops, truckers, and other locals grabbing a burger and fries. **Fidel's,** 120 E. Steuben St., Bingen, 509/493-1017, is perhaps the best dinner spot in the White Salmon-Bingen area, offering a reliable if predictable range of Mexican dishes. Prices are low to moderate, with dinner entrées only around $10.

The Logs Restaurant, Hwy. 141, BZ Corners, 509/493-1402, is a must stop for visitors who want a taste of local culture, history, and good fried chicken. A shrine of sorts to the area's proud and colorful history, the rustic log cabin has been serving locals since the 1920s. The place is full of logging camp photos, logging memorabilia, and atmospherics hinting at more rough 'n' tumble days in the not-so-distant-past. One imagines if the walls could talk, they'd tell tales of moonshine, cockfights, and epic brawls. The broasted chicken (secret family recipe—don't even think of asking) must be sampled with domestic beer on tap. Top off your meal with delicious, homemade pie à la mode. The whole experience will set you back about $10. Farther up the highway, **Serenity's,** Hwy. 141, Trout Lake, 509/395-2500, offers more refined dining at moderate prices in a shady roadside setting. In the heart of tiny Trout Lake, **KJ's Bear Creek Café,** Hwy. 141, 509/395-2525, is the place to find bacon and eggs or a burger and fries amid an unassuming country café ambience.

Information and Services

The **Columbia River Gorge Visitors Association,** 2149 W. Cascade St., Suite 106A, Hood River, OR 97031, 800/98-GORGE, www.gorge.net/crgva, provides informational packets on Gorge attractions and tourist services upon request. The helpful folks at the **Mt. Adams Chamber of Commerce,** Hwy. 14 at the Hood River Bridge, P.O. Box 449, White Salmon, WA 98672, 509/493-3630, www.gorge.net/mtadamschamber, can give you the best localized view of things to do and see in this area. The **Klickitat County Visitor Information Center,** P.O. Box 1220, Goldendale, WA 98620, 509/493-3630, www.klickitatcounty.org, also provides useful information, through their website, by phone, or in person. Good brochures and information are available at the **Washington/Oregon/Klickitat County Visitor Center at Maryhill,** in Maryhill State Park, P.O. Box 1220, Goldendale, WA 98620, 509/773-4395. Open daily May through October.

Amtrak, 800 NW 6th St., 509/248-1146, has a station and makes stops at Bingen. The station is one block south of Hwy. 14 in the middle of town (follow the sign). Daily passenger service is available to Vancouver, WA, and Portland, OR, as well as points east including Wishram, Spokane, and Chicago. For schedule and ticketing information, call 800/872-7245 or visit www.amtrak.com.

Skyline Hospital, 211 NE Skyline Dr. (just north of Jewett Blvd., Hwy. 141), 509/493-1101, offers 24-hour emergency room service in White Salmon. You can find a self-service **laundromat** in White Salmon at the White Salmon Laundromat, 423 Tohomish St., 509/493-1227.

Lyle to Maryhill

Heading east from White Salmon, visitors witness a rapid change in the look and feel of things. By the time travelers reach Lyle, they notice that the thick green carpet of forest clinging to the Gorge's west and central realms has been replaced by a much drier landscape. Scattered large pines tower above low, scrubby oak woods, interspersed with grassy openings. And then, just a few miles east of Lyle, the oaks all but disappear, yielding to the vast grassy expanses of the arid Columbia basin. This is "Big Country," where cattle ranches sprawl, houses are far apart, and towns are hamlets. In this part of the Gorge, the farther east you travel, the more it feels like the Old West. Real cowboys and Indians live here, along with lots and lots of cows.

That's not to say the area resembles a Remington painting of the western frontier. Excellent new wineries have sprung up here, and the area has some of the best wind-surfing sites in the country, as well as one of the best art museums in the entire Pacific Northwest. Those who discover the sunny side of Washington's Gorge with its stunning vistas will not leave disappointed.

Main towns in this region include Lyle, at the confluence of the Columbia and Klickitat Rivers; Wishram, an old railroad town and Native American village site; and Goldendale, the Klickitat county seat 12 miles north of the Gorge proper. All are small burgs; Goldendale is the largest with a population of just under 2,000.

This is "Big Country," where cattle ranches sprawl, houses are far apart, and towns are hamlets. In this part of the Gorge, the farther east you travel, the more it feels like the Old West. Real cowboys and Indians live here, along with lots and lots of cows.

HISTORY

The eastern section of the Columbia Gorge, especially along the Washington shore, may have had the highest concentration of continuous Native American settlements in the Pacific Northwest dating back over 10,000 years. The Columbia River's bountiful salmon were harvested at principal fishing sites between the present-day city of The Dalles and the now-inundated Celilo Falls. The Gorge's role as the only east-west, sea level passage through the Cascade Range was also extremely important to western Native Americans. Along with permanent villages next to the Columbia, temporary summer camps housing Natives from hundreds of miles away would spring up every summer. Huge gatherings of tribes, all bringing local products to barter, resulted in this area becoming one of the oldest and largest trading marts in the west.

Continual residents of the area consisted of several tribes from two distinct cultural and linguistic groups. Along the river, **Wishram, Wasco,** and other native peoples of upper Chinookan tribes dwelled in permanent villages. This area was the farthest inland extent of Chinookan speakers. Farther east, and in the uplands to the north and south of the river, Sahaptin-speaking tribes of the Columbia Plateau, including Yakama, Tenino, and Wyam inhabited vast territories.

The first white settlers arrived in the late 1850s and 1860s, brought west by the Oregon Trail and the promise of a better life. In the late 19th century, Lyle (originally called Klickitat Landing) became an important point for shipping wheat and sheep raised in the surrounding hills. When the main railway line came through in 1908, the town got a another economic boost. Many "sheep trains" shuttled thousands of animals eastward to Chicago's stockyards, where Mt. Adams lambs became prized commodities. Soon, the largest buildings in the county rose up near the tracks in Lyle. But by the 1920s, the sheep business sharply declined. Lyle slumped into a sleepy town until the 1980s when new life sailed in with the wind-surfers flocking to nearby Doug's Beach and other popular launch sites. As a result, several new businesses and a housing boom have infused Lyle with new energy.

Wishram is located along the banks of the Columbia several hundred feet below Hwy. 14. The site of a major switching yard, it was an important railroad town during the first half of the 20th century with its storefronts facing the tracks. With increased mechanization, modernization, and a decline in passenger travel, Wishram ended its career as a flourishing rail stop. Today, it is one of the quieter towns in the Gorge, bypassed by a parade of cars and big rig trucks whizzing along a highway above the rusty rails.

SIGHTS
Native American Heritage
The ancient Indian pictographs and petroglyphs at **Horsethief Lake State Park** are easily among the most compelling, powerful attractions in the Columbia Gorge. If you only have time to see a few sights, don't miss this one. Here you'll find the largest concentrations of ancient rock art in the Pacific Northwest. Pictographs (paintings on rock), petroglyphs (carvings in the rock), and combinations of the two vividly adorn cliff walls. The images once overlooked a major Wishram village. It and other ancient settlements were inundated by the Dalles Dam in 1957. A Chinookan-speaking tribe, the Wishram's culture is intimately intertwined with the river and the salmon. *Tsagaglalal,* or She Who Watches, the largest and best-known pictograph/petroglyph in the Northwest, awaits you at the end of the Pictograph Trail. This haunting, animal-like face with a mouth stretched wide in an exaggerated grin has great significance to native peoples. Information on the mythic legacy of *Tsagaglalal* can be found in the special topic She Who Watches.

An excellent, free, guided **pictograph tour** that finishes with a close-up view of She Who Watches is offered by Washington State Park rangers every Friday and Saturday at 10 A.M. from April to October. Because space is limited, you'll need to call ahead, 509/767-1159, for

reservations. This procedure was necessitated by past incidents of vandalism here.

Just shy of two miles up Hwy. 142 from Lyle, a left turn on Fisher Hill Road brings you to the **Fisher Hill Bridge,** located immediately west of the highway. The attraction here is both scenic and cultural. The bridge spans the Klickitat Gorge at a very dramatic stretch, where a large volume of rushing water is squeezed through an extremely narrow gash in the black basalt flows. The resulting rush of white water far below your feet is exhilarating and beautiful. This spectacular perch is also one of the only places where you can still see platforms for traditional Indian dip net fishing fastened into the rocks and hanging precariously over the churning waters below. Intrepid tribal fishermen stand over the water, secured by ropes tied around their waists and anchored to the rocks, fishing for salmon as their ancestors have done in the Gorge for thousands of years. You can see historic photos of dip net fishermen on platforms at Celilo Falls and other important sites along the river at the Gorge Discovery Center and Fort Dalles Museum, both in The Dalles (see The Oregon Gorge chapter).

an Umpqua Indian

Maryhill/Goldendale Area
Maryhill Museum of Art, 509/773-3733, is the crown jewel of Gorge museums, and quite an anomaly in the surrounding rangeland. *Time* magazine described it as "the loneliest museum in the world" when it first opened in 1940. It was originally built in the 1920s as a residence by railroad mogul, Sam Hill, who named it for his wife, daughter, and mother-in-law. Unfortunately, his wife refused to live in a 20,000-square-foot castle 800-feet above the Columbia in this remote region. She also gave up on living in the

WASHINGTON GORGE

SHE WHO WATCHES

Located at Horsethief Lake, *Tsagaglalal* (She Who Watches), in the language of the Wishram tribe of Native Americans, is the largest and most famous of the petroglyphs along the Columbia River. These images, carved in bone, stone, and antler, are often found among cremation burials in the region. They are believed to date from the early historic period—roughly the 18th century—just before and during the initial contacts with white explorers and pioneers settling the region. The association between these images and burials suggests the figures may represent a death cult guardian spirit. It is sad history that during this period quickly spreading epidemics of smallpox and other diseases were brought to the area by Euro-Americans. Native American populations with no immunities developed to fight these deadly maladies were decimated. Upon arrival in the mid-Columbia region, Lewis and Clark found diseased Indian populations sharply diminished in number. It is easy to imagine local tribes responding to the catastrophe by developing guardian spirits to ward off evil and cure the sick and dying. An old Wishram shaman woman told one researcher in 1957: "*Tsagaglalal* is for death. . . .People grin like that when they're sick."

Edward Curtis, a famous turn-of-the-century photographer and chronicler of Native American ways, recorded the following legend about She Who Watches, told to him by the Wishram: "A woman had a house where the village of Nixlu-idix was later built. She was the chief of all who lived in this region. After a time Coyote in his travels came to this place and asked the inhabitants if they were living well or ill. They sent him to their chief who lived up on the rocks, where she could look down on the village and know what was going on. Coyote climbed up to the house on the rocks and asked, 'Do you treat these people well or are you one of those evil women?' 'I am teaching them to live well and build good houses,' she said. 'Soon the world will change,' said Coyote, 'and women will no longer be chiefs.' Then he changed her into a rock with the command, 'You shall live here.' People know that *Tsagaglalal* sees all things, for those eyes are always watching them."

The area where *Tsagaglalal* watches is adjacent to what was, in the pre-dam era, a narrow, turbulent stretch of the Columbia known as the Long Narrows or Five-Mile Rapids. It once contained one of the densest concentrations of permanent Native American settlements on the continent. Clear archaeological evidence indicates that Native Americans have continuously inhabited this stretch of the Columbia Gorge for over 10 millennia.

The great river was "turned on its side" at the Long Narrows, squeezing down from over a mile wide to a fraction of this width as it sliced through a trough-like gorge. This meant that salmon, spawning up the rapids in thick clusters, could be harvested by Indian dip netters more easily than at any other location along the mighty Columbia. It's been said that during that era, even a spear thrown blindly couldn't miss harpooning a big one.

The natives viewed the salmon as spiritual deities, sacrificing themselves to feed the tribe. As such, descriptions from sources such as Lewis and Clark depict the ceremony welcoming the first salmon upriver as a high holy day. One band would give the bones to a strong swimmer who would deposit them on the river bottom, in the belief that this would compel the return of more fish. Due to these copious salmon harvests and a location along the east-west corridor between coastal and interior regions, this stretch of the river became an important trading center for Native Americans throughout western North America. Shells from British Columbia and California, turquoise from the Southwest, and pipestone from Minnesota found near here attest to the area's critical importance to Native American life.

agrarian-based, 7,000-acre utopian community that Hill envisioned at Maryhill. When the Quakers whom Hill hoped would populate his commune ("where the rain of the west and the sunshine of the east meet") followed suit, his dreams of making a home here died. Instead, Hill embellished his baronial mansion with an eclectic mix of artwork and exhibits. Now open to the public, it houses the largest collection of sculptures by Auguste Rodin west of the Mississippi. Also on display is an extensive collection of Native American artifacts, including beautiful baskets in the distinctive style of the Columbia Basin tribes. Note too the impressive array of chess sets spanning centuries and the globe, Russian icons, and memorabilia from Queen Marie of Romania. Hill, a personal friend of the queen, timed the dedication of his palace to coincide with the arrival of her royal highness in 1926. Fourteen years later, thanks to the efforts of California sugar heiress Alma Spreckels, the museum finally opened its doors.

In good weather, stroll the impeccably landscaped grounds and enjoy the outdoor sculptures and resident peacocks who call this their little chateau on the prairie. The museum has a good café and gift shop. It's located on Hwy. 14, three miles east of the U.S. 197 junction. Check for special events and exhibitions. Open daily 9 A.M.–5 P.M. from mid-May to mid-November; admission is $7 adults, $2.50 for seniors and children 6–16.

History and road engineering buffs will enjoy walking or bicycling the **Maryhill Historic Loops Road** dating back to 1909. It is three miles east of Maryhill Museum off Hwy. 14. Now closed to vehicular traffic, this was the first paved road in Washington. Sam Hill's innovative snaking of the road up the steep Klickitat Hills at gentle grades was a precursor to techniques used in designing the Historic Columbia River Highway. In any case, another remarkable example of Hill's impact on the Gorge territory is a replica of England's ancient, mysterious **Stonehenge,** built between the two world wars. A few miles east of the museum and south of Hwy. 14 (just east of Hwy. 97), this circle of upright poured concrete slabs is dedicated to Klickitat County World War

I dead. Reportedly, this replica of the site in England (when it stood intact) was inspired by Hill's idea that the original was also a sacrificial monument. In recent years, the monument has seen numerous druidic gatherings and harmonic convergences under a full moon. Hill had planned this place as a venue for such events but opinion is divided if the stones actually line up correctly with celestial bodies during equinoxes.

The sparsely settled area north of Goldendale offers dark night skies, utilized to full advantage at the **Goldendale Observatory,** 509/773-3141. The observatory, run by the state of Washington as a state park, has one of the largest public telescopes in the United States. Call for information on special astronomy programs offered periodically. The observatory is located along Hwy. 97, just north of town.

The classically Victorian Presby Mansion houses the **Klickitat County Museum,** just north of downtown Goldendale at 127 W. Broadway, 509/773-4303. Museum holdings include pioneer furnishings, tools, and artifacts in a tableau of turn-of-the-century daily life. It's open daily 9 A.M.–5 P.M. from April 1 to November 1. Twenty-one well-preserved old homes in Goldendale can be seen on the **Historic Homes Driving Tour.** The brochure is available through the chamber of commerce or at the County Museum.

Scenic Drive

A delightful loop starting and ending in Lyle runs along portions of Hwy. 142, U.S. 97, and Hwy. 14. From Lyle, drive north on Hwy. 142, which closely parallels the Klickitat River for the first 15 miles of the journey. Enjoy the unspoiled beauty of the lower Klickitat's dramatic canyon. Here you can observe the climatic and ecological transition between the forests of the Cascade Range and the arid expanse of the Columbia Plateau. Due to precise amounts of rainfall and microclimatic variations caused by the steep canyon terrain, you can turn your head 180 degrees and see these two worlds a stone's throw from each other. Shady, north-facing slopes are blanketed with woodlands that include towering Ponderosa pines. Across the canyon, arid hillsides covered with grasses and scrub vegetation bake in the sun.

The road eventually leaves the canyon, heading across farmland towards Goldendale, the Klickitat County seat. After enjoying a stop in Goldendale's quaint historic downtown, head south on U.S. 97 towards the Columbia. Just out of town, stop at the side of the road to marvel at the unobstructed view (weather permitting, of course) of several high Cascade peaks visible in the distance to the west. Closer Mt. Adams looms large on the horizon from this roadside perspective. After descending the slope of the Columbia Hills, head west on Hwy. 14, through a dramatic landscape of cliffs and 2,000-foot grassy ridges and vineyards. Periodic views of the wide Columbia River with Mt. Hood as a snowy backdrop are breathtaking. Excluding the stops, driving time for this loop should take about one hour and 45 minutes.

RECREATION AND ACTIVITIES
Hiking and Mountain Biking

Two nice hikes (one short and easy, the other a bit longer and moderately strenuous) can be made in the Lyle area. The easy one, the **Klickitat River Rails-to-Trails** hike, follows an abandoned railroad bed that parallels the first mile of the Klickitat River. Park on the south side of Hwy. 14 just east of the bridge over the Klickitat River, cross the road, and find the old railbed (now a graveled trail) just west of the junction of Hwys. 14 and 142. A mile-long, level walk runs alongside this major tributary of the Columbia past quiet pools and modest rapids. The route ends at a small, undeveloped park where it's not uncommon to glimpse waterfowl at rest in the river. Long-term plans to continue the trail up the scenic Klickitat Canyon are being developed by the U.S. Forest Service and State Parks Department.

The **Cherry Orchard Trail** takes hikers up the steep face of the Columbia Hills until it levels off over 1,000 feet above the river. Views from the top are spectacular, and the area abounds with multi-colored wildflower blooms in the spring. This trail passes through open grassland and oak woodlands rich in endemic plant and animal species. Typical of the Gorge's climatic transition zone, this oak woodland ecosystem is an impor-

tant habitat that is diminishing due to clearing for grazing, firewood cutting, and conversion to residential use. The entire trail traverses private land, so use common sense and respect; keep on the trail and heed No Trespassing signs. The trailhead is not easy to find. Go east on Hwy. 14; immediately after passing through two small tunnels just east of Lyle, park in the broad shoulder area on the north side of the highway. You'll see a small break in the fence at the north end of the parking area—that's the trailhead. Watch out for ticks and poison oak, particularly in spring. In summer, beware of rattlesnakes.

Dalles Mountain Ranch State Park consists of over 3,000 acres of grasslands covering the undulating slopes of the 2,500-foot high Columbia Hills, a long-time cattle ranch known as Dalles Mountain. It is one of the newest state parks in the Gorge. "The Ranch" has no formal hiking trails. Instead, two dirt roads traversing its length and width provide access for hikers and cyclists. In addition, hikers are allowed to set out cross-country within the boundaries of the park. Highlights include impressive wildflower displays between March and early summer, peaking in late spring when the hillsides are awash in purples (lupines), yellows (balsamroot), reds (paintbrush), and other delightful hues. Another draw is the spectacular panorama visible from the ranch's grassy hills, which are unobstructed by trees. On clear days from high points, you can see several Cascade volcanoes, a large stretch of the Columbia, and the rolling wheat fields of north-central Oregon receding in the distance. To get there, turn north off Hwy. 14 onto Dalles Mountain Road, about a mile east of the junction of Hwy. 14 and U.S. 197. The park boundary is about two miles up the road. A fork in the road, where you'll see the original ranch house and some farm buildings, marks the middle of the park. You can continue along the main road, or take the left fork up the ridge, and head into the hills from there.

Columbia Hills Natural Area Preserve comprises the ridge-top lands directly above Dalles Mountain Ranch. It was primarily established to protect rare plants, including species of buttercups and penstemon, and rare, unspoiled native grassland. Hiking is only allowed on existing roads in the preserve. For more information, contact the Washington Department of Natural Resources at 509/925-6131. To protect it from overuse, it is recommended that only those interested in local botany visit the preserve. All others can enjoy essentially the same hike at the adjacent Dalles Mountain Ranch.

Horsethief Lake State Park offers the only well-known rock-climbing opportunities in the east Gorge. Go approximately one mile east of the main entrance to the park on Hwy. 14. Here, you'll see a small (really small) roadside pullout and trailhead sign for Horsethief Butte Trail on the south side of the road. Experienced climbers will enjoy scrambling up the columnar basalt to savor the views from the top.

White-water Rafting

While the nearby White Salmon River is the most famous white-water run in the Gorge, stretches of the lower Klickitat River offer exciting rides down its scenic canyon. Some of the rapids here are Class III to Class IV, which should provide a sufficient rush for all participants. All Adventures in the Gorge, 877/641-RAFT, www.alladventures.net, offers 4 and 4-and-a-half hour raft trips down a 15-mile stretch of the Klickitat. This river is best run in early to mid-summer, when flows are still sufficient and the water not too cold. The cost is $75, including gear and lunch.

Fishing, Boating, and Swimming

Just behind The Dalles Dam, adjacent riverfront Hess Park and Spearfish Park are operated by the Army Corps of Engineers. Both offer fishing access, picnicking, camping, and restrooms. Spearfish Lake has a launch directly into the Columbia. Both parks can be reached from U.S. 197, just north of The Dalles Bridge. About five miles east of there, the Army Corps also operates another riverfront site, Avery Boat Launch, with picnic and overnight camping facilities. For more information, call the Army Corps office at The Dalles Dam at 541/296-1181. Just east of the Sam Hill (or Maryhill-Biggs) Bridge on U.S. 97, Maryhill State Park, 509/773-5007, has excellent boat launch facilities and a swim beach on the Columbia.

Windsurfing

Doug's Beach State Park is renowned among boardheads everywhere as one the top windsurfing spots in the nation. Located three miles east of Lyle next to Hwy. 14, Doug's combination of wind exposure and subsurface river contours make it a hot spot for hot doggers seeking high winds and waves. Exuberant sailors catching "air time" is a common site at Doug's. Park amenities include portable toilets and a few picnic tables. It's also a beautiful place to ponder the splendor of the Gorge on off-season or windless days.

Avery Park, located on the south side of Hwy. 14 three miles west of Wishram, offers good high-wind windsurfing, and has a bathroom, a boat launch, and limited camping facilities. Maryhill State Park features the full spectrum of amenities for sailors, including showers, rigging areas, restrooms, and picnic grounds. It is located off U.S. 97 (first right after crossing the Sam Hill Bridge). Currents and waves can be strong, but this is usually a good intermediate sailing site. Peach Beach provides a good alternative when the state park is too crowded. Conditions are similar, and the beach is a bit rocky. To get there, go east past Maryhill State Park. Restrooms and showers are available.

Wineries

The sunny slopes and rich soils of this area's volcanic terraces along the Columbia Gorge make it one of the best grape-growing regions in the Northwest. In recent years, many new vineyards and wineries have cropped up. Cascade Cliffs Winery, 8866 Hwy. 14, 509/767-1100, is a small winery with a commanding view of the Gorge, about midway between the Hwy. 97 bridge and the bridge at The Dalles. Fine wines, including nebbiolo, barbera, merlot, and syrah, are uncorked at the tasting room to treat your palette. It's open daily 10 A.M.–7 P.M. March through December. The Gorge's newest winery, Maryhill Winery, 9774 Hwy. 14, 509/773-6951 or 877/MARYHILL, rests on a high bluff overlooking the Columbia and distant Mt. Hood, about a mile west of Maryhill Museum. The large, new tasting room offers samples of full reds such as syrahs and merlots, along with the delightfully fruity chardonnays and other white varietals. A small deli sells specialty food items and gifts. Visitors are welcome to stroll among the vineyards and orchards, and picnic under a covered arbor. You can visit them on the web at www.maryhillwinery.com.

Fruit Stands and Pick-Your-Own Farms

The arid east end of the Gorge features excellent soils along the terraces flanking the Columbia, which, when irrigated, produce fine cherries, peaches, nectarines, and apricots. Just east of Maryhill Park, down in the townsite of Maryhill, **Gunkel Orchards,** 89 Maryhill Hwy., 509/773-4698, sells all those fruits. Delectable, juicy peaches—grown locally—give their name to nearby Peach Beach. You can get there by turning off Hwy. 97 (just east of Maryhill State Park) or by going south off Hwy. 14 near the Stonehenge Memorial. The **Maryhill Fruit Stand and Orchard,** at 65 Maryhill Hwy., 509/773-4695, offers similar delights next door.

Events

Maryhill Museum puts on special events each year, ranging from outdoor evening concerts to temporary exhibitions. Check for the latest schedule of events by calling the museum at 509/773-3733. July 4th in Goldendale features a **Demolition Derby** at the Klickitat County Fairgrounds, 1–5 P.M. The auto racing is complemented by food booths; call 509/773-3550 for more information.

A scenic, 10-minute drive from Lyle up the Klickitat Canyon on Hwy. 142 brings you to the small timber-based community of Klickitat. Here, the **Klickitat Canyon Days,** 509/369-2322, held on the last weekend in July, bring an art show, parade, food and local crafts to town. The **Klickitat County Fair and Rodeo,** at the county fairgrounds in Goldendale, is usually the third weekend in August. It lasts for three days with professional and junior rodeos, a timber carnival, livestock auctions, exhibits, and a parade. Call 509/364-3526 or 509/773-3400 for information.

PRACTICALITIES
Accommodations

One of the sweetest surprises in the Gorge is the charming, turn-of-the-century **Lyle Hotel,** 100 7th St., 509/365-5953, fax 509/365-2668, www.lylehotel.com, in the unassuming town of Lyle. With a gourmet-quality restaurant (see Food, below), it is a lodging bargain. Lovingly restored, this little hotel (c. 1905) offers rooms, some with antique furniture, for a mere $49–59. The atmosphere is decidedly laid back, with no TVs or phones in the rooms (there is a phone for guest use in the hall). Bathrooms down the hall, as in times past, and often-noisy rooms facing the railroad tracks make up the only hitches. Hosts Jim and Penny Rutledge will treat you right, and clue you into nearby attractions and sights not always found in tour guidebooks.

The only other budget options in the vicinity are two motels in Goldendale, 15 minutes north of Maryhill along U.S. 97. Both provide standard roadside motel rooms. **Ponderosa Motel,** 775 E. Broadway, 509/773-5842, has rooms for $49 in town. **Farvue Motel,** U.S. 97, 509/773-5842, will put you up on the highway for $59.

Morning Song Acres, 6 Old Knight Rd., 509/365-3600, www.morningsongacres.com, is located seven miles northeast of Lyle. It offers bed-and-breakfast with a twist: full board and three delicious homemade meals. Fifteen minutes north of the Columbia, downtown Goldendale's aptly-named **Victorian House,** 415 East Broadway, 888/426-7281 or 509/773-5338, features properly primped rooms with shared bath for $55 or $65 (with full breakfast). A bit farther afield, **Three Creeks Resort,** 2120 U.S. 97 (nine miles north of Goldendale), 509/773-3325, 3creeks@goldendale.net, boasts full resort facilities in the wooded Simcoe Mountains. Accommodations include cabins for $59 (midweek specials for $49), or suites with decks overlooking the creek for $89 ($69 midweek). For families or larger groups, town homes with private hot tubs are $189, or $169 during the week. An on-site restaurant adds to the attraction of this new resort.

Camping

Three state parks in this area offer full-service campgrounds, two of which are located on or adjacent to the Columbia River. All three have picnic areas, restrooms, and RV dump stations. **Horsethief Lake State Park,** 509/767-1159, lies south of Hwy. 14 a few miles east of its junction with U.S. 197. The small campground here includes 12 campsites overlooking an enclosed bay of the Columbia River (Horsethief "Lake"), near the boat launch and the ancient Native American pictograph trail (see Sights, above). **Maryhill State Park,** 509/773-5007 or 800/452-5687, 50 Hwy. 97, just east of the Sam Hill (Maryhill-Biggs) Bridge, offers one of largest campgrounds in the area. In addition to 50 full hookup sites and 20 tent sites, Maryhill has other amenities such as a group camp, kitchens, concession stand, and direct beach access to the Columbia. **Brooks Memorial State Park,** 2465 U.S. 97, 509/773-4611, 12 miles north of Goldendale, also has kitchens, group camps, and 23 trailer/campsites with hookups—all nestled in tall pines.

Three small parks run by the U.S. Army Corps of Engineers offer overnight camping with basic amenities. **Hess Park** and **Spearfish Park** are both located just east of U.S. 197, near The Dalles. **Avery Boat Launch** has a few campsites along the Columbia, and is located about five miles east of the other two parks. Call 541/296-1181 for reservations and other information.

Just east of Maryhill State Park, try **Peach Beach** for riverside camping next to a great windsurfing beach. Shade trees, picnic tables and fresh fruit at nearby farm stands make this an attractive alternative to the adjacent state park. For information, call 509/773-4927. Full-service, private **Columbia Hills RV Park** is located in Dallesport, north of The Dalles, 111 Hwy. 197 (a mile north of The Dalles Bridge), 509/767-2277. It has everything you'd ever want in an RV park, including 32 full hookup sites, laundry, showers, and a convenience store. Its Dallesport location, while not terribly scenic, is close to attractions in The Dalles and vicinity.

Food

The **Lyle Hotel,** 100 7th St., 509/365-5953, is an oasis for gourmet palates in an arid, culinary landscape. The hotel's constantly changing menu leans toward nouvelle cuisine. One night you'll dine on filet au poivre or honey citrus tuna, while later in the week you'll savor a bouillabaisse or excellent medallions of pork. Entrées typically run $12–20. Finish your sumptuous repast with a selection of enticing, sizable desserts. The hotel offers one of the best Sunday brunches in the Gorge, served until 3 P.M. Brunchers can enjoy breakfast-style entrées. Try the succulent oyster-bacon-egg mix of the Hangtown Fry. Brunch includes a small buffet with an unusual, tasty filet mignon sausage, fresh fruits, and juices. While in downtown Lyle, you can score down-home biscuits and gravy, burgers, or a sandwich at the **Country Cafe,** 605 Hwy. 14, 509/365-3883. Fare and prices are modest.

Cafe Maryhill, 509/773-3733, is the restaurant at the Maryhill Museum. It provides tasty if limited offerings. Lunches include homemade desserts. In good weather, one can dine outdoors and enjoy the view. If you're lucky, you'll catch a glimpse of resident peacocks struttin' their stuff on the surrounding, manicured grounds. The museum and cafe are located just south of Hwy. 14, three miles west of U.S. 97. Hours are 10 A.M.–4:30 P.M.

Information and Services

The **Columbia River Gorge Visitors Association,** 2149 W. Cascade, Suite 106A, Hood River, OR 97031, 800/98-GORGE, www.gorge.net/crgva, dispenses information on Gorge attractions and tourist services upon request. Providing useful information through its website, by phone, or in person, the **Klickitat County Visitor Information Center,** P.O. Box 1220, Goldendale, WA 98620, 509/493-3630 or 800/785-1718, www.klickitatcounty.org, is a good resource. You'll also find helpful brochures and information at the **Washington/Oregon/Klickitat County Visitor Center at Maryhill,** in Maryhill State Park, P.O. Box 1220, Goldendale, WA 98620, 509/773-4395. It's open daily May through October. The **Mt. Adams Chamber of Commerce,** Hwy. 14 at the Hood River Bridge, P.O. Box 449, White Salmon, WA 98672, 509/493-3630, www.gorge.net/mtadamschamber, provides information about attractions and activities around Lyle and up the Klickitat Canyon. For Goldendale attractions and events, contact the **Goldendale Chamber of Commerce,** P.O. Box 524, Goldendale, WA 98620, 509/773-3400. Their offices in downtown Goldendale, at 903 E. Broadway, are open Monday through Friday 9 A.M.–3 P.M., or visit them on the web at www.gorge.net/community/goldendale.

If you need medical attention, there are three hospitals in the area, all far from each other. In the west end of this area near Lyle, your closest hospital is **Skyline Hospital** in White Salmon, 509/493-1101. If you are near The Dalles, use the **Mid Columbia Medical Center,** 1700 E. 19th St., 541/296-1111. This is the largest, best-equipped hospital in the area. For those venturing northward, the **Klickitat Valley Hospital** is located in Goldendale at 310 S. Roosevelt, 509/773-4022.

Lyle has a self-service laundromat at the **Lyle Mercantile,** 615 Hwy. 14, 509/365-2323; it's on the north side of the road in the center of town.

Portland — Gateway to the Gorge

In shadows cast by 100-year-old trees and buildings, the new Northwest is taking shape in Portland, OR (metro area pop. over 500,00; greater Portland pop. 1.7 million). Amid greenery seldom seen in an urban environment, high-tech business ventures, a full cultural calendar, and an activist community are carving out a vibrant image. A latticework of bridges over the Willamette River adds a distinctive profile, while parks, malls, and other people-spaces give Portland a heart and a soul. The overall effect is more European than American, where the urban core is equal parts marketplace, cultural forum, and working metropolis.

Such a happy medium is the result of progressive planning and a fortunate birthright. Patterns of

Portland

PORTLAND

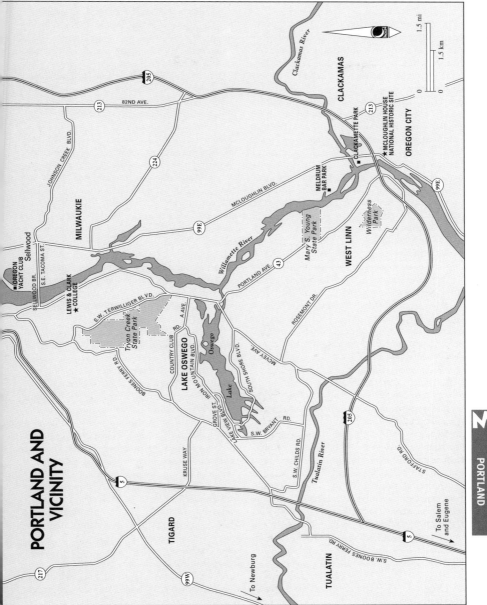

PORTLAND AND VICINITY

1.5 mi
1.5 km

Clackamas River

CLACKAMAS

★ MCLOUGHLIN HOUSE NATIONAL HISTORIC SITE

OREGON CITY

99E

CLACKAMETTE PARK

213

MELDRUM BAR PARK

Wilderness Park

WEST LINN

Mary S. Young State Park

MCLOUGHLIN BLVD.

99E

MILWAUKIE

224

82ND AVE.

213

205

JOHNSON CREEK BLVD.

OREGON YACHT CLUB Sellwood

SELLWOOD BR. S.E. TACOMA ST.

LEWIS & CLARK ★ COLLEGE

Willamette River

PORTLAND AVE.

43

ROSEMONT DR.

S.W. TERWILLIGER BLVD.

Tryon Creek State Park

BOONES FERRY RD.

COUNTRY CLUB RD.

A AVE.

Oswego Lake

IRON MOUNTAIN BLVD.

SOUTH SHORE BLVD.

MCVEY AVE.

LAKE OSWEGO

GROVE ST.

LAKE VIEW BLVD.

S.W. BRYANT RD.

205

STAFFORD RD.

KRUSE WAY

S.W. CHILDS RD.

Tualatin River

5

TIGARD

To Newburg

99W

217

TUALATIN

S.W. BOONES FERRY RD.

5

To Salem and Eugene

PORTLAND

© AVALON TRAVEL PUBLISHING, INC.

growth in this one-time Native American encampment at the confluence of the Willamette and Columbia Rivers were initially shaped by the practical midwestern values of Oregon Trail pioneers as well as by the sophistication of New England merchants. Rather than the boom-bust development, which characterized Seattle and gold-rush San Francisco, Portland was designed to be user-friendly over the long haul. During the modern era, such utopian refinements as the most advanced and extensive mass-transit systems in the U.S. and an urban plan that places strict limitations on the height of buildings and the space between them were added. Aesthetically pleasing and historic architecture as well as America's most extensive tract of city parkland have been preserved during Portland's last decades of growth. Over time, the place that was once called "Stumptown" has become the poster child for cities that work. At the end of 2000, *Money Magazine* rated Portland as the nation's most liveable city.

Another blessing is Portland's auspicious location at the confluence of two rivers, one of which supports oceangoing vessels. Even though the city's port sits 110 miles from the Pacific Ocean, the volume of wheat, potash, and other commodities makes Swan Island the nation's number one bulk-products exporter. It is also considered the second leading grain export site in the world.

Portland's waterways are her lifeblood in other ways. Mt. Hood's Bull Run watershed supplies some of the purest drinking water anywhere in the U.S., and the printing, textile, papermaking, and high-tech industries (the Portland area has over 1,100 such companies) place a premium on Portland's clean-running aqueous arteries. What has historically been low-cost and abundant Columbia River hydropower has provided an incentive for many other industries to locate here.

Along with a location easily reachable by air, land, and sea, Portland's proximity to rural retreats will please the traveler. With hiking and windsurfing in the Columbia Gorge, year-round skiing on Mt. Hood to the east, and the jewel of the Oregon Coast, Cannon Beach, to the west, relief from urban stress is little more than an hour away. To the north, Mt. St. Helens National Vol-

canic Monument can be enjoyed on a leisurely day trip. Closer to home, Portland's Forest Park is the largest urban wilderness in the country. Washington Park's Japanese Gardens and Rose Gardens are other internationally renowned places of beauty and contemplation. And if you need inspiration right in the downtown core, the Classic Chinese Garden uses centuries-old landscape architectural principles to induce a sense of well-being.

The cultural offerings in this city are noteworthy for their scope and excellence. Whether it's the wine, cheese, and camaraderie on first-Thursday-of-the-month gallery walks or the smorgasbord of live theater and state-of-the-art concert halls, Portland's music mavens and culture vultures enjoy a full table. In like measure, bibliophiles revel in one of the world's largest bookstores, Powell's, as well as many other outlets for rare editions. The Portland Symphony Orchestra under the baton of James De Priest has gained an international reputation through its compact disc recordings and world travels. As for popular music, top rock acts regularly hit Portland, while the local pub scene showcases many fine blues and jazz players.

On a smaller scale, readings by local literati Ursula Le Guin, Philip Margolin, Chuck Pahlaniuk, and Craig Lesley, or equally prominent visiting authors, present a treat for Portland's book lovers. The flame of knowledge is also kept burning by Portland's museums. The Portland Art Museum has risen to regional prominence by hosting an impressive roster of visiting shows and its own Grande Ronde Center for Native Art. Adding to this cultural mix are more movie screens, radio stations, bookstores, and dining spots than any American city of comparable size.

A scant 15 miles away from the Historic Highway, this urbane yet laid-back city is the most popular gateway to the Columbia River Gorge. We've restricted this book's Portland coverage to the downtown core and the east side in the interests of brevity and relevance. While it highlights all the essentials a Gorge-bound traveler needs to know for a gourmet taste of the city, those who plan an extended stay should consult *Moon Handbooks: Oregon* by Stuart Warren and Ted Long Ishikawa.

PORTLAND—THE CITY THAT WORKS

Oregon's progressive traditions of land use began in Portland during the mid-19th century. At a time when Americans were told it was their "manifest destiny" to expand the nation's borders and settle the West, this town chose to ignore the expansionist impulse and preserve the Park Blocks, a mile-long stretch of greenery in the heart of downtown. Over the first several decades of the next century, Portlanders who owned significant tracts of land in the Gorge surrounding what was to become the Columbia River Highway donated much of it to the Portland City Parks system. A prime example of this largesse was Simon Benson's gift of hundreds of acres surrounding Wahkeenah and Multnomah Falls. During other eras when wilderness was something to be subdued instead of preserved, the city has also demonstrated a desire to be more than just a center for commerce. As a result, today over 10 percent of its environs are people-friendly spaces. The latter includes Forest Park, whose 5,000-plus acres comprise the world's largest urban wilderness.

The legacy of the **Portland City Park** system was continued by progressive planning iniatives from the 1970s, which gave impetus to the growth of the best mass transit system in America and a vital downtown. What had been the Harbor Freeway in the '60s became Waterfront Park in the '70s. The creation of Pioneer Courthouse Square, a European-style piazza in the city center also helped get people out of their cars. On the heels of these developments, the "one percent for art" provision, dedicating a portion of any new construction costs to public art became a prototype for similar programs in other cities. A more recent statement of Portland's priorities came with the central library's 1998 multimillion dollar restoration to turn-of-the-century elegance.

Region-wide land use has also been characterized by innovation. Metro, a tri-county regional planning commission, has overseen efforts to ease Portland's growth-related stresses. The extension of the light rail transit system (MAX) into distant suburbs, citywide recycling, and the urban growth boundary are all overseen by Metro. The idea of the urban growth boundary is to stop leapfrog development across the open countryside by confining the new subdivisions and commercial enterprises to agreed-upon areas. In so doing, it also preserves Willamette Valley farmland from being exploited by real estate interests for quick profit. The latter concern inspired statewide land use planning statutes in the early '70s that spawned the urban growth boundary concept. Portlanders voted to establish the boundary and Metro in 1979. This embrace of innovation has enabled Portland to place second in the country in *Utne Reader's* 1997 ranking of "enlightened" cities, first among large cities. At the end of 1996, *The New York Times* selected Portland as the only large population center with a chance of weathering the transition into the next century gracefully thanks to utopian urban planning. With the arrival of the 21st century, Metro will be making the city's first major land annexation in two decades. By 1999, Portland had incorporated only two square miles in 20 years, counteracting the nationwide trend toward urban sprawl.

While the urban growth boundary has saved on the cost of providing emergency services to farflung locales and solidified the city's tax base while creating a human-scale large city, the limitations on available acreage for expansion has created escalating land prices. According to a Harvard University study, new homes were 44 percent more expensive here in 1998 than they were in 1991. And increased urban density is not necessarily to everyone's liking. In like measure, the expansion of light rail is also problematic. Planners have bet on higher ridership due to increasing gas prices in the era of declining oil supplies. If that happens, light rail would mitigate the smog problems and depersonalization plaguing big cities built around the car. If not, taxpayers will foot a high bill for empty MAX seats while continuing to deal with rush hour gridlock. Mass transit advocates counter such concerns by pointing out the higher costs of freeways in dollars as well as their negative effects on quality of life.

However history will judge Portland's land use planning legacy, travelers will immediately recognize that this is more a place to live than to sightsee. Rather than a Golden Gate Bridge or a Space Needle, visitors come here to enjoy a clean, compact city in the midst of spectacular natural surroundings with enough worthwhile cultural attractions, dining spots, and shopping to merit an extended stay. In November 2000, *Money* magazine concurred, rating Portland America's most liveable city.

EARLY HISTORY

England's 1824 establishment of Fort Vancouver across the Columbia brought French trappers into the area, some of whom retired around what would eventually become Portland. The city was formally born when two New Englanders, Pettygrove from Portland, Maine, and Lovejoy from Boston, Massachusetts, flipped a coin at a dinner party to decide who would give a name to the 640-acre claim they co-owned. The state-of-Mainer won and decided in the winter of 1844–45 to name it after his birthplace. The original claim is located in the vicinity of southwest Naito Parkway (also known as Front Avenue).

The trade that grew up along the Willamette River and the so-called plank road south of the city enabled Willamette Valley produce and lumber from the interior to find an outlet to the sea at Portland's Columbia River port. This was especially important in the mid-19th century since San Francisco needed these resources to sustain a housing boom fueled by the California Gold Rush. Portland was thus able to make the transition from a sleepy village (called "Stumptown" because it was so dominated by logging) to the major trade center and population vortex in the state, becoming incorporated in 1851. Another defining event was the coming of the railroads in the late 19th century, linking the city to the eastern U.S. However, the single greatest impetus contributing to the emergence of Portland as Oregon's leading city was the Lewis and Clark Exposition in 1905. Over three million people attended this centennial celebration of the famed expedition, establishing the city in the minds of the American business community as the gateway to the Orient as well as paving the way for significant population growth in the years following the fair. By 1910, a metropolis of almost a quarter million people had grown up at the confluence of the Columbia and Willamette Rivers, almost tripling the town's population over a period of five years.

After the 1905 Expo, the Rose City emerged as a commercial hub with the expansion of railroads, farming, and livestock raising east of the Cascades. The shift of America's timber industry from the Great Lakes states to the Northwest also occurred during this era. In response to this deluge of commodities, new wharves and factories were built at the northern end of the Willamette Valley. On the periphery of the original Expo site, northwest Portland became a center of housing and commerce. Not surprisingly, city leaders have hopes for a bicentennial celebration of the Lewis and Clark Expedition to once again showcase the town in a beneficial way.

Getting Oriented: Downtown Neighborhoods

Portland's revival picked up steam in the 1970s, turning a city mostly known for rain, roses, and run-down buildings into a showplace of eye-catching art and architecture. Included in this legacy were the renovations of the historic Old Town neighborhood and Pioneer Courthouse Square, as well as a law requiring that 1 percent of all construction costs go toward public art projects.

Before getting started on your travels, keep in mind the following worthwhile tips. Most Portlanders sleep east of the Willamette River. The business district, shopping areas, museums, and theaters west of the Willamette can be easily reached from east-of-the-river residential areas by mass transit. Buses and light rail are preferable to cars because of streets closed to traffic and the dearth of parking in the city. You'll find a complete mass transit schedule at the Tri-Met Office in Pioneer Courthouse Square, the central branch of the public library, and other such venues. Call 503/238-RIDE for more information.

Walkers have it best of all according to *Walking* magazine, which in 1996 rated Portland among the top 10 cities in the country, citing blocks that are half the size (200 feet) of those in most other urban population centers and a cityscape flat enough to let you log miles on foot relatively painlessly. A compact downtown area (about 13 blocks by 26 blocks) also invites strolling, so ditch your car and put on your walking shoes.

PORTLAND

The Transit Mall

Sometime in your downtown meanderings, you'll find yourself within the 11-block Transit Mall, on 5th and 6th Avenues. Thirty-one shelters (color-coded by their region) make up Transit Mall. Southbound buses pick up passengers on SW 5th Ave.; northbound travelers board on SW 6th Avenue. These two streets are largely banned to downtown vehicular traffic other than Tri-Met buses. Tri-Met, along with MAX light rail, comprises the most far-reaching and cost-effective inner-city transportation system in the nation according to the American Transit Association. Be that as it may, restrictions on car traffic in the downtown bus lanes might be partially lifted in the future to help area merchants.

Bus commuters, cyclists, and pedestrians on the go appreciate the variety of street carts (purveying burritos, bento, and the like) in the heart of the bus mall around SW 5th and Stark. The bus stops here feature brick-inlaid promenades and glass-canopied pavilions garlanded with floral displays. But the aesthetics don't stop there. These waiting areas have so many ornate statues and fountains that former Portland Mayor Bud Clark exhorts you to "expose yourself to art" here. A famous poster depicts his honor flashing the female nude statue *Kvinneakt*, on 5th Avenue between SW Washington and SW Stark, underscored by the aforementioned invitation. Bus and light-rail travel is free throughout much of downtown (see Inner City Transportation under Getting There and Getting Around in the Practicalities section, following).

Finding Your Way

Before you arrive, you might want to contact the **Portland Oregon Visitors Association** (POVA), 26 SW Salmon St., Portland 97204-3299 or 877/678-5263, www.travelportland.com, for free maps and their informative *Portland Book*. The latter might be Northwest Oregon's single most useful tourist information medium. In addition to in-depth Portland coverage, coastal and Columbia Gorge highlights are briefly detailed. Once in the center city, helpful information sources throughout the downtown core are the **Portland Guides**, 503/295-0912. Their distinctive green baseball caps make it easy to spot these free, walking information centers.

Heeding some observations can also help get your Portland travels off to a good start. The line of demarcation between north and south in addresses is Burnside Street; between east and west it's the Willamette River. These give a reference point for the address prefixes southwest, southeast, north, northwest, and northeast.

Another useful thing to keep in mind is that avenues run north-south and streets run east-west. Many street names on one side of the river continue across to the other. Twelve bridges connect east to west. Almost every downtown address will carry a southwest or northwest prefix.

Other aids to orientation include the fact that Naito Parkway (SW Front Avenue) is the road nearest the Willamette River downtown and Water Avenue is the nearest on the east side. Thereafter, numbered avenues begin.

Expect most streets downtown to run one way, alternating with the next going in the opposite direction. Streets in northwest Portland are named alphabetically (i.e., Burnside, Couch, on through Wilson). Finally, addresses increase by 100 each block, beginning at the Willamette River for streets and Burnside for avenues. More detailed orientation information is provided at chapter's end in the Getting There and Getting Around section.

DOWNTOWN WALKING TOUR

The best introduction to Portland is a walking tour that also takes advantage of the city's excellent mass transit. Despite the convenience of car travel, we feel the flavor of this compact downtown is better appreciated on foot, supplemented by bus or bike. Otherwise, Portland's mix of people, parks, and public art are too easy to miss. And no matter how fast you move, it's not possible to do all of the different portions of this tour in one day, so slow down and savor each part of town.

Portland Building, Ira's Fountain, and Public Art

We'll begin our tour below a statue that is said to symbolize the city, Raymond Kaskey's ***Portlandia,*** which ranks right behind the Statue of

PORTLAND

WESTSIDE PORTLAND SIGHTS

N.E. GRAND AVE.

MARTIN LUTHER KING JR. BLVD.

ROSE GARDEN ARENA/ MEMORIAL COLISEUM

Willamette River

STEEL BRIDGE

BROADWAY BRIDGE

LIGHT RAIL

BURNSIDE BRIDGE

Tom McCall Waterfront Park

FRONT AVE.

1ST AVE.

CLASSICAL CHINESE GARDEN

2ND AVE.

Old Town

3RD AVE.

Chinatown

4TH AVE.

5TH AVE.

★ SATURDAY MARKET

OREGON MARITIME MUSEUM ★

Skidmore Historic District

S.W. ANKENY ST.

★ CHINATOWN GATES

S.W. PINE ST.

S.W. OAK ST.

UNION STATION (AMTRAK)

GREYHOUND BUS STATION

6TH AVE.

BROADWAY AVE.

N.W. GLISAN ST.

N.W. FLANDERS ST.

N.W. EVERETT ST.

N.W. DAVIS ST.

N.W. COUCH ST.

6TH AVE.

TRANSIT MALL

BROADWAY AVE.

POST OFFICE

7TH AVE.

8TH AVE.

NORTH PARK BLOCKS

W. BURNSIDE ST.

PARK AVE.

9TH AVE.

The Pearl

10TH AVE.

S.W. STARK ST.

S.W. WASHINGTON ST.

S.W. ALDER ST.

★ BLITZ-WEINHARD BREWERY

POWELL'S BOOKS

★ McMENAMINS CRYSTAL BALLROOM

N.W. LOVEJOY ST.

N.W. HOYT ST.

11TH AVE.

12TH AVE.

13TH AVE.

14TH AVE.

15TH AVE.

405

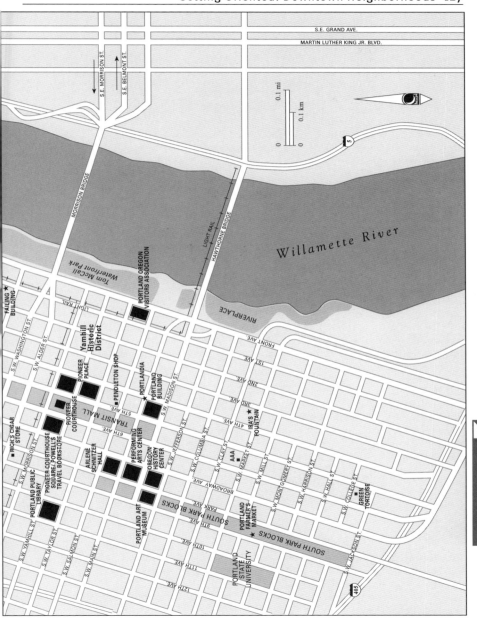

S.E. GRAND AVE.

MARTIN LUTHER KING JR. BLVD.

S.E. MORRISON ST.

S.E. BELMONT ST.

0.1 mi

0.1 km

5

MORRISON BRIDGE

Light Rail

HAWTHORNE BRIDGE

Willamette River

Tom McCall Waterfront Park

PORTLAND OREGON VISITORS ASSOCIATION

RIVERPLACE

TAILING BUILDING

CITY HALL

FRONT AVE.

1ST AVE.

2ND AVE.

3RD AVE.

Yamhill Historic District

S.W. WASHINGTON ST.

S.W. ALDER ST.

PENDLETON SHOP

PORTLANDIA

PORTLAND BUILDING

PIONEER PLACE

S.W. MADISON ST.

IRA'S FOUNTAIN

TRANSIT MALL

5TH AVE.

6TH AVE.

PIONEER COURTHOUSE

RICH'S CIGAR STORE

PIONEER COURTHOUSE SQUARE, POWELL'S TRAVEL BOOKSTORE

ARLENE SCHNITZER HALL

PERFORMING ARTS CENTER

OREGON HISTORY CENTER

S.W. JEFFERSON ST.

S.W. COLUMBIA ST.

S.W. CLAY ST.

S.W. MARKET ST.

S.W. MILLS ST.

S.W. MONTGOMERY ST.

S.W. HARRISON ST.

S.W. HALL ST.

COLLEGE ST.

GREEN TORTOISE

BROADWAY

AAA

PORTLAND PUBLIC LIBRARY

S.W. MORRISON ST.

PORTLAND ART MUSEUM

SOUTH PARK BLOCKS

PORTLAND FARMER'S MARKET

PARK AVE.

9TH AVE.

S.W. YAMHILL ST.

S.W. TAYLOR ST.

S.W. SALMON ST.

S.W. MAIN ST.

SOUTH PARK BLOCKS

10TH AVE.

11TH AVE.

12TH AVE.

PORTLAND STATE UNIVERSITY

S.W. JACKSON ST.

I-405

N

PORTLAND

© AVALON TRAVEL PUBLISHING, INC.

Liberty as the world's largest hammered copper sculpture. Located outside Michael Graves's post-modern Portland Building, SW 5th Ave. between SW Main and SW Madison, the golden-hued female figure holding a trident re-creates the Lady of Commerce on the city seal. Locals refer to it as "Queen Kong," and sometimes practical jokers from Portland State University will dangle a giant yo-yo from her outstretched finger. Inside the Portland Building on the second floor is the **Metropolitan Center for Public Art,** 1120 SW 5th Ave., where you can pick up a brochure annotating a walking tour of the city's murals, fountains, sculptures, and other art forms. This profusion of statues and other public art pieces comes from the "one percent for art" program, which began in the early 1980s and allocates a percentage of construction costs for the purchase and display of public art.

A few blocks away from *Portlandia* is another eye-catching creation, the simulated cascades known as **Ira's Fountain.** To get to the fountain (also known as Forecourt Fountain), walk south on SW 4th Avenue to Clay Street. Walk down the hill (east) to Portland's **Civic Auditorium** (also known as Keller Auditorium) at SW 3rd and Clay for a full frontal view of the fountain. The sights and sounds of this kinetic sculpture with its multitiered cooling waters anticipates your next stop. Arrive at the waterfront by walking around the southern end of the Civic Auditorium where a left at Main Street and several blocks takes you to a riverside park where Portland has its most prominent festivals and celebrations.

Tom McCall Waterfront Park
Your introduction to the mile-long Tom McCall Waterfront Park begins at **RiverPlace,** an attractive area of restaurants, specialty shops, and boating facilities. The boutiques, brewpubs, and ornate piazza on the southern edge of this com-

Walking magazine, in the late '90s, rated Portland among the top 10 cities in the country for walking, citing blocks that are half the size (200 feet) of those in most other urban population centers and a cityscape flat enough to let you log miles on foot relatively painlessly.

plex overlook the Willamette River in the shadow of the Marquam Bridge. It's hard to imagine that 1894 floodwaters were high enough here to totally submerge many of RiverPlace's present-day storefronts. It's equally difficult to conjure hundreds of citizens volunteering to pile sandbags along this part of the waterfront in 1996 to hold back what threatened to be a reprise of the disaster from the previous century.

In any case, you can follow the paved walkway north to a more benign encounter with water at the **Salmon Street Springs Fountain,** a few minutes north of RiverPlace bordering Front Avenue/Naito Parkway. This is often the centerpiece of Portland's many festivals and provides a refreshing shower on a hot day. The fountain water's ebb and flow is meant to evoke the rhythms of the city. If you have any questions about Portland at this point, stop off at **POVA** across Front Ave. (hereinafter known as Naito Pkwy.) from the Salmon Street Springs Fountain. Maps and other sightseeing literature are available free here, and attendants are available to answer questions. There is also a discount theater seats outlet here where walk-ins can get half-price day-of-the-show deals. Ticketmaster, Fastixx, and Artistix tickets are also available.

Tom McCall Waterfront Park is named for the governor credited with helping to restore Oregon's rivers as well as other environmental initiatives. In the early 1970s the park's grassy shore replaced Harbor Drive, a freeway that impeded access to the scenic Willamette River. To go back to the time when the town's destiny was entwined with the Willamette and the Columbia, walk north along the waterfront till you are just south of the Burnside Bridge. Across Naito Parkway at the Ash Street stoplight is the oldest part of town.

The Skidmore Historical District
A block south of the corner of Ash Street and Naito Parkway, the **Oregon Maritime Muse-**

PORTLAND

um, 113 SW Front Ave., 503/224-7724, has photos of the era when sternwheelers plied the rapids of the Columbia River Gorge that are alone worth the $4 admission price. Also, don't miss the **USS** *Portland,* the last steam-operated tug on the West Coast. It is moored in the harbor across from the museum and like its parent facility is open Fri.–Sun. 11 A.M.–4 P.M.

After the museum, go back to Ash Street (look for the historic firehouse) and head west a block. Make a right on SW 1st and Ash, and walk along the cobblestones through the Skidmore Historic District. Along with this neighborhood's classic architecture, heritage markers can help inspire historical reverie. A little south of the Burnside Bridge you'll read that the **Skidmore Fountain,** SW 1st Ave. and SW Ankeny St., is named for a man who intended that it provide refreshment for "horses, men, and dogs." Local brewery owner Henry Weinhard offered to fill the fountain with beer for its grand opening, but the city leaders declined, fearing the horses would get drunk. Just south of the fountain, read the Ankeny Block placard on the wall for a good, concise description of Portland's architectural evolution. Despite the spouts and animal troughs, the 1888 bronze-and-granite fountain is still purely decorative. It does serve, however, as a portal to the largest continuously operating open-air handicrafts market in the United States. **Saturday Market** is an outdoor potlatch of homegrown edibles, arts, crafts, and excellent street performers. The market takes place every Saturday and Sunday from mid-March through Christmas in the shadow of the Burnside Bridge. On Saturday, the hours are 10 A.M.–5 P.M.; on Sunday the market operates 11 A.M.–4:30 P.M.

The 26 food booths at the market are a street-eater's delight. Particularly recommended are Cajun shrimp, elephant ears (deep-fried whole-wheat slabs immersed in butter, cinnamon, and sugar), and the seafood crepes at **Nutritious Delicious Crepes.** The handicrafts range from exquisite woodwork (at reasonable prices) and feather jewelry to homemade fire-starter kits and juggling toys. What's astonishing is the high quality that's been maintained here for over two decades. Travelers on a budget should note that prices at food booths drop as closing time approaches.

Across SW 1st Avenue and cobblestoned **Ankeny Square** from the Skidmore Fountain is the **New Market Theater,** constructed in 1872 as a theater and produce market.

A few blocks south of the market (double-back along 1st) the **Failing Building,** 235 SW 1st Ave. and Oak St., typifies the influences and use of cast iron so popular during the 1880s. Today it houses McCormick and Schmick's restaurant. Writer Gideon Bosker asserts you can trace the evolution of American architectural style on a stroll through Portland. This is easy to believe if, from the Failing Building, you walk three blocks east to SW Front Avenue and turn left to a prime location of elegant restorations. Prior to Portland's era of expressways and bridge building, this whole neighborhood was filled with cast-iron facades and Italianate architecture. Back on 1st Avenue catch the MAX light rail going south to Morrison Street, exiting blocks west at 5th Avenue, close to a more contemporary expression of Portland's mercantile instincts. Note that all mass transit within the 300-block area of "Fareless Square" (See Getting There and Getting Around in the Practicalities section, following) is free of charge.

Downtown Shopping

Pioneer Place is an attractive, upscale shopping atrium housing such shops as The Sharper Image, The Nature Company, The Museum Company, Godiva Chocolates, Eddie Bauer, and Banana Republic. Downstairs you'll find a food court with dozens of quality concession stands purveying an array of cuisines. Shoppers might also want to note the Pendleton shop, 900 SW 5th Ave., 503/242-0037, near the corner of 4th and SW Salmon. If the famous retailer of quality wool blankets and clothing is too pricey, their discount factory store across the Columbia River in Washington can be accessed by driving north on I-5 across the bridge and following Hwy. 14 10 miles east to the outlet's roadside Washougal outlet.

Pioneer Courthouse Square

If you follow Morrison across 5th Avenue you'll be on the north side of **Pioneer Courthouse,** 555 SW Yamhill, the oldest public building in the state, constructed between 1869 and 1873. This landmark is surrounded by statuary with small bronzed beavers, ducks, and sea lions congregating near a series of pools on the north side of the Pioneer Courthouse. On the south side of the courthouse on Yamhill Street, a bear with a fish in his mouth may be seen. The classic contours of this gray granite structure contrast with the blue-tiled, mauve-and-beige tuxedo-patterned facade you saw at the Portland Building. On the first floor of the Hall of Justice is a post office with historic photos on the wall. Period furniture and brass lamps line the hallways on the way to the Ninth Circuit Court of Appeals, located upstairs in room 204. If court is not in session, ask a security guard to let you in, 8:30 A.M.–5 P.M. weekdays, to see the Victorian courtroom. Also, from the cupola atop the courthouse peer out the same window from which President Rutherford B. Hayes viewed the city in 1880.

One block west, outside the front door of the building, is Pioneer Courthouse Square, bordered by Yamhill, Morrison, 6th Avenue, and Broadway—the cultural vortex of the city. On the south side of the square is *Allow Me,* a life-sized statue of a businessman with an umbrella hailing a cab. Also within the amphitheater-like confines of the square is **Powell's Travel Bookstore,** 701 SW 6th Ave. at SW Yamhill St., 503/228-1108, down the hall from which you'll find Tri-Met offices, where mass transit information can be procured and questions answered weekdays 9 A.M.–5 P.M. You can also call 503/238-RIDE or visit www.tri-met.org.

Diagonally across the square is a 25-foot column known as the **weather machine.** Every day at noon the forecast is delivered by one of three creatures: a dragon if it's stormy, a blue heron in overcast weather, or a sun figure. As if that's not enough, the machine also emits a small cloud accompanied by a fanfare while colored lights display temperature and air quality. In summer, the red-bricked square hosts jazz, folk, and other types of music every Tuesday through Thursday noon–1 P.M. On Monday summer evenings, 5–7 P.M., you'll find another free concert series here, **Starbucks by Starlight.** On warm spring and summer nights the music and crowds return, augmented by symphony-goers departing the

Performing Arts Center just up Broadway. The Birkenstocks and Gore-Tex of casual Northwest attire mingle easily with business suits here.

Should you tire of people-watching, inspect the bricks on the square, each of which bears the name of one of the 50,000 donors who anted up $15–30 for the privilege. From the northeast corner of the square gaze up at the white-brick and terra-cotta clock tower of the **Jackson Tower** on SW Yamhill and Broadway, and over at the copper sheathing of the Guild Theater building on 9th and Salmon to experience the glory that was Portland in the early part of this century.

Another part of the Pioneer Courthouse Square experience can be had in the middle of the amphitheater located on the northwest corner of the square. Here you might notice people talking to themselves. If you follow suit, you'll be treated to a perfect echo bouncing back at you.

The South Park Blocks Cultural District

Two blocks west of Broadway and the square are the **Park Blocks,** created in 1852 and comprising a 25-block spread between Park and 9th Avenues. To get to the heart of the Park Blocks cultural district from the Broadway side of Pioneer Courthouse Square, head south a block to Salmon Street and turn right. Two blocks west are the city's oldest and most esteemed museums and performance venues, flanking a broad tree-lined mall. Here, note the four drinking fountains put in by early 20th century lumber magnate Simon Benson to promote a teetotaling outlook among his workers. Close by is the Italianesque Shemanski Fountain with its *Rebecca at the Well* statue. A decade ago, the city increased the number of brighter period-style lampposts to make this neighborhood inviting after dark. Come to the South Park Blocks in the fall and you can sense Portland's New England heritage. One-hundred-year-old elm trees with their bright yellow leaves line a series of small parks down the middle of the South Park Blocks. These sentinels tower above cast-iron benches, bronze statues, and neatly trimmed grass fronting the **Portland Art Museum,** the **Portland Center For The Performing Arts,** and the **Oregon Historical Society.** Be sure to check out the murals portraying Lewis and Clark, Sacajawea, fur traders, and Oregon Trail pioneers on the south and west walls of the Historical Society on Main Street. **Portland State University** is at the end of the South Park Blocks.

The **Oregon History Center,** 1230 SW Park Ave., 503/222-1741, unfurls a pageant of Oregon's patrimony with interactive exhibits, artifacts, paintings, and historical documents relating to early explorers and pioneers as well as vintage photos of native tribes. The extensive collection of photographs, maps, documents, and artifacts from the center's second-floor library is cataloged onto an electronic database linked to the Internet, and is accessible by the public via research terminals within the exhibit galleries and library. The center's hours are Tues.–Sat. 10 A.M.–5 P.M., SUNDAY NOON–5 p.m., closed Monday. The museum's admission price—$6 adults, $3 students, and $1.50 kids 6–18—allows patrons to use the photo archives (the best collection of historic Oregon photos in existence) and library. Consult local media outlets to keep up on revolving exhibits here. The Historical Center will be one of five locales in the country to host a traveling exhibit of Lewis and Clark artifacts during the bicentennial celebration. This venue will also be a vortex of Portland's own Lewis and Clark Exposition in 2005 with expedition artifacts of its own such as a branding iron, a sewing kit and a medal from Thomas Jefferson.

The other big chapter in the state's history, The Oregon Trail, has an oddly muted presence here. Museum personnel are likely to refer you to The End Of The Trail Interpretive Center, 12 miles away in Oregon City.

Across the street, the **Portland Art Museum,** 1219 SW Park Ave., 503/226-2811, designed by famed architect Pietro Belluschi, can complete a perspective on the Northwest Native Americans in the **Grand Ronde Center For Native Art** on the 2nd and 3rd floors of the museum's Hoffman Wing. The masks and baskets displayed here are not merely ornamental but are intimate parts of tribal ritual. The totem animals represent archetypal presences in native belief systems and are rendered with loving detail. Eons-old basalt carvings as well as the 19th century beaded bags and reed baskets by Columbia River Gorge natives

are on the third floor while the second floor highlights Alaskan and western Canadian coastal art. It also has plateau tribe and Mesoamerican pieces. The Native American art exhibits make a nice lead-in to the third floor art scene of the pioneering generations of 20th century Portland. The fourth floor houses work from the last 40 years of Oregon art. Northwest themes are also breathtakingly displayed in the following works: Albert Bierstadt's historic painting of Mt. Hood (European and American Collection) and in the century-old photos of Oregon on the lower level below the first floor. Hours are Tues.–Sun. 10 A.M.–5 P.M., and open until 9 P.M. the first Thursday of each month. Admission is $7.50 adults with discounts for seniors and students.

Each Memorial Day Weekend the median mall of the South Park Blocks in front of the museum hosts the only annual art festival in the country organized by Native Americans. With over 250 Native American artists exhibiting and selling everything from ceramics to beadwork to basketry and weaving, this is a regional "take" on the famed Santa Fe Indian Market in New Mexico. Music, arts demonstrations, ceremonial dances, and a food court featuring fry bread tacos, alder-smoked salmon, and other indigenous dishes also make this a worthwhile event. The outdoor marketplace runs Sat.–Sun. 10 A.M.–6 P.M. The marketplace suggests a $2–5 donation and some cultural events charge admission. For more information call 503/224-8650. At press time, the festival's future was uncertain.

Close by the art museum is a bus stop on the corner of SW Jefferson and 10th where you can catch Tri-Met bus #63 which will take you up into the West Hills to Washington Park. Here, you'll find two world-famous botanical gardens and a highly regarded zoo.

WASHINGTON PARK AND VICINITY

The colorfully painted Tri-Met bus #63/Zoo/OMSI (Washington Park) route includes Washington Park—the hillside home of the International Rose Test Garden, the Japanese Gardens, and the Washington Park Zoo. In addition, there's the Portland Children's Museum, a historic carousel, the World Forestry Center, the Hoyt Arboretum, the Vietnam Memorial and nearby, the Pittock Mansion (see Portland Viewpoints, below).

You can also get to Washington Park by MAX light rail via the Washington Park Zoo station. In summer, there is free shuttle from the terminal elevator in the zoo parking lot that'll go about a mile down the hill to the Rose Garden. By car from downtown, you can begin your tour of Washington Park by going west on Burnside about a mile past NW 23rd, hang a fishhook left at the light onto Tichener. Follow the hill up to Kingston and make a right. Follow Kingston a quarter-mile into Washington Park and park at the tennis courts. Just below the tennis courts is the Rose Garden, and the Japanese Gardens sign and access road should be visible up the hill from where you parked. Another way to reach Washington Park is by taking U.S. 26 to the zoo exit. Drive past the zoo and World Forestry Center. Make a right and follow the road over the hill and through the woods down to the Rose Garden.

International Rose Test Gardens

The Rose City's welcome mat is out at this four-acre garden overlooking downtown. With more than 400 species and over 10,000 rose plants, it's the largest rose test garden in the country. "Rose test" refers to the fact that the garden is one of 24 official testing sites for the All American Rose selections, a group of leading commercial rose growers and hybridizers in the United States. The blossoms are at their peak in June, commemorated by the Rose Festival. But even if you're down to the last rose of summer, there's always the view of the city backdropped by (if you're lucky) Mt. Hood. The best vantage point for the latter is the east end of the garden along the Queen's Walk, where the names of the festival's Rose Queen winners are enshrined (since 1907).

If you enter from the parking lot west of the restrooms near the center of the garden, look for the rose labeled Fragrant Cloud to the left of the walkway at the beginning of the row. As its name suggests, this is *the* place to stop and smell the roses. On the right-hand side of the walk is the all-

International Rose Test Gardens

© OREGON TOURISM COMMISSION/DAVE DAVIDSON

star lineup of award winners. This floral fantasia can be enjoyed from dawn to dusk at no charge.

Japanese Gardens

From the Rose Garden head west up the steps that go past the parking lot and tennis courts on the way to the Japanese Gardens, off Kingston Avenue in Washington Park, 503/223-4070. You can walk up the short but steep road that leads to the Japanese Gardens, or hop the free open-air shuttle that climbs up the hill every 10 minutes or so.

The Japanese Gardens so moved the Japanese ambassador in 1988 that he pronounced it the most beautiful and authentic landscape of its kind outside Japan. Ponds and bridges, sand and stone, April cherry blossoms, and a snowcapped Fujiyama-like peak in the distance help East meet West here. This is always an island of tranquility, but connoisseurs will tell you to come during the fall-foliage peak in October. Many people in Japan feel these gardens are at their best when it's raining. In any case, it's open daily in summer 10 A.M.–6 P.M. and thereafter, Sept. 16–April 4, daily 10 A.M.–4 P.M. The gardens are closed on Thanksgiving, Christmas, and New Year's Day. Admission is $6 for adults, discounts for students and seniors; children under age three get in free.

Washington Park Zoo

After the Japanese Gardens, you can catch the Zooliner train (terminal located south of the Rose Garden on a bluff—or you can be board in the zoo itself), which goes four miles to the zoo. The train costs $2.75 for ages 12–64 (discounts for seniors, free with zoo admission) and runs 10:30 A.M.–6:15 P.M. at 40-minute intervals. Figure on 35 minutes for a round-trip. The ride itself is worth your time if only because the Zooliner is a 30-year-old steam engine. But that's not all. The forested ridge defining the route features 112 species of birds, 62 kinds of mammals, and hundreds of plants. Unfortunately, the English ivy covering many of the trees might kill off some of the forest unless it is somehow controlled. During a brief stopover, you may see some peaks of the Cascade Range. The train may not run when the weather is rainy or attendance is low.

The Washington Park Zoo, 4001 SW Canyon Rd., 503/226-1561, itself predates the Rose Garden (1887 versus 1917), and it exerts almost as ubiquitous a presence within the city. This is evident from the array of zoo animals depicted on the multicolored bus #63, front page newspaper articles announcing the birth or death of tigers, elephants, or other coveted species, and the fact that the zoo is continually ranked among the top attractions in the state. The city is justly proud of the zoo's award-winning elephant-breeding program and the nation's largest chimpanzee exhibit. Also noteworthy are a colony of Humboldt penguins from Peru and an Alaskan tundra exhibit featuring grizzlies, wolves, and musk oxen. The latter exhibit is supplemented by polar bears swimming in pools of simulated Arctic ice. Whenever possible, animals are kept in enclosures that re-create their natural habitats. The most recent example is the African Grasslands exhibit, which houses impalas, zebras, giraffes, and a black rhinoceros.

You also shouldn't miss the zoo's **Elephant Museum,** which takes a lighthearted look at pachyderms. Along with elephant jokes, elephants in literature and art are depicted with dioramas and masks. A look at the ivory trade injects a somber note into the proceedings. The exhibit is completed by the zoo's collection of the world's largest and most prolific herd of captive Asian elephants. In 1994, Rose Too was born, allowing zoo-goers the rare treat to watch a baby elephant grow up. In this vein, the zoo also specializes in breeding rare and endangered species, such as orangutans and red pandas. The Great Northwest exhibit, with its focus on indigenous species, is also recommended. At press time, Steller Cove showcased gargantuan sea lions, sea otters, tide pools, and other creatures evocative of the state's shoreline. The seemingly real coastal caves and simulated blowhole here also hint at the quality of local color exhibits to come.

There are several food service outlets at the zoo. The major restaurant is the Africafe, which offers a good selection of moderately priced cafeteria food. The chance to dine overlooking a glassed-in aviary is the big attraction, however.

The zoo is open 9:30 A.M.–5:30 P.M. April–Memorial Day, 9:30 A.M.–6 P.M. June–Labor Day, and 9:30 A.M.–4 P.M. the rest of the year. Admission is $6.50 for adults, with discounts for seniors and kids 3–11. Since many of the animals are nocturnal, it's usually best to get to the zoo early in the morning. But if you go late in the day on the second Tuesday of every month, you can enjoy the zoo at a reduced price. Just be prepared to jog, given just two hours you'll have to enjoy the expanse of the exhibits here.

Looking for the place to stop and smell the roses? Enter the International Rose Test Gardens from the parking lot west of the restrooms near the center of the garden and look for the rose labeled Fragrant Cloud to the left of the walkway at the beginning of the row.

World Forestry Center

Before heading over to Northwest Portland on mass transit, it is worth stopping at a place that highlights what has been Oregon's essential enterprise for most of its history. Up the hill from the MAX elevator in the zoo parking lot, you'll see the **World Forestry Center,** 4033 SW

Canyon Rd., 503/228-1367, which features exhibits on the natural processes of trees, the types of forests in the world, fighting forest fires, silviculture, and timber industry activities. Also featured is the Jessup Wood collection which displays examples from the 505 trees native to North America. Dioramas, films, and mechanized exhibits are complemented by lectures, shows, and special events. The center's best-known (and after five minutes, most boring) attraction is the 70-foot talking tree.

Worth more of your time is the second-floor rainforest exhibit. Perhaps the best way to understand the mixed conifer forests of the region is by taking in "The Old Growth Forest: Treasures In Transition." The museum is open daily 9 A.M.–6 P.M. in summer, 10 A.M.–5 P.M. in winter (closed Christmas day). Admission is $3.50 for adults with discounts for children and seniors. Outside the museum note the old growth stump of impressive girth and a steam engine that began hauling logs in the Coast Range in 1909. Also, don't miss the unique wooden items in the gift shop.

NORTHWEST PORTLAND

The zoo has a MAX stop that facilitates the next part of the tour. An elevator ride from the parking lot can take you to a Civic Stadium–bound train (also known as PGE Stadium) where the #15 bus takes you to northwest Portland's Nob Hill.

Nob Hill

Nob Hill is north of Burnside between NW 18th and NW 27th Avenues. In the heart of the neighborhood, NW 21st–NW 23rd Avenues, Victorian homes have been remodeled into boutiques to join stylish shopping arcades, bookstores, restaurants, and theaters. Given the profusion of brewpubs and coffee spots here, it's easy to see how northwest Portland garnered the reputation as "latte-land" and "beer-vana."

An impression of growing gentrification is especially defined on NW 21st and NW 23rd Avenues, where, at last count, each street boasted almost two dozen dining spots. The area encompassed by these thoroughfares is also referred

to as Nob Hill. On NW 21st alone, several eateries have earned accolades from the likes of *Zagat Guides, The New York Times,* and *Bon Appétit.* The neighborhood's artsy shops and café society also attract strollers en masse, creating a people-watcher's paradise. A mile northwest of this neighborhood is **Forest Park** looming over industrial northwest Portland, the largest urban wilderness in the United States.

The Pearl District

If you proceed west down Burnside by vehicle or on foot and cross above I-405 on the overpass, you'll find yourself in the Pearl District (encompassed in the area north of Burnside to Marshall and from NW 8th Avenue until NW 15th Avenue to the west). Here, old warehouses have become art galleries as well as studios and offices of Portland's creative community. High-priced condos are also starting to proliferate. First-Thursday-of-the-month gallery walks feature hors d'oeuvres and 8 P.M. closing times at neighborhood galleries. On the southern fringe of the Pearl, **Powell's Books** is on 10th Avenue and Burnside (see the special topic A City of Books).

From the heart of the Pearl—NW 10th and Everett—walk a quarter of a mile east to Broadway and go five blocks north, looking for the tile roof of Union Station with Broadway Bridge in the background. From here begin your tour of what Portlanders call Old Town.

Old Town/Chinatown

The tile-roofed clock of the **Union Station,** NW 6th Ave., has been a beacon since the 1890s, when passenger trains first rolled into the red brick terminal. This is the second oldest operating major passenger terminal in the U.S., the oldest big city depot west of St. Louis. Inside, check out the ornate high ceilings, marble floors, and vintage photographs. While Portland has always had a reputation as a port city, much of the shipboard cargo arrived or departed behind a locomotive. By the late 19th century, it was served by no less than three major rail lines. Theory has it that the city decided to build Union Station on top of the lakefront landfill donated by prominent sea captain John Couch rather than have

A CITY OF BOOKS

Powell's Books, 1005 W. Burnside, 503/228-4651 or 800/878-7323, is a Portland institution as well as the largest independent bookstore in the world. Add such accolades as author Susan Sontag calling it "the best bookstore in the English-speaking world" and you can believe tales of famous writers finding books here that were impossible to find elsewhere. Over a million new and used books are housed in a labyrinth of hallways that take up a city block. A helpful staff and maps of the stacks help locate whatever you might be looking for in 50 sections ranging from automobiles to Zen. Hours are Mon.–Sat. 9 A.M.–11 P.M., Sun. 9 A.M.–9 P.M.

To make it even more appealing, there is the **Ann Hughes Coffee Room,** 503/228-4651, at the west side of the store, which sells espresso drinks, pastries, salads, soups, and snacks. The Coffee Room is a favorite place for singles to make connections. *The New York Times* and other papers on library-style posts and the chance to look over prospective book purchases while sipping coffee makes many Portlanders regard Ann Hughes (and Powell's) as kind of a spiritual home. Free parking in a special garage on the side of the store and the world's leading authors reading their works several nights a week enhance this impression. Browse the store's website, www.powells.com, to get a sense of what *The Wall Street Journal* describes as "one of the most innovative and creative enterprises in the country."

Of special interest to Gorge-bound travelers is a book that is in Powell's rare book collection, but can't be viewed at the store. If you go online to www.powells.com/lewisandclark, however, you can view the first edition of *The Journals of Lewis and Clark,* edited by Nicholas Biddle in 1809 and published by Bradford and Inskeep in Philadelphia five years later. A variety of photos are included as well as detailed maps. The actual book is kept in a safe deposit box because its value exceeds $100,000.

northwest of the city (previously the leading candidate for a townsite due to exploration by Lewis and Clark and a location near the confluence of the Willamette and Columbia Rivers).

If you walk southeast from Union Station to SW 4th, you pass through Old Town/Chinatown, a compact area of restaurants, galleries, and exotic Asian grocery stores. In 1890 Portland had the largest Chinatown on the West Coast. The Chinese came to work on the railroad and in eastern Oregon gold mines. Back then, opium and gambling dens and houses of negotiable affection proliferated the neighborhood. Perhaps the most notorious corner of Old Town/Chinatown was SW 2nd and Couch, the location of Erickson's Saloon. Here sailors would partake at a bar that stretched 684 feet around. Occasionally, bartenders would conspire with work contractors to drug a seaman's drink. When unconscious, the sailor would then be transported to a waiting ship by means of underground tunnels that extended down to the waterfront, later waking to find himself "hired" and at sea. Rumor has it that one of these tunnels is being opened up for visitors. Check POVA (800/345-3214) for details.

Shanghaied seamen were not the only ones down on their luck in Portland's rough-and-tumble waterfront. In fact, the term "skid row" is sometimes said to have originated here. This expression came from the "skid roads," paths on which logs were slid downhill to waterfront mills. After logging booms went bust, folks down on their luck would "hit the skids" in these parts of town. Today, the area puts its best foot forward two blocks west at the **Chinatown** gates. The gargoyled gate at 4th Avenue and Burnside is always good for a photograph. Notice that the male statue is on the right with a ball under his foot, while the female has a cub under her paw. Also note the red lamp posts. These are traditional Portland gaslight posts, but they have street names on them written in Chinese. Acupuncture houses, herbal shops, and traditional groceries keep the old ways alive next to the galleries of Portland's contemporary art scene.

In spring, the cherry blossoms on 5th and Davis become the highlight of Chinatown along

several different depots controlled by the rail lines. Some historians also credit Couch with the selection of Portland's townsite, which he favored over the area near present-day Linton, with the contemplative repose found at the **Classical Chinese Garden.** This intricate landscape is located on a block bounded by NW 2nd and 3rd Avenues and Everett and Flanders Streets. Three-hundred tons of cloud-shaped rock and elaborate carvings were imported from China to help shape the hemisphere's largest and most authentic garden of this genre. Decorative pavilions, a teahouse, a large reflecting pool, and other motifs were inspired by gardens in the 2,500-year-old city of Suzhou, the Venice of China. Admission is $6 with discounts for seniors, students, and children. Hours are 9 A.M.–6 P.M. in spring, summer and fall. After Halloween, winter hours are 10 A.M.–5 P.M. For more information call 503/228-8131.

Overlapping this neighborhood are the museums, galleries, restaurants, and shops of **Old Town.** Many of the buildings here date from the 1880s, despite the fact that Portland's beginnings stretch back four decades earlier. This is because an 1872 fire razed much of what was then the commercial district. Cast-iron buildings with Italianate flourishes went up in the wake of the fire. While a large number of these foundry facades were torn down in the 1940s to make way for a Willamette River bridge and a waterfront freeway, a few (more than in any other place in the U.S. except New York City's SoHo district) survive in Old Town and the adjoining Skidmore Historical District. Old Town runs predominantly north of West Burnside between Front and 4th Avenues.

While these neighborhoods are adorned with antique street signs, newly touched-up "old brick," and lots of iron and brass meant to evoke old Portland, such accoutrements aren't always necessary to induce a historical reverie. There are enough turn-of-the-century, white terra-cotta building facades and other period architecture for that. Fires caused enough of a problem throughout the 19th century to compel the introduction of white terra-cotta in the early 20th century.

PORTLAND VIEWPOINTS

These excursions are best undertaken by car as mass transit is sometimes problematic in the West Hills behind the city.

Pittock Mansion

Featured as the first stop on many bus tour itineraries because of its history, the mansion is also known for its architecture and an all-encompassing view of the city. Mass-transit access from downtown is provided by bus #77 to NW Barnes and Burnside Street, at which point you'll have to walk the steep half mile up Pittock Avenue. To get there by car, head west up Burnside past the turnoff to Washington Park. Turn right at the sign for the Pittock Mansion, 503/823-3624, onto Pittock Avenue and follow the signs. From here, it's a quarter-mile drive up steep and curving switchbacks. Situated at nearly the highest point in the west hills, 1,000 feet above sea level, this French Renaissance mansion completed in 1914 also stands above the rest of the grand edifices in the city for other reasons. *Oregonian* founder Henry Pittock spared little expense in furnishing his 22-room shack with such accoutrements as modern showers with multiple shower heads, a central cleaning system, room-to-room telephones, and a Turkish smoking room. The whorl-pattern wooden floors in some of the public rooms here are a must-see as are the views of the city from the bedrooms upstairs. The antique furniture, access to Forest Park trails, and fair-weather views of the Cascades (Mts. Hood, St. Helens and Rainier are potentially visible) from the lavishly landscaped backyard also make this place a fixture on many itineraries.

The mansion is also a movie location and TV backdrop favorite, most recently for *Imaginary Crimes,* starring Harvey Keitel (1994), as well as *Good Morning America* and several evening magazine shows. Lunch and afternoon tea are available in the Gate Lodge, the former caretaker's cottage behind the mansion. Lunch is served at 11:30 A.M., 1–2:30 P.M. tea and dessert are served. For $7–10 you get soups, salads, and sandwiches on the lunch menu (reservations suggested). Regular tours are conducted daily, 1–5 P.M., except Sunday, and the grounds are open to the public until dark. The mansion is especially nice to visit when it's bedecked in Christmas finery. Be that as it may, the summer flowers surrounding the structure and the vistas in back of the mansion may well offer the most compelling reasons to come up here. Admission is $5 adults, $4 seniors, and $2 children ages 6–18. In the north corner of the Pittock parking lot, there's a trailhead that leads two miles down to Cornell Rd. through an old-growth forest.

Council Crest

Considered to be among Portland's preeminent vistas, Council Crest can be enjoyed from atop a butte in a ridge-top neighborhood in the posh West Hills. At 1,073 feet above sea level, this is the highest point within the city limits. Purportedly named during an 1898 National Council of Congregational Churches conference that met here, Council Crest later gained notoriety in its early decades as an amusement park at the end of a streetcar line. Today, Council Crest is home to such Portland luminaries as award-winning film director Gus Van Sant.

To get there from Burnside, take a left (go south) on Vista (NW 23rd), a left on Greenway, then take the right fork, Council Crest Way, into the park. Just follow the Scenic Drive signs. The bluff looks out on snowcapped volcanoes and 3,000 square miles of territory. As you circle the summit, out to the west the panorama of the Tualatin Valley and Washington County is worth a gander, particularly at sunset. On the eastern side, steps lead up to an observation platform with arrows indicating locations of five Cascades peaks (check out the echo here). Even if they are not visible, the view of downtown and the rest of the city to the east is breathtaking.

The Skyline from Council Crest

From atop Council Crest you'll note the two tallest buildings in the Portland skyline. In case you're wondering which of the two bank towers is the highest in Portland, consider the following stats, then decide upon your frame of reference. The **Wells Fargo Tower,** the whitish building in the center of the city, has 40 stories. Sitting to the north is a big pink structure, the 42-story **U.S. Bank** tower. Number crunchers might take interest in the fact that the top of the Wells Fargo tower is still a tad higher (despite a shortfall of two stories) when the slope of downtown Portland is taken into account.

TOURS

In a guide for independent travelers a listing of tours may seem out of place, but sometimes organized outings provide insights unavailable elsewhere.

One such perspective is provided by a harbor cruise on a sternwheeler. This mode of transport opened up the Willamette River a century ago, and the 599-passenger **Columbia Gorge** and the smaller **Cascade Queen,** 503/223-3928, both cruise the waterway today. The *Cascade Queen* handles the cruises in Portland Harbor (departing from Riverplace Marina) and the *Columbia Gorge* does the trips in Cascade Locks (see the Oregon Gorge chapter for information on the sterwheeler as well Gorge-bound cruise ships) in the region for which it is named. River cruises on the Willamette visit the Willamette greenway, an untouched area south of the city. Downriver trips pass city lights and ships bound for Pacific Rim ports. The *Cascade Queen* departs Riverplace Marina May 1–Sept. 30, 3–5 P.M. Cruises run on weekends with sightseeing packages ($12.95 adults, $7.95 children) and brunch cruises at roughly double the sightseeing rate. There's also dinner cruises for $33 adults, $21 children.

Ecotours of Oregon, 1906 SW Iowa St., 503/245-1428 or 888/TOURS-33, www.Ecotours-of-Oregon.com/Ecotours/, runs tours emphasizing ecological understanding while having a good time. Door-to-door van transport from anywhere in the Portland area, lunch, and commentary are included in itineraries that cost $30 (city tour)–60 (whale-watching) per person per day. Trips are usually confined to vans of six with a professional naturalist-historian guide.

Finally, there is **Grayline of Portland,** P.O. Box 17306, 21320 N. Suttle, Portland 97217, 503/285-9845 or 800/422-7042. Grayline in most cities runs competent tours with experienced drivers. Portland's outfit is no exception. In addition to day trips to such locales as Mt. Hood, the Oregon Coast, and the Columbia River Gorge, three- and seven-hour city tours depart all year long from Union Station. Half-day trips such as the Multnomah Falls/Columbia Gorge tour (about $25 per person) and full-day trips

PORTLAND

like the Mt. Hood Loop (about $45 per person) are highly recommended. While calling to reserve is handy, consider stopping by their downtown offices at the Embassy Suites on 319 SW Pine. Not only will you be able to talk directly to a helpful ticket agent, but you'll also be able to pick up brochures and a free Portland tour map, an information-filled user-friendly layout of the city. Finally, be aware that Grayline offers free hotel pickups in conjunction with their tours in selected locations.

EVENTS

While Portland's event calendar doesn't lack for variety, there is one festival with special relevance to Gorge-bound travelers.

On the second weekend in October, watch the **salmon spawn** at Oxbow Park in the Sandy River Gorge outside Gresham. Old-growth walks, an eight-km run, and a salmon barbecue as well as arts and crafts round out this fete. To get there from downtown, take I-84 east to the Wood Village exit. Turn south on Division and follow the signs seven miles to Oxbow Park. Or, take I-84 to Exit 17, drive east a mile, then make a right on 257th Street and follow it to Division where the previous directions take effect. There's a $6 fee per vehicle and a $7 additional charge for lunch and activities. Festival participants will tell you that a rainy day seems to encourage salmon-spawning activity. Call 503/248-5050 for more information. Anglers are kept busy with spawning runs of coho, fall, and spring chinook salmon, and winter and summer steelhead trout. Hours are Sat.–Sun. 10:30 A.M.–5 P.M.

Practicalities

ACCOMMODATIONS

Portland poses no problem for those seeking accommodations at a good dollar value. The neighborhoods profiled below each have something to recommend them. Whether it's the luxury of downtown accommodations, the convenience and tradition of Historic Landmark northeast Portland B&Bs, or the rockbottom rates in a southeast Portland hostel, these lodgings offer the best of the city near the best of the rural splendor of the Gorge. Contact POVA, 800/345-3214, for the free *Portland Book*. For air travelers, we've also profiled some choices near the airport.

Southeast

Hawthorne Boulevard is a part of town that recalls the hip gourmet ghettos of Cambridge and Berkeley and is easily incorporated into a trip out to the Gorge. To get there from downtown, follow Madison Street east. At the Willamette River cross the Hawthorne Bridge.

The Hawthorne neighborhood's Hostelling International **hostel**, 3031 SE Hawthorne Blvd., 503/236-3380, offers proximity to Clinton, Belmont, and Hawthorne "hip strips" as well as area eateries. Folks more inclined to spend their money on cultural pursuits and dining adventures will forsake some comforts and privacy to patronize these lodgings. It's all possible at rates of $15–20; private rooms available for $36. Hostellers also like easy access on mass transit. From downtown take bus #14 down Hawthorne Boulevard; from the airport take bus #12, then transfer to #75/Hawthorne Boulevard. Kitchen privileges as well as breakfasts and summertime barbecues for a small additional charge are appreciated extras here. Next door, **At The Hop's** patty melts and milk shakes seem especially popular with foreign visitors on a budget. Make reservations well in advance for this 38-unit, rambling white hostelry in summer due to the influx of folks from other countries. A spacious screened-in back porch provides a cool place to sleep in July and August. It should also be mentioned that a day-use fee of $3 is invoked and some chores are required. In summer, the hostel sometimes organizes van trips to the Columbia Gorge, the coast, and other getaways.

Another hostel at 1818 NW Glisan, 541/241-2783, offers 10 units in a stimulating neighborhood (Nob Hill) as well as such extras as washing machines and private rooms ($40) if the $15 units don't offer enough privacy.

Northeast

This neighborhood's bed-and-breakfast options combine easy access to a local restaurant row, moderate rates, and lodgings rich in amenities. Convenient mass transit linkages to downtown and the charm of northeast Portland's early 20th century architecture also make this area a good base for further exploration. Those that want a quieter, albeit slower route to the Gorge can follow Sandy Boulevard 15 miles east.

An excellent alternative to downtown hotels, **Portland Guest House,** 1720 NE 15th, 503/282-1402, offers proximity to excellent restaurants on Broadway, and boasts a locale of broad tree-shaded avenues. While the high-ceilinged Victorian elegance and summer blueberries from the garden for breakfast are enticements to many, it's the room tariff that often closes the deal: $55 single, $65–95 double. The owner says there's always quite a run on the single rooms from business travelers footing their own bill, so be sure to book well in advance. The availability of rooms with private baths as well as easy access to the bus line are also appreciated.

McMenamin's Kennedy School, 5736 NE 33rd, 503/223-0109, is a bed-and-breakfast set in an old elementary school that has been transformed into a complex parlaying a theater, restaurant, and concert venue with the brewpub experience. Madcap mosaics, carvings, and paintings festoon the hallways along with historic photos from the days when the building was a citadel of education. The rooms are also lavishly decorated with art as well as antique furniture. Add a phone, modem, and private bath to such included perks as admission to the movie theater, use of the pool, and breakfast and you can understand why this place is more than just a chance to sleep soundly in a classroom. Be sure to inquire about lodging/dining packages that feature discounts and/or extra amenities. Weekday rates, Sun.–Thurs., run $99; Fri.–Sat. you'll pay $109. For more information, contact www.kennedy@mcmenamins.com.

The opulent **White House Bed and Breakfast,** 1914 NE 22nd, Portland 97212, 503/287-7131, gives you the presidential treatment. Located just off Broadway near an avenue of shops and restaurants, only 5–10 minutes from Lloyd Center and downtown, this lovingly restored 1912 lumber baron's mansion with Greek columns evocative of its namesake in Washington, D.C. has rates ranging $100–150, double occupancy. Beyond the tall mahogany front doors here, hand-painted murals in the huge foyer usher guests into the crystal chandeliered dining room. Antique guest room furnishings and claw foot tubs may sustain the illusion that you're staying in the Lincoln Bedroom but the innkeeper's baked scones and other goodies at breakfast (sautéed apple French toast) and tea, together with complimentary sherry nightcaps, impart the touch of home.

Downtown

Due to soaring occupancy rates, six new upscale hotels were built for the downtown business district and extended stay residence hotels constructed near the airport, taking pressure off of other sectors of the market. Even still, travelers of all descriptions need to reserve well in advance for June, July, and August.

The listings below reflect a cross section of desirable places to stay in the city center. Other choices can be found in the lodging guide *Where To Stay In Oregon,* available free from POVA, 800/345-3214.

$50–100: It's hard to find rooms downtown below $80 that are clean, safe, and in a good location—reflecting Portland's recent transition into a more expensive city. Nonetheless, it's still cheaper than Seattle or San Francisco with less traffic and crime.

Days Inn, 1414 SW 6th Ave., 503/221-1611 or 800/899-0248, is centrally located near Portland State University, downtown shopping, and cultural venues. Amenities range from a heated outdoor pool to free covered parking. There is also a decent on-site restaurant. While nothing special, the rooms, $70–130 (the majority of the doubles are below $80), cover the basics well enough to make it a cost-effective downtown lodging.

PORTLAND

WESTSIDE PORTLAND FOOD & LODGING

N.E. GRAND AVE.

MARTIN LUTHER KING JR. BLVD.

84

5

5

405

ROSE GARDEN ARENA/ MEMORIAL COLISEUM

Willamette River

STEEL BRIDGE

BROADWAY BRIDGE

BURNSIDE BRIDGE

Tom McCall *Waterfront Park*

LIGHT RAIL

FRONT AVE.

1ST AVE.

2ND AVE.

3RD AVE.

4TH AVE.

5TH AVE.

6TH AVE.

UNION STATION (AMTRAK)

GREYHOUND BUS STATION

POST OFFICE

BROADWAY AVE.

N.W. GLISAN ST.

N.W. FLANDERS ST.

N.W. EVERETT ST.

N.W. DAVIS ST.

N.W. COUCH ST.

W. BURNSIDE ST.

PARK AVE.

8TH AVE.

9TH AVE.

10TH AVE.

11TH AVE.

12TH AVE.

13TH AVE.

14TH AVE.

15TH AVE.

N.W. LOVEJOY ST.

N.W. HOYT ST.

FONG CHONG ▶

OBAI ▶

BRIDGEPORT BREW PUB ▶

Old Town

Chinatown

LA PATISSERIE

▶ ALEXIS

CAFE AZUL

NORTH PARK BLOCKS

The Pearl

BROADWAY AVE.

PARK AVE.

6TH AVE.

IMPERIAL ▶

PAZZO

TRANSIT MALL

BIJOU CAFE

S.W. ANKENY ST.

S.W. PINE ST.

S.W. OAK ST.

S.W. STARK ST.

S.W. WASHINGTON ST.

S.W. ALDER ST.

Skidmore Historic District ▶

MCCORMICK & SCHMICK'S ▶

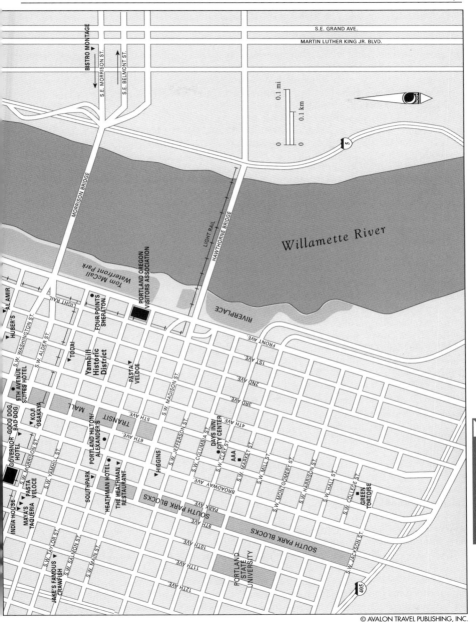

S.E. GRAND AVE.

MARTIN LUTHER KING JR. BLVD.

BISTRO MONTAGE

S.E. MORRISON ST.

S.E. BELMONT ST.

0.1 mi

0.1 km

0

0

5

MORRISON BRIDGE

LIGHT RAIL

HAWTHORNE BRIDGE

Willamette River

Tom McCall
Waterfront Park

PORTLAND OREGON
VISITORS ASSOCIATION

FOUR POINTS
SHERATON

RIVERPLACE

AL AMIR

HUBER'S

LIGHT RAIL

S.W. WASHINGTON ST.

TODAI

S.W. ALDER ST.

Yamhill
Historic
District

PASTA
VELOCE

FRONT AVE.

1ST AVE.

2ND AVE.

3RD AVE.

4TH AVE.

5TH AVE.

6TH AVE.

S.W. MADISON ST.

5TH AVENUE
SUITES HOTEL

GOVERNOR
HOTEL

GOOD DOG/
BAD DOG

KOJI
OSAKAYA

MALL

TRANSIT

PORTLAND HILTON/
ALEXANDER'S

HIGGINS

S.W. COLUMBIA ST.

S.W. JEFFERSON ST.

DAYS INN/
CITY CENTER

AAA

S.W. SALMON ST.

S.W. MARKET ST.

BROADWAY AVE.

S.W. MILL ST.

S.W. MONTGOMERY ST.

S.W. HARRISON ST.

S.W. HALL ST.

COLLEGE ST.

GREEN
TORTOISE

S.W. JACKSON ST.

405

INDIA HOUSE

MAYA'S
TAQUERIA

PASTA
VELOCE

S.W. MORRISON ST.

S.W. YAMHILL ST.

S.W. TAYLOR ST.

S.W. SALMON ST.

S.W. MAIN ST.

SOUTHPARK

HEATHMAN HOTEL

THE HEATHMAN
RESTAURANT

SOUTH PARK BLOCKS

PARK AVE.

9TH AVE.

10TH AVE.

11TH AVE.

12TH AVE.

SOUTH PARK BLOCKS

PORTLAND
STATE
UNIVERSITY

JAKE'S FAMOUS
CRAWFISH

PORTLAND

© AVALON TRAVEL PUBLISHING, INC.

Despite moderate rates, the **Mallory Hotel,** 729 SW 15th Ave. at Yamhill, Portland 97295, 503/223-6311 or 800/228-8657, at first glance suggests a luxury lodging, with a lobby boasting ornate plaster, crystal chandeliers, and an elegant, skylit interior. The dining room's (try the German pancakes for breakfast) marble pillars and chandeliers sustain the four-star facade along with the elaborate jungle motif of the Driftwood Room Lounge. Somehow, it all feels very British, especially when it's raining outside. A location on the MAX line not far from the boutiques of the northwest district and South Park Blocks cultural attractions also recommend it. With an address like this, the Mallory's free parking is especially appreciated. Only the smallish rather plain rooms might justify low prices of around $85 for a double. And if you're lucky enough to score one of the king-sized suites for $150, you'll probably walk away shaking your head in disbelief at this lodging value. A sister hotel, the **Imperial,** 400 SW Broadway, 503/228-7221 or 800/452-2323, is another good buy in a comparable price range. The Imperial shares a location with hotels that charge double its own rate, close by the best of downtown shopping, galleries, and Pioneer Square. The Cameo Cafe and Typhoon, two quality Portland eateries (see Food, below) are on-site and Powell's Books is a five-minute walk away. There's a lot of street noise near here at night however so book an upper floor room if possible.

The **Four Points Sheraton,** 50 SW Morrison, 503/221-0711, ranges $89–140 and overlooks Waterfront Park and the Willamette River through large windows. Sheraton renovated the guest rooms and lobby here in a stylish, ultramodern motif (they advertise "contemporary lodging with European flair") and the hotel is ideally located for morning joggers and folks who want to visit Saturday Market or shop and dine near Pioneer Square.

The MacMaster House B&B, 1041 SW Vista Ave., 503/223-7362, wwww.macmaster.com, is located near Washington Park, northwest shopping and Council Crest viewpoint. In one of the city's ritziest neighborhoods, the eight rooms in this mansion include two units with private bath-

room ($100). The other rooms ($80) share facilities. Some rooms have fireplaces or interesting murals and one has a claw foot tub. The public rooms also have objets d'art and decor that are the essence of Victoriana. Rooms here might fetch a higher price but for the steep flight of steps at the entrance. However, the latter may in truth be appreciated after the included full breakfast.

$100–150: The **Portland Hilton,** 921 SW 6th Ave., 503/226-1611, has doubles for $109–185. Business travelers will enjoy the newly remodeled rooms, generous corporate rates, frequent flyer plan compatibility, a complete business center, a state-of-the-art health club, and a miracle-working concierge. An exceptional rooftop restaurant (see Food, below) and a location in the heart of the theater district across the street from Niketown are other extras that rate thumbs up with the modern-day road warrior.

The **Northwest Silver Cloud Inn,** 2426 NW Vaughn St., 503/242-2400, charges $100–150 for comfy, aesthetic surroundings with such amenities as refrigerators, microwaves, and a location near Portland's best shopping and restaurants in Nob Hill. There's also a fitness room and spa. While the Silver Cloud abuts an industrial district to the north, thankfully, the boutiques and eateries to the south cast a bigger shadow here.

$150–250: The **5th Avenue Suites Hotel,** 506 SW Washington, 800/711-2971, is the latest big player in the luxury hotel sweepstakes. With rooms beginning at $150 it tends to be a little less expensive than its downtown upscale counterparts with more spacious rooms and such extras as a complimentary regional wine tasting every evening in the lobby. A mix of classical and contemporary art and indoor greenery decorate the public rooms but the plush furnishings in the guest units are what grab most travelers. It has one of the more central locations in town and an affordable restaurant, The Red Star Grill, emphasizing gourmet interpretations of American food.

The **Heathman Hotel's,** 1009 SW Broadway, 503/241-4100, interior exudes understated old world elegance with generous use of teak paneling and marble. There's also art ranging from Andy Warhol to turn-of-the century prints in the public rooms. Rooms begin at $160 and the location amid theaters and museums has attracted everyone from John Updike, Alice Walker, and Luciano Pavarotti to presidents and foreign dignitaries. While they are usually a little smaller than similarly-priced accommodations, the rooms, filled with antiques and other appointments, set the Heathman apart. A first-class restaurant, a 400-film video collection, a library, and afternoon tea comprise appreciated extras. At night, the Heathman bar has jazz, and while it's more expensive than many spots in River City, you'd be hard-pressed to find better mixed drinks, appetizers, and atmosphere anywhere else in Oregon.

History buffs and downtown explorers will all find something to appreciate at the lovingly renovated **Governor Hotel,** SW 10th at Alder, 503/224-3400 or 800/554-3456. Built in 1909 during one of the city's exponential growth spurts, the old Governor has emerged from its 1990 facelift with its sparkling terra-cotta facade and old-style charm intact. Inside, high ceilings, arts-and-crafts-style furnishings, and the lobby's sepia-toned mural depicting scenes from the Lewis and Clark Expedition all contribute to the turn-of-the-century sense of taste, proportion, and sanity. Rooms begin at $185. In addition to modern amenities and a central location in a classic setting, you're also paying for numerous, worthwhile extras. With a bar featuring music most nights of the week (usually jazz), a good restaurant (Jake's Grill), and an excellent health club, the Governor is a good choice for business and pleasure.

The Airport

The expansion of Portland's airport (PDX) has been paralleled by the growth of nearby lodging alternatives. Many of these lodgings are equidistant from downtown and the Gorge.

A 12-minute ride from the airport (by free shuttle), you'll find **Quality Inn,** 8247 NE Sandy Blvd., 503/256-4111 or 800/246-4649. Located near The Grotto (old growth trees and contemplative surroundings) and the Cameo Cafe (see Food, below), it's a world away from terminal traffic snarls. Better yet, it's halfway between the airport and downtown with easy access via city bus. While the rooms are typical of moderately priced ($60–130) chains, the free breakfast and other amenities make it a good choice.

The Alderwood Inn, 7025 NE Alderwood Rd., 503/255-2700 or 888/987-2700, is a 150-room hotel with a pool, spa, and fitness center and well-appointed rooms for $69–106. A free airport shuttle and breakfast are also available.

A comparably-sized hotel, **Courtyard By Marriott,** 11550 NE Airport Way, 503/252-3200 or 800/321-2211, offers somewhat more modest rooms in the same price range (beginning at $72 double) as well as suites ($115) with microwaves, wet bars, and other appreciated extras. A restaurant, pool, and spa facilities are also on-site. Located three miles east of the airport, the motel features 24-hour free shuttle service to the terminal.

The Silver Cloud Inn Airport, 11518 Glenn Widing Rd., 800/205-7892, is a more upscale choice with doubles for $91–105. All 100 rooms face a lake, helping you forget the proximity of the terminals and freeways. In-room computer dataports, microwaves and refrigerators, free coffee and continental breakfast, and on-site whirlpool and exercise facilities also rate thumbs up with the busy travelers. Noteworthy, too, are the courtesy airport shuttle and nearby airport restaurants.

CAMPING

In case the wealth of sites in the Gorge are full or the prospect of train or highway noise at Ainsworth, Viento, and Memaloose campgrounds presents too great an obstacle for light sleepers, the following option has been included.

Oxbow County Campground, 503/663-4708, sits 10 miles southeast of Troutdale in Gresham's Sandy River Gorge. To get there, follow Exit 17 off I-84 to 257th Avenue, turn right and head several miles south to Division Street. Turn left on Division and drive seven miles east, make another left and follow the entrance road to Oxbow Park. The 1,000 acres of this preserve feature trails along the Sandy River and old-growth forests as well as fishing, swimming, and a 10-mile float trip. Campers can choose between 45 sites for tents, trailers, and RVs for $10–13.

PORTLAND

Flush toilets, picnic tables, and other amenities combine with activities and a beautiful setting (convenient to the Gorge and Portland) to rate our highest recommendation. No reservations are taken. Bans on pets and motorized boats are strictly enforced. This year-round facility is prone to flooding and features a popular salmon spawning festival (see Events, above).

FOOD

Portland's renaissance has resulted in the highest number of restaurants per capita of any city in the country. Perhaps more impressive is the fact that you can have a singular dining experience for much less than you'd pay for a gourmet outing in either Seattle or San Francisco. Even the traditionally overpriced bland food served in many hotel dining rooms can often turn out to be affordable and tasty.

Similarly, downtown sidewalk food carts serve what is often gourmet fare at fast food prices. The latter can be found in three main areas: around the Portland building (between 4th and 5th Avenues and Main and Madison Streets); at the south end of Pioneer Courthouse Square; and in a row at the edge of a parking lot on 5th Avenue between Stark and Oak Streets. There are other, smaller concentrations around downtown.

Portland restaurant coffee will probably be stronger than what you're used to if you aren't from Seattle or San Francisco. According to news analysis from the previous decade, Portland has the highest percentage of white to minority citizens of any large U.S. city but an increase in the number of ethnic eateries here shows this is changing. What also might surprise newcomers to Portland dining is the large number of places that give breakfast a higher profile than lunch or dinner.

The establishments reviewed below reflect neighborhoods that are commonly visited by travelers on the fly as well as a cross section of cuisines and price ranges. The focus is on diversity, dollar value, and a sense of fun.

Downtown

Downtown Portland features a wealth of carts purveying gourmet food as well as a cross sec-

tion of restaurants expressing the city's growing sophistication.

Carnivores: For a great meal for less than $5, try **Good Dog, Bad Dog,** 708 SW Alder, 503/222-3410. The Oregon Smokey, $4, is a spicy introduction to Northwest cuisine. Choose from 10 meaty sausages at this budget diner's dream. These are often best enjoyed with a microbrew.

Japanese: Several blocks north of Pioneer Square, **Koji Osakaya,** 606 SW Broadway, 503/294-1169, is a reliable choice for Japanese food. This outpost of sushi, soba, and teriyaki can accommodate everyone from hard-core devotees of fresh raw fish to the most finicky vegetarian. The best value for most people are the donburi dinners ($6.50–11), featuring fish, beef, or chicken with vegetables cooked in the special house sauce over rice, served with miso soup. There are also curry and noodle dishes in this price range. Dinner entrées are highlighted by prawn tempura ($13.95) and assorted sashimi ($17.95) and come with miso soup and salad. Close quarters and no reservations may occasionally create a wait for a table, but you'll leave satisfied.

Italian: A chain found throughout the Portland area, **Pasta Veloce** serves up quality pasta dishes in the $4–7.25 range, backed up by moderately priced soups and salads as well as affordable beer ($2.75 per bottle for a microbrew) and wine (under $4 a glass). Two downtown outlets can be found at SW Morrison at 10th, 503/916-4388, and at SW Salmon at 3rd, 503/223-8200. The Morrison Street outlet has a two-tiered restaurant allowing for more intimacy than the expansive dining room on Salmon Street. Exposed brick walls and tall windows looking out on a brick-inlaid section of Morrison Street, backdropped by old-time architecture, adds to an ambience rarely seen in a local chain. Such dishes as cheese tortellini with sun-dried tomato pesto or penne with roasted squash, spinach, tomatoes, and herbs in a light cream sauce also are more in keeping with a high-end place than Veloce's family-friendly prices indicate. This illusion is fostered by the bruschetta accompanying each meal and all the pestos and sauces made fresh daily. Complete your foray into fast food fine dining with tiramisu ($3.25) washed down by cups of full-bodied Torrefazione coffee.

Indian: A small northern Indian restaurant on the corner of 11th Avenue and SW Morrison has become the talk of Portland's cost-conscious gourmets. The $6.95 buffet lunch at **India House,** 1038 SW Morrison St., 503/274-1017, lets you load up your plate with a variety of vegetable curries, samosas (triangular potato pastries with flaky crust), tandoori chicken, basmati rice, and salads.

Indian food connoisseurs will tell you this cuisine is distinguished by the diner's ability to taste a number of individual spices in one dish—a quality in ample evidence in many India House specialties. You'll even notice this fanfare of flavors in a kind of bread served here. Naan is an unleavened bread cooked in a tandoor oven, which is a superhot barbecue pit lined with clay. The toasty texture and slight mesquite aftertaste come through with your first bites, and thereafter, the complexities of other flavors assert themselves. The Keema naan, for example, is redolent with cumin and mustard seed beneath flecks of lamb and butter on top. You can cool your tongue off with the Darjeeling tea and rice pudding for dessert, well-chosen accompaniments to finish off this budget banquet.

Mediterranean: Next to the Art Museum and nearby the Portland Center for the Performing Arts, **SouthPark,** SW Salmon and Park, 503/326-1300, bills itself as a seafood grill and wine bar but it is much more. Here, Northwest ingredients stylishly accompany recipes from Spain, Portugal, Italy, Turkey and Morocco. Begin by choosing one of several shellfish appetizers ($7.50–10), prior to indulging in paella ($17.95) or paprika-rubbed pork loin chops ($16.50), and you'll soon be humming along with the restaurant's muted Gypsy Kings or Segovia mood music. Lighter appetites might prefer such tapas plates as green-lipped mussels, crab cakes, pizza, or hummus with marinated olives (averaging $7.50) at the wine bar. A highlight at lunch is the

roast pork sandwich with pear chutney and aoli for $8. Sunday brunch offers a choice of dishes in the $8–14 range. Tall windows onto the city's theater district, a spectacular wine list, and the buzz of downtown culture vultures give South-Park an excitingly urbane pulse.

Mexican: While not as down-home as Portland's many *taquerias,* **Maya's Taqueria,** 1000 SW Morrison, 503/226-1946, offers well-rendered Mexican fast food ranging from *chiles rellenos* to chicken mole enchiladas, $6–8. Lighter appetites can enjoy taco plates with rice and beans for around $3. The Mexican beer and refrescos and the best array of salsas in Portland also make this elaborate taco stand seem closer to the Guadalajara marketplace than to Pioneer Courthouse Square. On warm days, sit outside to people-watch and admire the Mexican-style murals.

Santa Fe Taqueria, 831 NW 23rd Ave., 503/226-0406, is Maya's outlet in the northwest district. **Aztec Willie's** carries the banner for Maya's on Broadway and NE 15th.

Lebanese: Portland is starting to see many quality middle eastern restaurants, but we'd like to recommend an old reliable. **Al Amir,** 223 SW Stark, 503/274-0010, a long-time dinner favorite, is located on the periphery of Old Town in the dark-paneled Gothic elegance of the former home of Portland's archbishop (circa 1879). Its down-to-earth prices belie the fancy digs. The menu emphasizes Lebanese specialties, and there's live jazz Friday 10 P.M.–1 A.M. The lentil soup with plenty of cumin, *babaghanoush* (an eggplant dip), lamb kabobs, and rich, garlicky hummus are standouts. A mezza plate for two, $13, lets you sample a variety of items including falafel, hummus, *babaghanoush,* and tabouleh.

Comfort Food: Although lunch is also served at the **Bijou Cafe,** 132 SW 3rd Ave., 503/222-3187, it has built its reputation on breakfast. While fried cinnamon bread and red snapper or roast beef hash, $7.25, are morning mainstays in this cheery cafe, ordinary breakfast food like scrambled eggs, hash browns, muffins, and oatmeal are done perfectly here with the freshest and most nutritious ingredients. As for the latter, Bijou patrons appreciate the restaurant's emphasis on organic produce (seen to great advantage in lunchtime salads) and whole-grain products for no more than it would cost to eat at a highway truck stop (breakfast and lunch entrées $4–9).

Seafood: Famous for those lobster-like denizens of the Oregon freshwater deep, **Jake's Famous Crawfish,** 901 SW 12th St., 503/226-1419, is also renowned for the widest-ranging seafood menu in the Northwest and one of the most extensive Oregon wine lists. The largest, privately owned fine art collection in the region also graces the mahogany-paneled confines of Jake's. Nevertheless, it's the local crawfish (available May–September) that let the restaurant make a name for itself. Other specialties include clam chowder, smoked salmon and sturgeon, steamed butter clams, spring chinook salmon, bouillabaisse, and the best Irish coffee in town. You can also get a good steak and meat loaf here. In fact, their roasted half-chicken is a favorite with locals. For the best luck, order one of the two dozen or so specials off the "fresh sheet," $13–20. Lunch and dinner entrée prices run $9–25. Whatever you choose for your meal, leave room for the chocolate-truffle cake. Getting reserved seating in this 100-year-old plus landmark is often difficult, but not enough to deter dozens of people *without* reservations who might wait over an hour for an opening. Inexpensive ($1.95) but excellent bar food is also available 3–6 P.M., if you can ever penetrate the crowd there to order.

McCormick and Schmick's, 235 SW 1st Ave., 503/224-7527, has venerable roots—it's the offspring of century-old Jake's restaurant and enjoys a location in the historic Failing Building. Despite these bloodlines and Victorian digs, this place is inclined to experiment with such avant garde ingredient combinations as Cajun seared rockfish with lime cilantro butter sauce or seafood stir-fry with lemon ginger glaze. More straightforward fare can also be found on this restaurant's extensive menu and "fresh sheet." Expect to pay at least $20 pp for a full dinner. Lunch prices run $7–14 but there are also $4.95 specials. Better yet, for $1.95 enjoy a bar menu

4:30–6:30 P.M. that might feature Greek or Caesar salad, shrimp stir-fry, Cajun cheeseburger, pizza, and more.

Northwest Cuisine: Normally one of the more expensive places in Portland, **The Heathman Restaurant,** 1001 SW Broadway, 503/241-4100, can still be affordable thanks to their nightly special for theater-goers. The Heathman dining room's award-winning chef Pierre Boulot's creations can be had in a prix fixe dinner ($20 for three courses) 5 P.M.–6:30 P.M. The fare may be described as French meets Northwest in a constantly changing menu. This might manifest in a marinated sea bass salad for lunch or a pistachio-stuffed leg of rabbit for dinner. The creative use of local ingredients can be seen with salmon which may be served smoked in a hash for breakfast or seared with wasabi béarnaise sauce later in the day. For dessert, the bread pudding ($6) is noteworthy as is the ubiquitous presence of local berries and fruit. Entrée prices run $13–24.

A few blocks down the street, **Higgins,** 1239 SW Broadway, 503/222-9070, is another temple of Gallic-influenced Northwest cuisine that takes the adjectives "fresh, home-grown and organic" seriously while catering to a variety of tastes. As a result, vegetarians revel in such dishes as asparagus and morel risotto with goat cheese and red onion vinaigrette or an eggplant potato torta with oyster mushrooms and sundried tomatoes, while the rest of us can enjoy a spectacular sirloin burger on the lunch/bistro menu and fresh fish that's never overcooked. Everyone appreciates the menu's extras such as crisp produce from the best local purveyors around, bar delights like honey-roasted hazelnuts with chile washed down by Belgian ales, and desserts with homemade ice cream ($6.50). The wood-paneled tri-level dining room with big windows on Broadway is as inviting as the food. Dinner prices on the seasonally/monthly rotating menu run $16–27; lunch is about half that price. A bistro menu with many dishes under $10 expands the offerings.

Northwest Portland

The neighborhood called Nob Hill and defined by NW 21st and NW 23rd Avenues features the closest thing to a restaurant row as there is in Portland. Amid art galleries and boutiques are temples to Northwest cuisine and ethnic food with flair. Also in the mix are places serving down-home food that could be appreciated anywhere.

Carnivores: For over 50 years, the **Ring Side,** 2165 W. Burnside, 503/223-1513, served predominantly steak and prime rib until menu changes in the last decade made some concessions to the culinary trends of the "heart smart" '90s. Caesar salad (with a seafood option) as well as grilled salmon and halibut (also consider the lamb chops and chicken livers) now come highly recommended for those who can forsake the legendary prime rib, $20, and one of the best hamburgers in town ($7.25—or try it for $2.25 after 9:45 P.M. and Sunday 4–6 P.M. along with other appetizers in the bar/lounge).

Epicurean taste trends and health regimens may come and go, but when all is said and done, it's still the plump Walla Walla sweet onions that put the restaurant's name up in lights. These delicately battered yet crisp onion rings ($4.50) with a hint of spice are as much an American classic ("The best I've ever had," quoth James Beard) as the Hemingway-esque decor of faded boxing photos and hunting trophies, flaming red booths, and big stone fireplace. In 1996, The American Academy of Restaurants rated this place among the top 10 steakhouses in the country.

Middle Eastern: For late-night middle eastern food, you can't beat **Garbonzo's,** 2074 NW Lovejoy St., 503/227-4169. Falafel, spinach pie, and other specialties are prepared à la carte (averaging $4) or come with such "salads" as hummus and tabouleh (with entrée, around $7). The most expensive item on the menu is lamb kebobs with salad for $8.50. For a lighter meal, Garbonzo's own veggie burger or lentil soup with an order of tabouleh is recommended. Eastside diners can also enjoy this healthy fare at 3343 SE Hawthorne, 503/239-6087. These places are open Fri–Sat. till 3:30 A.M., and till 1:30 A.M. the rest of the week.

Italian: Portland's culinary version of Little Italy, the Nob Hill district, encompassing the blocks between NW 21st and NW 23rd Avenues, has almost a half-dozen Italian restaurants. **Il Fornaio,** 115 NE 22nd Ave., 503/248-9400, has an ambitious menu that tries to tour the different regions of Italy (pasta entrées $10–20) backed up by an excellent on-site bakery (*il fornaio* means the oven). In addition to the pricey dinner menu—$30 or more for antipasti, entrée, dessert, and wine—humbler lunchtime fare can be enjoyed in the same bright, airy setting of brick and wood, white tiles, and white linen. Sandwiches on delicious pan marino bread can be had here for less than $5 and many dinner entrées are half the price you'll see later on in the day.

Caffe Mingo's, 807 NW 21st Ave., 503/226-4646, nine entrées ($8–18) deliciously stretch a dollar and your stomach. In a menu that rotates seasonally, the Northwest mushrooms (or clams) cooked in olive oil, garlic, and lemon then sealed in parchment is a Tuscan appetizer that is not to be missed. The polenta with mushrooms and Italian sausage is also a signature dish but don't overlook the penne and braised beef infused with espresso and chianti. In any case, this small popular trattoria doesn't take reservations so misanthropes beware: even if you get here when the restaurant opens at 5 P.M., you'll still find yourself rubbing elbows (literally) at the rustic wooden tables with an interesting cross section of savvy diners.

Thai: Typhoon!, 400 SW Broadway in the Imperial Hotel, 503/224-8285, or at 2310 NW Everett St., 503/243-7557, has graced the pages of national gourmet magazines and other high profile media. What all the fuss is about is Thai food reflecting the culinary and aesthetic sensibilities of the chef/owner Bo Kline. This as evident from the boldly colorful decor and ornate presentation on each plate as it is from one bite of *miang kum* ($8). Inspired by Thai street food, this build-it-yourself dish consists of fresh spinach leaves wrapped around toasted coconut, dried shrimp, shallots, ginger, and Thai chilis, topped with plum sauce. Seafood dishes like Fish on Fire (halibut flambé with curry sauce)., Call Me Ginger (a salmon filet doused in black bean sauce), and Bags of Gold (shrimp wontons tied up with chives) also might want to make you forget *pad Thai* noodles ($9) and other common incarnations of this cuisine. Prices range $6–8 for lunch, $9–20 for dinner.

Comfort Food: For decades, breakfast at **The Stepping Stone Cafe,** 503/222-1132, NW 24th and Quimby, has meant quality eats in the formica-decorated confines of a well-kept '50s hash house. This reinvented corner cafe serves up tasty, filling breakfasts for prices more commonly seen in Mexican bus stations and Las Vegas casinos than in Portland's trendy Northwest district. For instance, the Birdwatcher's Special (available before 9 A.M.) features two eggs, new potato hash browns, toast and coffee for $3. There's also pancakes and three-egg omelettes ($4–6). Breakfast is served everyday until 2 P.M.

The **Foothill Broiler's,** 33 NW 23rd Pl., 503/223-0287, clientele of construction workers, suits, and dot-commers line up at the counter every day except Sunday, 7 A.M.–9 P.M., to order well-prepared comfort food with no frills at low prices ($4–8). Caesar salad, Greek salad, gyros, homemade pies, and one of the best hamburgers in the city compel an early arrival to avoid the queue. The latter, along with meat loaf sandwiches and BLTs, are less than $5. This is the place to grab a quick bite before hitting Cinema 21 or last-minute shopping. Should you get caught in the mealtime rush, **Elephant's Delicatessen** a few doors down has pricey multi-ethnic gourmet take-out items that are often a justifiable splurge.

N.Y. Deli: Kornblatt's, 628 NW 23rd, 503/242-0055, may be the only Oregon outpost of Jewish deli food that would be recognizable to East Coast transplants jaded from too many Portland-style five-grain bagels. By contrast, Kornblatt's sticks to what works in New York. Here the "Nova" (mild lox) is thin sliced, the whitefish salad smokey, the kugel (noodle pudding) is heavy with cinnamon, the bagels boiled and chewy, and the pickles extra sour. Triple-decker sandwiches—10 ounces of meat—average $7–9, and good bargains on baked goods can be found in the day-old basket. Try corned beef hash served with egg and bagel ($7.95) and cheese blintzes ($7.50) for filling breakfasts.

Northwest Cuisine: Started by French-Canadian loggers at the turn of the century, **Besaw's,** NW 23rd and Savier, 503/228-2619, is a meat-and-potatoes meets brie-and-chablis kind of place, where comfort food shares the menu with dishes prepared with house-smoked salmon, wild mushrooms, and other gourmet ingredients. This orientation is in evidence at breakfast with the prosciutto and egg scramble and the omelette made with shiitake, oyster, and button mushrooms (both $8). At lunchtime in the same price range, you'll find such sandwiches as grilled salmon in a horseradish-caper *rémoulade* and an eggplant and provolone combo. For dinner, similar epicurean turns show up in the weekly specials ($12–18), exemplified by pepper-glazed pork with apple chutney and coq au vin. Homemade desserts ($4) like apple raspberry bread pudding and berry brown Betty can conclude your meal of high-class comfort food at reasonable prices. Ports, cognacs, well-made Irish coffee, and other after-dinner drinks (averaging $5) at Besaw's century-old mahogany bar can make waiting for a table here eminently bearable.

Paley's, 1204 NW 21st Ave., 503/243-2403, is the quintessential Northwest bistro and according to many Portlanders, the most enjoyable dining experience in town. This intimate restaurant (16 tables seating maybe 50 people) has a few stalwart dishes backing up a seasonally rotating menu featuring foods in season. The latter might include grilled chinook with chanterelles, arugula salad with goat cheese, and other culinary expressions of the region. Entrées run $18–26, and elaborate salads and small plates $10–12. Hand-cut french fries with mustard aoli ($3.50) is a delicious side dish. Desserts ($7–9) are all spectacular, but the crème brûlée and warm chocolate soufflé cake are the grandest finales of all. The great wine regions of the world are explored Wednesday nights with the chance to sample by the glass and enjoy a wine-bar menu. The front porch of Paley's turn-of-the century Victorian makes outdoor dining on a summer night here (and other times of year thanks to radiant heat from overhead lights) a pleasure, particularly for those who find the tight fit of the restaurant's interior inhibiting.

Across the street from Paley's, **Wildwood,** 1221 NW 21st Ave., 503/248-9663, is yet another shrine to Northwest cuisine. Appropriately, dishes bear such regional monikers and flavors as Painted Hills rib eye ($27) or Clatskanie quail with blackberry hash and Walla Walla onion confit ($24). In the same vein, local produce purveyors are often mentioned on the menu. While entrée prices run high, such signature starters as skillet-roasted Washington mussels in a tomato saffron garlic broth and wood-oven baked sweet onion and bacon pizza let you enjoy lunch or a light dinner for around $10. This warm, inviting space is on the dance card of every visiting foodie, so make reservations in advance.

The Pearl District

This is Portland's latest "buzz" neighborhood. Of the many new places (a preponderance of first-rate Italian spots) here we've chosen two that embody the dynamism of this emerging culinary scene.

Cafe Azul, 112 NW Ninth Ave., 503/525-4422, is not just another *taqueria.* Chances are you've never had Mexican food like this before. *Tinga pie* (a chicken and vegetable pastry seasoned with herbs, currants, and smoked chipotle chiles) and *cochinita pibil* (marinated pork tacos with stringy red onions doused in orange juice) typify what may be best described as gourmet interpretations of peasant fare. Little known ingredients, often indigenous to central and southern Mexico, spice up complex moles (a chocolate-based sauce), stews, and other dishes in a menu that changes with the seasons. Such Northwest versions on this theme as wild mushroom empanada use the regional bounty of fresh produce to full advantage. Reassuringly familiar accompaniments like cinnamony Mexican hot chocolate, guacamole, and flan may help you get your culinary bearings here, but most of the time only your taste buds will be your guide. In like measure, your server will encourage wine instead of the beer that traditionally complements Mexican food. The end result is a memorable meal created by a chef trained at the venerable Chez Panisse. Dinner prices can total $25–30 pp here, high for Mexican food, but you won't experience a tastier intro to the flavors of the sun anywhere.

The most trendy dinner spot in the avant garde Pearl District is **Oba!,** 555 NW 12th Ave., 503/228-6161. Upon entering the restaurant's high-ceilinged burgundy- and buff-colored confines, a wave of sound hits you that pulsates throughout the several dining rooms and bar here. The animated talk and laughter might be catalyzed by fresh fruit–mango margaritas or diners commenting on such over-the-top appetizers as crispy coconut prawns with jalapeno citrus marinade ($7) and seared rare ahi tuna with mango tomatillo salsa ($11). Whether it's melted cheese with spicy sausage from Spain, arepa corn cakes from Colombia, Brazilian black bean pork Feijoada, or yuca—the starchy tuber ubiquitous throughout equatorial South America—the focus is on Latin cuisine, albeit with new world interpretations. Such entrées as butternut squash enchilada in walnut sauce ($13) and grilled salmon in a banana-lime vinaigrette ($18) exemplify these nuevo Latino juxtapositions. Great desserts ($5–7) and a late-night bar menu are other reasons to make the scene at Portland's current late-night mecca.

Old Town

The former speakeasies, opium dens, and houses of negotiable affection of what is now a National Historic District house a variety of restaurants. Here are several with distinctive personalities and good food at low-to-moderate prices.

At the edge of Old Town is a Portland institution. Joie de vivre is in the air when you step into **Alexis,** 215 W. Burnside, 503/224-8577, but it's not just the retsina, Greek music, and folk dancing that keep people coming back. This is the best Greek food in Oregon. Appetizers like calamari or *saganaki* (fried cheese) might start your meal here. You can spend an evening just ordering appetizers and enjoying the crusty bread, but it would be a shame to forgo such entrées as the moussaka and oregano chicken ($9–13). On weekends this moderately priced taverna features belly dancing and an atmosphere that'll bring out the Zorba in anyone.

La Patisserie, 208 NW Couch, 503/248-

N

PORTLAND

PORTLAND BY THE SLICE

Pizza styles from Chicago, New York, and other locales are represented in the Pacific Northwest. When you're heading out for piece of pie in the Rose City, expect to pay $2.25 a slice, on the average, and get a greater variety of toppings than what's usually seen elsewhere.

Pizza in Portland means **Escape From New York,** 622 NW 23rd Ave., 503/227-5423—if you're an East Coast purist who likes foldable crust, copious cheese, and conventional toppings. If you're not averse to paying a little more for your pizza (from $2.75 a slice), head to one of **Pizzicato's** six outlets around town—such as 705 NW Alder, 503/226-1007, and 28 NE Burnside, 503/236-0045—where exotic condiments on the order of lamb, sausage, chanterelle and shiitake mushrooms, and rock shrimp make a meal out of a slice. For price, selection, and a stimulating campus ambience, **Hot Lips Pizza,** 1909 SW 6th, 503/224-0311, near Portland State University is a good choice. On the eastside, **It's a Beautiful Pizza,** 3341 SE Belmont, 503/233-5444, has psychedelic decor, live music, and some of the best pies in the city (from $2.50 a slice). These also might be the most filling slices around.

Another place for pizza is the **Bridgeport Brew Pub,** 1313 NW Marshall St., 503/241-7179. The malt-based pizza crust with olives, chorizo, yellow peppers, and eggplant washed down by Blue Heron or Coho Pacific ale can only be described as quintessential Portland. The best pizza slice deal in the city ($1.25) is available here after 9 P.M. on Monday, Tuesday, and Wednesday. For $3 you can sample seven distinct beers made by Oregon's first microbrewery. On warm days, the outdoor loading dock that serves as the brewery's "picnic area" feels like a millionaire's patio after the second glass.

goods and moderately priced lunchtime soups and sandwiches ($7) also are claims to fame.

While not for the faint of palate, the dim sum at **Fong Chong,** 301 NW 4th, 503/220-0235, is one of the more exotic low-cost dining adventures in the city. It all begins at 11 A.M. every day, when carts of steaming Cantonese delicacies come whooshing down the aisles. Even if the mumbled explanations of the barely bilingual staff don't translate, the array of crepes and buns stuffed with chicken, shrimp, pork, and other fillings are so varied and cost so little ($2–5 a plate) that you can't miss. After 3 P.M., the restaurant reverts to unexciting Cantonese fare.

Northeast

Northeast Sandy and northeast Broadway are alternative routes to I-84 to and from the Gorge. Breakfast at area restaurants is a highlight.

Spanish: Colosso, 1932 NE Broadway, 503/288-3333, is a tapas bar and "meet" market where small plates of Spanish delicacies ($3–12) with wicked cocktails (especially vodkas and citrus juice concoctions) facilitate the get-acquainted process for yuppies and tattooed creatures of the night. The tapas menu tops out with Seafood Vatapa, a mélange of shellfish in a Brazilian sauce with lots of peanuts and coconut ($12). The menu is full of other tempting fish plates as well standbys (paella) and intriguing surprises (tenderloins in a mango citrus marinade). Desserts are served here as well.

Mexican: A good way to judge a Mexican restaurant is by its *chiles rellenos.* If a place can make this popular dish with a light, crisp batter so as not to mute the taste of the chile pepper and melted cheese, chances are it can pull off the whole enchilada in fine style. **Chez Jose,** NE 22nd and Broadway, 503/280-9888, passes this test and probably meets any other standard you might use to judge a Mexican restaurant. You'll also enjoy the fact that a sumptuous combination plate can feed two people for around $9. Longtime patrons here tout the Mexican chicken soup ($4.95) and lime chicken enchiladas ($8) as "must-haves." If you want to stray from the old

9898, is a second-floor walk-up coffeehouse whose windows overlook Old Town, one of the best people-watching neighborhoods in the city. You can also enjoy a tasty and sumptuous breakfast for little more than $5. Housed in a turn-of-the-century structure (with intricate woodwork) that was once a speakeasy, spectacular baked

reliables of Mexican food, try such entrées as squash enchilada with peanut sauce, or marinated prawns with chile and honey sauce. For a few bucks more you can order a serving of Mexican chocolate ice cream with a cinnamon aftertaste that recalls the flavor of hot chocolate south of the border. Another branch of Chez Jose is located at 8502 SW Terwilliger Blvd., 503/244-0007.

Italian: Paparazzi's, 2015 NE Broadway, 503/281-7701, features almost two dozen pasta dishes (especially delicious is the ravioli with smoked salmon or forest mushrooms), Neapolitan pizza (thin crust, light toppings), great minestrone soup, and the friendliness of a neighborhood trattoria. Despite parchment menus written in Italian and other down-home touches, be forewarned that bills are not paid in lira here. Enough pasta dishes cost $14 to destroy any illusion of family-friendly prices.

Pan-Asian: Although Vietnamese flavors predominate at **Saigon Kitchen,** 835 NE Broadway, 503/281-3669, Thai dishes like beef in coconut juice and basil leaves and ginger chicken are highlights. The $4.95 lunch specials Monday–Friday are an especially good value. Dinner combination plates in the $8–10 range might include such uncommon specialties as garlicky salted squid or charcoal chicken rolled up in rice papers with lettuce, mint, cilantro, and peanut sauce. Another exotic mainstay is coconut lemongrass soup (feeds several people for $7.45). This restaurant has always been the darling of Portland's alternative weeklies, which rightfully extol its spring rolls. A serving of three spring rolls at lunch comes to your table all chopped up and ready for dipping into the restaurant's hot-sweet fish sauce—a wonderful light meal ($4.25).

The neighborhood between NE 50th and NE 70th along Sandy Boulevard is the vortex of Portland's Asian business community. Here, at **Zien Hong,** 5314 NE Sandy Blvd., 503/288-2743, and at **Yen Ha,** 6820 NE Sandy Blvd., 503/287-3698, Vietnamese, Chinese, and Thai influences assert themselves in the cuisine of each kitchen. Extensive menus, low prices, and high quality distinguish both restaurants. Zien Hong's soups,

$4–7, are meals in themselves, and Yen Ha's meat dishes (the house specialty is *bo nuong vi*—marinated beef grilled tableside for $11.95) are particularly noteworthy. Zien Hong's late-night hours are especially appreciated on the east side of the Willamette River, where most restaurants close by 10 P.M. Several other restaurants nearby are dedicated to *pho,* a Vietnamese beef noodle soup. For just a few bucks, you get a big bowl (other soups and entrées are also offered) that's sure to satisfy. **Pho 54,** 6852 NE Sandy Blvd., comes recommended. In any case, Portland's large Vietnamese community has graced the Rose City with some of the best purveyors of this cuisine outside Saigon, so sayeth *New Yorker* food philosopher Calvin Trillin.

Comfort Food: If the **Cadillac Cafe's,** 914 NE Broadway, 503/287-4750, Fleetwood-fin-shaped logo and shocking-pink color scheme don't wake you up in the morning, the first-rate breakfast will. The thematic continuity of the restaurant's decor, along with fresh flowers and clean architectural lines, bespeak the same attention to detail that greets northeast neighborhood breakfastgoers and lunchtime devotees of the menu's expertly prepared fare. Here you'll find a light omelette batter that doesn't overwhelm the taste of the ingredients inside, as well as perfectly done hash browns. We recommend an early arrival to get a seat for Henry's North American (sweet Italian sausage scrambled with eggs, spinach, and Swiss cheese) and hazelnut custard French toast. Breakfast here is in the $7–10 range. Later, tuna melts, BLTs, and other expertly rendered classics anchor a similarly priced afternoon menu.

Dollar value is a term usually not associated with breakfast tabs than can range $9–11, but the **Cameo Cafe,** just west of The Grotto near the corner of 82nd and Sandy (other locations are the Imperial Hotel lobby, SE 6th and Broadway and one on the corner of NW 23rd Place and Westover), is an exception. Portions and quality here more than justify this description. The homey cafe is always busy with devotees of its "acre" pancakes (try the strawberry banana) and waffles, "real" homefries, and homebaked multigrain bread. Everything else here showcases the restaurant's commitment to excellence, from large jugs of Vermont maple syrup gracing each table to the smiling wait staff who seem able to guess just when you'll need a warm-up to your morning coffee. Lunch ($9–11) and dinner ($14–16) offer generous smatterings of Asian and Italian dishes to complement American comfort food.

Northeast Portland's new breakfast hot spot is **Milo's**, 1325 NE Broadway, 503/288-6456. One bite of smoked salmon hash ($8) or French toast with spicy sausage and cheddar cheese ($6.50) should explain this popularity, but a half-dozen creative omelette combinations along with a passel of eggs Benedict variations (all around $7) and scramble options ($4–8.50) can also win converts. These are supplemented by hash-and-egg combos ($7) and French toast and waffles ($4–6). East Coast diners who've had trouble finding decent crab cakes out West can confidently order this dish here, which occasionally shows up on the specials list. Lunch here boasts salads, sandwiches, and pasta in the same price range as breakfast.

North Portland

A popular route with Gorge-bound locals who are not in a hurry and who wish to escape traffic jams on I-84 is to take Marine Drive (from downtown, take I-5 about 10 miles north to Exit 307) east. Gorge-bound travelers have the option of following Marine Drive to I-84 or crossing the I-205 Bridge to pick up Hwy. 14 through Washington's Gorge. Here are two dining options along the way.

Jubitz Truckstop, 10310 Vancouver Way, 503/283-1111, might be a useful place to grab a bite and take care of other traveler needs if you're in North Portland near the Columbia River. In addition to scarfing down such deals as two pounds of baby-back ribs for $16 or a mound of beef stew for $6 in the Cascade Grill, you can enjoy a movie in the theater here, take in or dance to country acts in one of the largest venues for country music in the city, or shop in a 6,000-foot retail space. The Oregon Welcome Center is also located within this complex, with dozens of free travel publications and pamphlets of use to

the Gorge-bound traveler. The truck stop's **Ponderosa Motel,** 800/523-0600, has comfortable, reasonably priced rooms ($60) and jacuzzi suites ($80) to ease the pain of the road. You can also wash clothes and fill up your tank here round-the-clock. Pick up Vancouver Way off Marine Drive.

Salty's on the Columbia, 3839 NE Marine Dr., 503/288-4444, is a great choice for those headed to the Gorge. The river frontage and fish-on-ice displays that greet you set the mood for a seafood feast. Bills can run high ($30 pp for dinner is common), so save this one for a special occasion. Otherwise, lunch prices ($12–16) might fit better into your budget. Many fresh specials supplement the menu, which offers such imaginative dishes as a Caesar salad garnished with bits of blackened or smoked salmon (smoked alderwood salmon is a specialty here). Rich desserts and a nautical-theme bar well stocked with Northwest microbrews also recommend this place. If it's warm, the outdoor seating above the river is a special treat but airplane noise can occasionally stifle conversation. When you emerge from the restaurant, fair-weather views of Mt. Hood can provide the finishing touch to your dining pleasure.

Hawthorne District

Easily incorporated into a Gorge excursion, the Hawthorne Boulevard neighborhood recalls the hip gourmet ghettoes in Cambridge, MA and Berkeley, CA. To get there from downtown, take Madison Street east to the Willamette River and cross the Hawthorne Bridge, where Tommy Lee Jones chased Benicio del Toro in a climactic scene from *The Hunted,* filmed in Portland and nearby Silverton in 2001.

Multiethnic: The **Hawthorne Cafe,** 3354 SE Hawthorne, 503/232-4982, carries the banner for a neighborhood long known for its Bohemian feel and ethnic flair. Therefore, it shouldn't be surprising that this restaurant serves up hearty breakfasts and lunches whose nutritional concerns are reminiscent of the '60s—but with the tastiness of Mediterranean cuisine. The latter comes courtesy of such garnishes as the restaurant's homemade hummus, tabouleh, and strips of seasoned lamb known as gyro. Moderate prices and cozy dining rooms in a refurbished old mansion also make this place a winner. The farmer's omelette and eggs Florentine typify the first-rate breakfast fare ($6–7), and keep an eye out for the pancakes or coffeecake made with marionberries that frequently appear on the "specials" board. In the same price range as breakfast, a grilled chicken sandwich with bacon and gruyère cheese ($6.25), rock shrimp pasta salad ($7) and the like rate a thumbs up for lunch.

Mexican Northwest: Dingo's, 4612 SE Hawthorne, 503/233-3996, is what happens when you cross the hip Hawthorne ghetto with the fish taco stands so popular in Baja, Mexico. This place receives salmon, tuna, and halibut trimmings from a supplier who purveys the filets to gourmet restaurants. Anyone who orders such dishes as the grilled ahi or spicy salmon or halibut burrito (all $4.35) will appreciate the flavorful results of this practice as well as the price. Other well-prepared seafood and traditional Mexican entrées, outdoor seating, and microbrews on tap are other enticements.

Mexican: A newly emerging hot spot for Mexican food is **La Calaca Comelona,** 1408 SE 12th, 503/239-9675, located on the fringe of the Hawthorne District. Those who still have the unfortunate image of Mexican restaurants as places of burritos and Day-Glo velvet paintings will be pleasantly surprised by Frida Kahlo–style murals and Day of the Dead puppets festooning the walls here as well as a distinctive bill of fare without a burrito in sight. Instead of just the usual tacos and tostadas with either chicken, beef, or pork seen on menus in these establishments north of the border, this place also includes combination taco platters ($8) consisting of several kinds of cooked meats and vegetables served with homemade tortillas. There are also quesadillas filled with your choice of ingredients ($1–6). Spicy homemade chorizo sausage with melted cheese on a tortilla ($4) typifies the latter. To ease the fire of spicy dishes, fresh-squeezed tropical juices are worth the

few extra bucks, that is if you can forego a bottle of Negra Modelo, any true Mexican beer connoisseur's choice. By the time you leave, you should understand why the restaurant's translated name—The Hungry Skeleton—refers only to the decor.

Italian Northwest: As its name implies, **Three Doors Down,** 1429 SE 37th Ave., 503/236-6886, is several doors away from Hawthorne Boulevard. It also presents a refined dining experience that stands apart from its neighboring bento and pizza joints. Such dishes as roasted salmon or halibut with pancetta and chanterelles (19.50), baked steamer clams with garlic and wine ($11.50), and penne with Italian sausage in a vodka-based sauce with plum tomatoes and chili flakes ($15) have made the Italian-accented menu here a favorite. This restaurant does not accept reservations and is filled to overflowing Tuesday–Saturday, so get here early (before 6 P.M.) or prepare to wait for a table.

Ethiopian: Jarra's, 1435 Hawthorne, 503/230-8990, was Portland's first introduction to Ethiopian food and its mouth-burning stews known as *wat.* This may be the hottest food in the state, but the flavors of lamb, beef, and chicken assert themselves through the peppers. The spongy *enjera* bread that accompanies your meal also manages to soak up some of the heat. Dinner will cost less than $9 here, but be prepared to buy an extra drink to cool off your taste buds.

Lebanese: For home-cooked Lebanese comfort food, try **Riyadh's,** 1318 SE Hawthorne Blvd., 503/235-1254. While the falafel, hummus and *babaghanoush* are as good here as we've had anywhere, lesser-known dishes like *kafta* (ground beef minced with parsley, onions, cilantro, and spices) and *manikish* (a cheeseless herbal pizza) deliciously expand gustatory horizons. Despite low prices ($3–6.50) and generous portions in this small cafe, leave room for homemade *halawa* (a ground sesame candy) and first-rate baklava.

Thai: The aptly named **Thai Thai,** 4604 SE Hawthorne, 503/236-1466, offers some standout dishes at good prices. *Som tum* ($5.95), a shredded green papaya salad with shrimp, peanuts, tomato, chile and lime juice, and fish sauce, and *tom ka gai* ($7.95 feeds several people), a coconut milk–based, hot-sweet soup with choice of meat or tofu, help this place set the standard among Portland Thai restaurants. The rest of the menu at this warm, welcoming family restaurant in the shadow of Mt. Tabor has a consistent level of quality with prices $5–9.

Pan-Asian: Thanh Thao, 4005 SE Hawthorne, 238-6232, is the favorite of Reed College students, Vietnamese families, and other devotees of pan-Asian food. In a vast menu of Vietnamese and Thai specialties, peanut chicken, eggplant in garlic sauce, and barbecue pork rice noodle (all at or near $7) typify the well-prepared moderately priced entrées. Accompaniments like chicken sour soup ($7 feeds a family of four) and salad rolls ($4 for 2) also explain lines outside the door here most nights of the week.

Comfort Food: The **Tabor Hill Cafe,** 3766 Hawthorne Blvd., 503/230-1231, is another dollar-wise Hawthorne mainstay. Berry pancakes and overstuffed omelettes comprise breakfast highlights, and inventive pasta dishes with fish and chicken proliferate the menu the rest of the day. Expect to pay $7–9 for breakfast and $10–12 for dinner.

Northwest Cuisine: The three-course, Jewish-style Sunday brunch has helped establish **Bread and Ink,** 3610 SE Hawthorne, 503/239-4756, as *the* gathering place in the Hawthorne neighborhood. If lox, borscht, and the like are not your weekend repast of choice, there's always an assortment of homemade breads and imaginative omelettes to sustain you. Later on in the week, lunchtime diners line up for a massive burger topped with gruyère cheese and Bermuda onion and locally esteemed salmon sandwiches. Dinner is a primer on Northwest cuisine—whatever is in season, the freshest ingredients, creatively prepared. Breakfast and lunch can run in the $7–11 range (with the complete Yiddish brunch $15), dinner $15–20.

GETTING THERE AND GETTING AROUND

In Portland, streets are named and run east and west, avenues are numbered and run north and south, and boulevards exist in the netherworld of thoroughfares that go in many directions. Adding to the confusion, Martin Luther King Boulevard, Portland's main route in town before the interstates, used to be called Union and the old name survives in some quarters. As it heads south, it becomes McLoughlin Boulevard. Broadway (in effect, 7th Avenue) is Portland's only undefined arterial, having an east-west orientation while carrying the prefix N.E.; with the prefix S.W. or when it's just plain Broadway, it runs north-south. Finally, no rules of logic seem to apply in the west hills when it comes to finding your way. Despite these idiosyncrasies, Portland is, for the most part, easily navigable.

Newcomers should note that the Willamette River determines east-west boundaries and Burnside Street delineates north-south address prefixes. Also, northwest Portland streets proceed in alphabetical order from Burnside moving north with streets keyed to names of early settlers. Back in midtown, Naito Parkway (also called Front Avenue, paralleling the Willamette) is in effect, "Zero Avenue," with numbers going up as you move west away from the river. These avenues are all one way. Finally, remember that traffic along 5th and 6th Avenues is largely restricted to mass transit.

By Car

Portland sits on or near the routes of Interstates 5, 405, 205, and 84. Interstate 5 runs from Seattle to San Diego and I-84 goes east to Salt Lake City, passing through the Gorge. I-405 circles downtown Portland to the west and south. I-205 bypasses the city to the east. A bridge over the Columbia River intersects with Washington's Gorge route Hwy. 14. U.S. 26 heads west to Cannon Beach on the coast and east to Mt. Hood.

The parking situation in Portland has its good news and bad news. First, the bad news: Even though parking meters and day parking proliferate in the city, it's often hard to find an empty spot. The good news is many of the parking garages accept merchant validation stamps (on the garage receipt) for free parking. As for parking on the street, it's free 6 P.M.–8 A.M. on weekdays and all day Sunday.

Finally, keep in mind that gas prices in Portland could well be higher than those found in other U.S. cities. Without self-service gas stations or oil refineries in the state, this trend will most likely, unfortunately, continue.

By Bus, Train, and Boat

The **Greyhound** bus station, 550 NW 6th Ave., 800/231-2222, has storage lockers available for 75 cents a day.

The **Green Tortoise,** 616 SW College St., 800/867-8647, goes to Seattle Tuesday and Saturday (as well as Thursday and Sunday June 1–Oct. 1) at 4 P.M. for $15 and to San Francisco at 12:30 P.M. Sunday and Thursday (plus Tuesday and Friday June 1–Oct. 1) for $49 (plus $4 for dinner and hot tub at a southern Oregon encampment). Departures are from the University Deli on 6th and College across from the Cheerful Tortoise. Eugene departures cost $10 and leave the same day as the San Francisco runs.

Amtrak runs Coast Starlight trains north and south to Seattle and Los Angelels respectively.

There are also several high-speed Cascades trains to Eugene and Seattle daily. Trips to Seattle begin at just $21, one-way. Laptop outlets and more pleasant scenery than I-5 are other inducements. Two Cascades trains run south to Eugene leaving 5:30 P.M. and 9 P.M. Visit www.AmtrakCascades.com for a virtual tour and exclusive online discounts or call 800/USA-RAIL. The Empire Builder leaves at 4:40 P.M. every day and heads east along the Washington shoreline of the Gorge, taking in spectacular vistas of waterfalls and windsurfers along a river-level track passing through picturesque rock tunnels. This line heads east to Chicago, stopping at such venues as Chicago, Minneapolis, and, in summer, Glacier National Park. Because there is also a westbound train, windsurfers can leave stations in Bingen or Wishram in the morning en route to Portland and return to the Gorge for dinner the next day for $18–30. For reservations, call 800/USA-RAIL. Several Portland city buses (nos. 31–35, 54, or 56–59) will take you to Amtrak. Pick up any one of them at the downtown transit mall. The following Tri-Met bus routes access Greyhound and Amtrak terminals (nos. 1, 5, 14, 32, 33, 35, 54, 56, 57, 58, and 59).

Hopes run high for the reinstatement of Amtrak Pioneer service on the Oregon side of the

© BRIAN LITT

freight train rounding a bend in the Gorge

PORTLAND

gorge. This line was terminated due to lack of revenue but if the route resumes it would feature stops in Cascades Locks, Hood River, and The Dalles. More reliance on freight and increased visitation are expected to make up the shortfall. Call Amtrak for details.

By Air

Portland International Airport (airport city code PDX), 877/739-4636, is among America's fastest growing airports. This increased traffic has spurred massive expansion, set to culminate in 2004. In the interim, transitional arrangements unfortunately render definitive listings about long and short-term parking impossible. Please contact the information number for updates.

The PDX airport is served by more than a dozen major airlines. Portland and Seattle are linked by commuter flights on **Horizon,** 800/547-9308, every half-hour during the day. **Air B.C.,** 800/663-0522, flies from Portland to Vancouver, British Columbia every two hours. **United Express,** 800/241-6522, competes with Horizon in the Pacific Northwest, and with **Southwest,** 800/435-9792, in California. East Coast travelers might note that **Continental,** 800/525-0280, goes nonstop from Portland to Newark, New Jersey. At press time, nonstop flights to New York's JFK airport via Delta and Continental were also reportedly in the works. Connections from abroad can be made via Continental's PDX connection with Houston and south-of-the-border locales and to Europe through Ohio airports. The only daily direct service out of the country are the Horizon and Air B.C. flights to Vancouver, B.C. in Canada.

Europeans interested in air connections to and from Oregon should note that a **Delta Airlines,** 800/221-1212, connection through Ohio now makes it possible to fly from Portland to Frankfurt, Germany. To get back to Europe cheaply, consult AirHitch (800/326-2009; www.airhitch.org) or Air-Tech (800/575-8324; www.airtech.com). Each of these firms finds an inexpensive flight within the window you specify.

The #12 Tri-Met buses from downtown run 5 A.M.–12:30 A.M. and leave from SW 6th Avenue and Main Street. From the airport, buses depart every 15 minutes, 5:30 A.M.–11:30 P.M. Catch #12 outside the baggage claim. It arrives downtown 40 minutes later via Sandy Boulevard.

The airport MAX train enables arriving and departing travelers to take light rail from the terminal. Just south and almost under the ramp from the terminal's departure level and just east of Alaska/Horizon luggage carousels is the MAX station. The airport train will merge with Eastside MAX at the Gateway Station. The train will turn around at SE 11th downtown to head back to the airport. Onboard are luggage racks.

Other ways of getting to town include free hotel courtesy shuttles and the **Grayline Airporter** bus, 503/285-9845, which stops at the Greyhound station as well as many hotels en route, $15 one-way. It runs 5 A.M.–midnight, stopping at each hotel on the route. Call Grayline for the exact arrival/departure schedule or ask hotel personnel or the airport information desk, which is on the first floor near the main terminal's baggage claim. Across the street from this desk, an Airporter leaves for downtown on the half-hour.

To drive to the city from PDX, follow the signs to downtown. This would take you first to I-205 South which would then flow into I-84 East. About 10 minutes later, you'll flirt briefly with I-5 south before quickly exiting onto the Morrison Street Bridge. This will take you across the river where the first cross street encountered is SW 1st Avenue.

Storage facilities at PDX include lockers (C and D concourses) that charge 75 cents a day, and D.J.'s Baggage Service (across the hall from Continental and American baggage claims), 503/281-9464, with nightly rates starting at $2 a suitcase. Lockers can accommodate only smaller items.

Finally, the Portland airport is situated a mere 20-minute drive from the western portal of the Columbia River Gorge in Troutdale. With car rental facilities, limousine services to Gorge resorts such as Skamania Lodge, and Tri-Met buses equipped with bicycle racks that can access Troutdale and the Historic Highway, you can be out of the airport and off on a Gorge adventure within an hour of landing.

Inner City Public Transportation

Begin your orientation to the Tri-Met bus system at Pioneer Square. The **Tri-Met office,** 1 Pioneer Courthouse Square, 701 SW 6th Ave., 503/238-RIDE, is open 9 A.M.–5 P.M. weekdays. Information can be obtained from Tri-Met drivers, hotel front desk clerks and concierges, or any branch of Willamette Savings. Or you can call these numbers: recorded information for call-a-bus, 503/231-3199; for bicycle commuter service, 503/239-3044. Adult fares begin at $1.25 (two zones). These fares also apply to **MAX,** the light-rail train, that does not make as many stops. MAX runs every 15 minutes. To ride it to its easternmost extremity, Gresham (17 miles from downtown), takes 45 minutes. Hillsboro is the western terminus. Buy tickets from machines at MAX stations before boarding. Tri-Met buses require exact change, and you can purchase tickets at the Tri-Met office or aboard the area bus.

Passengers in the downtown area can ride free anywhere in Fareless Square. This 300-square-block area is defined by I-405 to the south, NW Hoyt Street to the north, and the Willamette River to the east. Across the river, the Lloyd District might soon be added to Fareless Square.

A one-day pass is a good way to get oriented to Portland and environs. Purchase one at Tri-Met service centers (or some credit unions, banks, and supermarkets like Safeway and Albertson's) or at the main Tri-Met office beneath Pioneer Courthouse Square. In addition, bus drivers can issue a transfer good for all day and all zones, which is the equivalent of a one-day pass.

The first step in setting up your own personalized mass-transit tour is picking up a schedule at one of the Tri-Met service centers or bus-information racks scattered around town.

By Bike

For several years (most recently in 1999) *Bicycling* magazine selected Portland as the most bike-friendly major city (out of 226 contenders) in the country. Recent evidence of this has been the establishment of covered bike parking, showers, lockers downtown (call 503/823-7671 for information), and increased numbers of bike lanes on commuter thoroughfares. With bike racks available on many Tri-Met buses ($5 passes available at Pioneer Square in offices near Powell's Travel Bookstore) and publications such as the *From*

Here To There By Bike map and *Getting There By Bike,* published by Metro (a government agency) and sold at bookstores and bike shops, there is no shortage of available resources. For more information contact the **Office of Transportation Bicycle Program,** 1120 SW 5th Ave., Room 730, Portland 97204, 503/823-7082.

Gorge-bound travelers can bypass 17 miles of suburbs by taking MAX light rail from downtown to the Gresham stop. Here catch an 80, 24, or 81 Tri-Met bus to Troutdale and the western portal of the Historic Highway.

INFORMATION AND SERVICES

Portland's visitor-information resources are far-reaching and extensive. Begin at **Portland Oregon Visitors Association,** 26 SW Salmon St., Portland 97218, 877/678-5263 or 503/275-9750. This facility sits across Front Avenue from Waterfront Park's beautiful fountain. Hours are Mon.–Fri. 9 A.M.–5 P.M., Sat. 9 a.m.–4 P.M., and Sun. 10 A.M.–2 P.M. In addition to knowledgeable personnel, POVA has the most complete collection of printed traveler-information pamphlets in the state, as well as a discount theater ticket outlet. While Portland is naturally the focus of most of the office's publications, materials about every part of the state fill the racks here. The best free **maps** of the city are available nearby from Powell's at Pioneer Square and from Hertz on the corner of SW 6th Avenue and Salmon, 503/249-5727.

Helpful information sources throughout the downtown core are the **Portland Guides,** 503/295-0912. Their distinctive green baseball caps make it easy to spot these free walking information centers.

Several travel agencies rate a mention for cheap fares and helpful travel tips. **Council Travel,** 1715 SW Morrison, 503/228-1980 or 800/228-2854, and **ASA University Travel,** 1503 SW Broadway, 503/224-6659, serve the student community and are up on all the deals. For travel in the Northwest and an ecotourism orientation, **Journeys,** 1526 NW 23rd, 503/226-4849, is tops. Journeys also has a storefront at Powell's Travel store in Pioneer Square. Another agency well-versed in regional outdoor recreation is **Elephants Trunk,** 2312 Kearney, 503/223-2626.

A local **events hotline,** 503/233-4444, can supplement the media sources identified below to update you on what's going on, where, and at what time. Other useful numbers include a **Crisis Line,** 503/223-6161; **Women's Crisis Lines,** 503/235-5333; **Men's Resource Center,** 503/235-3433; **Drug Counseling and Intervention,** 503/320-9654; **Health Help Center,** 503/288-5995; and the **Aging Services Division,** 503/248-3464.

A convenient part of town for the traveler to take care of essentials is the Hollywood District north of Sandy Boulevard around NE 42nd. A mini-mall off NE 42nd and Hancock features a bank, a laundromat, and an excellent coffee shop, **Sweet Indulgences,** 1925 NE 42nd Ave., 503/249-0686. Across the street to the east is a post office subcontractor who has weekend hours when the "official" post office outlets are closed. A block south on Sandy is **Trader Joe's,** whose array of discount gourmet grocery items can provision a picnic. Sandy Boulevard can be followed 13 miles to Troutdale and the Columbia River Gorge if a calmer, albeit slower, alternative to I-84 traffic is desired.

The hours of the main **post office,** 715 NW Hoyt St., Portland 97208, 503/294-2124, are Mon.–Fri. 8:30 A.M.–8 P.M. and Sat. 8:30 A.M.–5 P.M. The Pioneer Courthouse might be more convenient to use if you're in midtown Portland.

The **Multnomah County Library** has 15 branches throughout the city with books, films, records, and at some branches, videos available for borrowing. The central branch, 801 SW 10th Ave., 503/223-7201, is a top-notch research facility with a newspaper and periodical section that's well organized and voluminous and 60 percent open stacks.

Medical care downtown can be most conveniently accessed through **Good Samaritan Hospital,** 1015 NW 22nd Ave., 503/229-7711. This hospital's **Convenience Care Center,** 503/229-8000, located on-site, offers quicker, less costly care than the main emergency room. The center is open during the week 9 A.M.–9 P.M., weekends 10 A.M.–9 P.M. Twenty-four hour pharmacies at chains like Walgreen's (39th and SE Belmont) and Rite-Aid (39th and SE Division, among other outlets) are also good to keep in mind.

Resources

Suggested Reading

In addition to the titles cited in the text, Gorge-bound travelers would do well to acquaint themselves with these books. We advise readers to search for out-of-print books at www.powells.com.

General Interest Guides

Jones, Philip N., ed. *Columbia River Gorge—A Complete Guide.* Seattle: Mountaineers, 1992. The best comprehensive coverage of the history, geology, and wildflowers of the Gorge as well as its recreational activities, this guide contains essays by the preeminent experts on every subject of interest (save for creature comforts) to Gorge travelers.

Gorge Native Culture

Rubin, Rick. *Naked Against the Rain.* Portland: Far Shore Press, 1999. Containing literature on Gorge natives, this self-published classic can be found in such independent Portland bookstores as Powell's or from the author at 2147 NW Irving, Portland 97210, 503/227-4207.

Williams, Chuck. *Bridge of the Gods, Mountains of Fire: A Return to the Columbia Gorge.* White Salmon, WA: Friends of the Earth, 1981. This excellent photo essay and narrative highlights the rich native culture of Gorge tribes.

Lewis and Clark

Ambrose, Stephen. *Undaunted Courage.* New York: Touchstone Press, 1996. A classic book on Oregon's and the country's seminal voyage of discovery, the Lewis and Clark Expedition, it gives a historical context to the journals in an entertaining, enlightening way. Read this before taking on *The Journals of Lewis and Clark* themselves. The latter work is available through many different publishers but the antiquated grammar and archaic English make it difficult reading.

Smith, Landon. *The Essential Lewis and Clark.* New York: Ecco Press, 2000. A version of *The Journals of Lewis and Clark* with much of the antiquated grammar and spelling edited out.

Natural History

Jolley, Russ. *Wildflowers of the Columbia.* Portland: Oregon Historical Society Press, 1988. An exhaustive study on Oregon's plant species, identifying 744 of the Columbia Gorge's more than 800 species of flowering shrubs and wildflowers.

Allen, Dr. John Eliot, Marjorie Burns, and Sam C. Sargent. *Cataclysms on The Columbia.* Portland: Timber Press, 1991. This is the seminal work on Gorge geology.

Photo Essays

Stirling, Linda. *Columbia River Gorge.* Woodburn: Beautiful America, 2001. With photos by Larry Geddis, this book contains remarkable photos and readable text.

Atkeson, Ray. *Oregon I, Oregon II,* and *Oregon III.* Portland: Graphic Arts Center Publishing, 1968-1987. Preeminent coffee-table books of Gorge photos. These once-costly hard-covered editions are now available in paperback.

Hiking and Recreation Guides

Sullivan, William L. *100 Hikes in Northwest Oregon.* Eugene: Navillus Press, 1993. Travelers to the Columbia Gorge will find the section on Gorge hikes provides the clearest directions. Also pertinent are observations on human and natural history.

Samson, Karl. *Frommer's Great Outdoor Guide To Oregon and Washington.* New York: Macmillan Travel, 1998. The Gorge chapters in this travel guide get our highest recommendation for launching an adventure by land or by sea.

Fiction

Hockenberry, John. *A River Out of Eden.* New York: Doubleday, 2001. A recent addition to Gorge literature, this novel centers on Chinook Indian Frances Smoholla, a government marine biologist hired to save salmon threatened by a dam supplying Washington's hydroelectric power. Having seen the effects of the disappearance of Celilo Falls salmon fishery on her people, her participation in this effort runs into political hot water. This is a good "read" and offers perspective on the dams versus salmon crisis.

Audio Tapes

If you're going to the Gorge with youngsters, a well-done audio tape is *Columbia Gorge Driving Tours,* sold at Powell's Books and the Oregon History Center in Portland—or you can order by calling 503/730-7495. For $15, you get a breezy, informative rundown of history, geology, and local color spiced up with dramatic (sometimes overly so) readings of native legends. The entertaining narration is kept simple enough for kids to relate to, but will satisfy older travelers as well.

Another tape, put out by Friends of the Gorge, is a more complete treatment of the region but is apt to be appreciated only by adults. Buy it at Powell's or by contacting Friends of the Gorge at 319 SW Washington, Suite 301, Portland 97204, 503/241-3762, www.gorge friends.org.

Acknowledgments

Moon Handbooks: Columbia River Gorge would never have seen the light of day without the backing of Avalon's acquisitions committee—thanks, Bill and Pauli! And were it not for the efforts of editor Erin Van Rheenen, you would not be holding this book in your hands.

Another heartfelt *gracias* goes out to Dave Johnson and Josephine Bridges for last-minute editorial help of stellar importance. We would also like to acknowledge Jeanette Kloos of The Oregon Department of Transportation for photos.

Stuart is grateful to his co-author Brian for his considerable expertise on all matters related to the Gorge as well a level of professionalism seldom seen during Stuart's two decades in the guidebook business. Brian just wants to say, "Thanks, buddy, for giving me the chance to write about a place I love more than anywhere in the world."

The input, good humor and encouragement of Lester and Lois throughout the project were always appreciated and even though Stuart is still recovering, he would like to thank his son Phineas and friend Douglas for dragging him up Dog Mountain. At a time when personal matters made continuing the project doubtful, the view of the Columbia River Gorge from the summit helped convince him to continue. Brian would also like to thank his good friends Jayne and Jim for being there in the pinch as well as BD for being the best pal in the world Finally, the inspiration and support of Kathleen and Sydney as well as our parents and siblings sustained us through many long days on the trail, behind the wheel, and at the computer.

Index

Hikes

Historical Sites

Parks

Waterfalls

Index

U.S.~METRIC CONVERSION

1 inch = 2.54 centimeters (cm)
1 foot = .304 meters (m)
1 yard = 0.914 meters
1 mile = 1.6093 kilometers (km)
1 km = .6214 miles
1 fathom = 1.8288 m
1 chain = 20.1168 m
1 furlong = 201.168 m
1 acre = .4047 hectares
1 sq km = 100 hectares
1 sq mile = 2.59 square km
1 ounce = 28.35 grams
1 pound = .4536 kilograms
1 short ton = .90718 metric ton
1 short ton = 2000 pounds
1 long ton = 1.016 metric tons
1 long ton = 2240 pounds
1 metric ton = 1000 kilograms
1 quart = .94635 liters
1 US gallon = 3.7854 liters
1 Imperial gallon = 4.5459 liters
1 nautical mile = 1.852 km

To compute celsius temperatures, subtract 32 from Fahrenheit and divide by 1.8. To go the other way, multiply celsius by 1.8 and add 32.

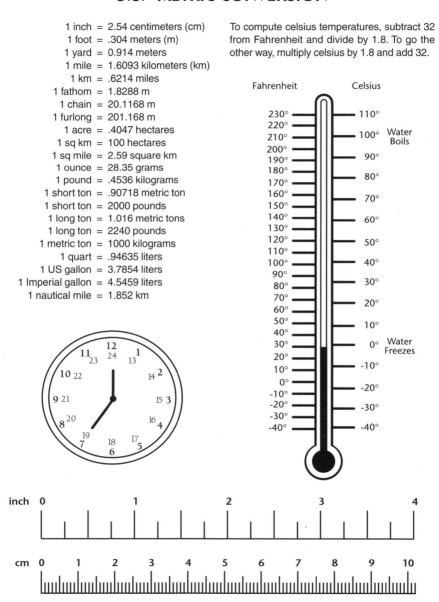

AVALON
TRAVEL
publishing

How far will our travel guides take you? As far as you want.

Discover a rhumba-fueled nightspot in Old Havana, explore prehistoric tombs in Ireland, hike beneath California's centuries-old redwoods, or embark on a classic road trip along Route 66. Our guidebooks deliver solidly researched, trip-tested information—minus any generic froth—to help globetrotters or weekend warriors create an adventure uniquely their own.

And we're not just about the printed page. Public television viewers are tuning in to Rick Steves' new travel series, *Rick Steves' Europe*. On the Web, readers can cruise the virtual black top with *Road Trip USA* author Jamie Jensen and learn travel industry secrets from Edward Hasbrouck of *The Practical Nomad*.

In print. On TV. On the Internet.

We supply the information. The rest is up to you.

Avalon Travel Publishing

Something for everyone

www.travelmatters.com

Avalon Travel Publishing guides are available at your favorite book or travel store.

MOON HANDBOOKS provide comprehensive

coverage of a region's arts, history, land, people, and social issues in addition to detailed practical listings for accommodations, food, outdoor recreation, and entertainment. Moon Handbooks allow complete immersion in a region's culture—ideal for travelers who want to combine sightseeing with insight for an extraordinary travel experience in destinations throughout North America, Hawaii, Latin America, the Caribbean, Asia, and the Pacific.

WWW.MOON.COM

Rick Steves shows you where to travel and how to travel—all while getting the most value for your dollar. His Back Door travel philosophy is about making friends, having fun, and avoiding tourist rip-offs.

Rick has been traveling to Europe for more than 25 years and is the author of 22 guidebooks, which have sold more than a million copies. He also hosts the award-winning public television series *Rick Steves' Europe*.

WWW.RICKSTEVES.COM

ROAD TRIP USA

Getting there is half the fun, and Road Trip USA guides are your ticket to driving adventure. Taking you off the interstates and onto less-traveled, two-lane highways, each guide is filled with fascinating trivia, historical information, photographs, facts about regional writers, and details on where to sleep and eat—all contributing to your exploration of the American road.

"[Books] so full of the pleasures of the American road, you can smell the upholstery."
~BBC radio

WWW.ROADTRIPUSA.COM